# Site Reliablity Engineers Handbook

*Understanding SRE core principles to build and operate reliable systems*

**Anupam Singh**

**bpb**

www.bpbonline.com

First Edition 2025

Copyright © BPB Publications, India

ISBN: 978-93-65893-601

To View Complete
BPB Publications Catalogue
Scan the QR Code:

# Dedicated to

*My husband*

# About the Author

**Anupam Singh** is a technology enthusiast and loves solving problems with technology. She is currently working as an engineering director- SRE for an international financial technology organisation. Anupam has around 16 years of experience working in the software industry across the globe, in various domains and has successfully delivered solutions. She is an experienced software developer and has a deep understanding of SDLC from different facets. She obtained a master's degree in management information systems from W.P. Carey School of Business, Arizona State University, in 2017. And she also holds a bachelor's of technology degree in information technology from G.B.P.U.A.T Pantnagar, India in 2008. Anupam is a featured speaker for AnitaB.org India GHCI 2024 on *Eliminating anti-patterns to build reliable system.* She is a mentor to fresh graduates in her organisation, helping them excel in the corporate world. Outside work, she is a volunteer of a global non-profit organisation, AnitaB.org India and has organised various events for women in technology. On the personal front, she loves travelling. In her free time, she spent her time gardening. Anupam is also a health enthusiast and loves to explore new adventures and activities.

# About the Reviewers

❖ **Ankit Sharma** is a seasoned technical manager with extensive experience managing large-scale applications. He is a generative AI enthusiast and a passionate advocate for leveraging cutting-edge technologies to solve complex business challenges. A postgraduate in data science from Deakin University, Australia, he also wears the hat of an author and enjoys exploring the evolving intersection of AI and software development. An active reader, he regularly engages with books across technology, data science, and innovation, and contributes as a technical reviewer for works in the AI and software engineering domains.

❖ **Varun Verma** is a seasoned full-stack engineer from India with 12 years of hands-on experience turning challenging business problems into elegant, high-impact software. Equally at home in the browser and the cloud, he builds end-to-end solutions with C#, .NET Core Web API, Angular / React, and modern JWT-secured architectures.

Varun specializes in domain-driven design and CQRS, designing systems that stay clean as they scale. On the infrastructure side, he is fluent in Azure, utilizing services such as Functions, Service Bus, Cosmos DB, Terraform, Docker, Kubernetes, GitHub Actions, and Jenkins to ensure fast and repeatable delivery. He has authored custom Terraform providers, automated golden-path GitHub templates, and migrated petabytes of IoT data across global energy devices without a hiccup.

A keen advocate of MLOps, he weaves machine learning pipelines and NLP-driven chatbots into production workloads, transforming unstructured sources such as PDFs into actionable insight. His code is continuously scanned, tested, and linted long before it hits production, reflecting his automate everything mantra.

Beyond client work, Varun blogs, contributes to open source, and mentors teams on cloud-native best practices, always exploring what is next and sharing what he learns.

# Acknowledgement

Writing this book has been a journey filled with challenges and growth. I would like to express my deepest gratitude to the editors, whose thoughtful feedback and dedication helped this book take shape.

My heartfelt thanks to BPB Publications for their guidance and assistance through the publishing process.

I am grateful to the technical reviewers whose valuable feedback and insights have been instrumental in shaping the content and improving the quality of this book.

I am thankful to my husband, Lokesh Sharma, for his unwavering support, patience and encouragement.

Last but not the least, I want to express my gratitude to the readers who have shown interest in the book, your support and encouragement is deeply appreciated.

Thank you to everyone who contributed in making this book a reality.

# Preface

SRE is a set of principles and practices that apply a software engineer's approach and help IT operations. SRE and DevOps follow similar underlying principles; however, they differ in practice. SRE aims to deliver a highly scalable and reliable software system; however, like any technology and practice, some roadblocks can lead to pitfalls for SRE also. It is not easy to build and deliver a highly available and reliable system. As not one solution fits all, however, some of the best practices can help achieve business goals.

This book will help readers identify and address roadblocks and find solutions to those. The solutions can help organisations to boost their development and quality delivery process.

This book will take readers through some real scenarios of SRE pitfalls and solutions to overcome these pitfalls. And best practices to help build highly reliable and scalable systems.

The key highlights of this book are various ways to avoid anti-patterns in the SRE approach to scale, explained in Chapter 5, and the relation between SRE and DevOps in Chapter 2. The book also highlights some of the best practices of SRE to elevate IT operations, along with real industry examples.

The book is designed to cater to software engineers, site reliability engineers, DevOps engineers, software architects, product managers and all those professionals working around technology and building software.

**Chapter 1: Site Reliability Engineering: Beyond Scalability-** This chapter is an introduction to SRE. It describes the high-level meaning of SRE, and emergence of SRE and its importance in today's SDLC. This chapter gives an understanding of how SRE is positioned in IT. The chapter also covers the continuous need for SRE in the IT industry and how SRE manages cloud-native complex problems to achieve business goals. The chapter highlights the need for SRE, the role of SRE in the software development lifecycle and various pillars of SRE. The chapter also explains the significance of SRE in the cloud-native era.

**Chapter 2: SRE and DevOps-** This chapter explains the role of SRE and how it's related to DevOps. The chapter describes various common practices between SRE and DevOps and also the differences between the two methodologies. By the end of the chapter, readers will gain an understanding of how SRE and DevOps are changing the software industry and modernizing the software development lifecycle model.

**Chapter 3: Build Effective Solutions with SRE-** This chapter will help readers understand various ways to deliver efficient and quality software and how SRE methodology can help build this effective solution. This chapter also explains some real-time scenarios of the SRE, DevOps and Agile approach that delivered robust software and the specific techniques SRE teams used to build efficient systems. Along with building scalable software, the chapter also highlights capacity planning and cost management. Readers will also get insights on some of the key features of SRE, such as the importance of testing, monitoring and observability, measuring the performance, incident management and automation. The chapter also explains the CAMS model as an SRE essential.

**Chapter 4: Understanding Anti-patterns-** This chapter explains the meaning of anti-pattern and what anti-patterns mean in software development. It also describes how recurring problems of software engineering and site reliability are related. The readers will gain insights on some of the known anti-patterns in SRE.

**Chapter 5: Types of Anti-patterns-** This chapter describes the different types of anti-patterns and ways to recognise these anti-patterns. It also explains measures to overcome anti-patterns in order to have an efficient SRE methodology. In this chapter, the reader will learn some of the hidden roadblocks along with known anti-patterns that lead to pitfalls. The chapter will help explain readers' real-time scenarios of roadblocks impacting software and solutions implemented to overcome roadblocks. The chapter will help readers gain insights on how to identify the anti-patterns in an ongoing software development project.

**Chapter 6: Real-world Examples of Successful SRE-** This chapter provides various real-world scenarios for successful SRE implementation. Readers will get insights on how various software organisations solved anti-patterns and improved system reliability. The chapter will help readers understand various phases of SRE practice and how these practices can help achieve software reliability. Some of the highlights of these practices are alert management, incident management, root cause analysis, defining metrics, chaos engineering and automation.

**Chapter 7: Best Practice for SRE-** This chapter explains some of the best practices for SRE. These practices are derived from real-world scenarios from organisations following SRE path. The chapter also explain the importance of good software design and software development for quality delivery. By the end of this chapter, readers will gain a comprehensive understanding of the approach to achieving quality delivery.

**Chapter 8: Tool Kit for SRE-** This chapter describes some of the best tools available in the market and can be used as an SRE tool kit throughout the book. This chapter gives readers a cheat sheet for successful SRE. Readers will gain an understanding of the diverse skill sets required to be a site reliability engineer. By the end of this chapter, readers will have a high-level understanding of SRE tools available in the market. The toolkit also helps readers design software systems.

**Chapter 9: Day in the Life of SRE-** The chapter explains the roles and responsibilities of an SRE and gives a glimpse of the daily tasks of the SRE team. The chapter also throws some light on SRE team skill sets. By the end of the chapter, the reader will gain an understanding of how to start a career in SRE and how an SRE team functions in today's Agile throughout the book approach.

**Chapter 10: Future of SRE-** This is the last chapter, which will conclude with key SRE features that readers learned through this book. It also gives a comprehensive SRE goal and some food for thought to readers on how and where to begin the SRE journey. The objective of this chapter is to focus on the SRE career path and how you can become an SRE.

# Code Bundle and Coloured Images

Please follow the link to download the
*Code Bundle* and the *Coloured Images* of the book:

# https://rebrand.ly/9da36d

The code bundle for the book is also hosted on GitHub at
**https://github.com/bpbpublications/Site-Reliability-Engineers-Handbook**.
In case there's an update to the code, it will be updated on the existing GitHub repository.

We have code bundles from our rich catalogue of books and videos available at
**https://github.com/bpbpublications**. Check them out!

# Errata

We take immense pride in our work at BPB Publications and follow best practices to ensure the accuracy of our content to provide with an indulging reading experience to our subscribers. Our readers are our mirrors, and we use their inputs to reflect and improve upon human errors, if any, that may have occurred during the publishing processes involved. To let us maintain the quality and help us reach out to any readers who might be having difficulties due to any unforeseen errors, please write to us at :

**errata@bpbonline.com**

Your support, suggestions and feedbacks are highly appreciated by the BPB Publications' Family.

## Piracy

If you come across any illegal copies of our works in any form on the internet, we would be grateful if you would provide us with the location address or website name. Please contact us at **business@bpbonline.com** with a link to the material.

## If you are interested in becoming an author

If there is a topic that you have expertise in, and you are interested in either writing or contributing to a book, please visit **www.bpbonline.com**. We have worked with thousands of developers and tech professionals, just like you, to help them share their insights with the global tech community. You can make a general application, apply for a specific hot topic that we are recruiting an author for, or submit your own idea.

## Reviews

Please leave a review. Once you have read and used this book, why not leave a review on the site that you purchased it from? Potential readers can then see and use your unbiased opinion to make purchase decisions. We at BPB can understand what you think about our products, and our authors can see your feedback on their book. Thank you!

For more information about BPB, please visit **www.bpbonline.com**.

# Join our Discord space

Join our Discord workspace for latest updates, offers, tech happenings around the world, new releases, and sessions with the authors:

https://discord.bpbonline.com

# Table of Contents

# CHAPTER 1
# Site Reliability Engineering: Beyond Scalability

## Introduction

This chapter is an introduction to **site reliability engineering** (**SRE**). It will cover the meaning and role of SRE in today's software development. This chapter will also highlight the emergence of SRE and its journey. We will understand how and where SRE is positioned in the **software development lifecycle** (**SDLC**). Along with this, the chapter will also cover the consistent requirements for SRE in the IT industry. As part of the need for SRE, you would learn how SRE principles manage to solve complex cloud-native problems to achieve business goals.

## Structure

The chapter covers the following topics:

- Understanding site reliability engineering
- Site reliability engineering in SDLC
- Need for site reliability engineering
- Pillars of site reliability engineering
- Significance of SRE in the cloud-native era

# Objectives

By the end of this chapter, you will understand the meaning of SRE and its journey in the IT industry. This chapter will frame a baseline to help you visualize the software development lifecycle model from an SRE perspective. You will understand the need for site reliability engineering and why site reliability is gaining importance in the IT industry.

# Understanding site reliability engineering

SRE is a set of principles and practices that applies aspects of software engineering to IT infrastructure and operations. SRE claims to create highly reliable and scalable software systems. Though there are various versions of these definitions, and they change as per the organization, type of software project, and the type of software system, each definition leads to one goal for the software system: high scalability and reliability.

The field of SRE was originated at *Google* in 2003. Since 2003, the concept of site reliability spread across broader software development organizations. Though not many organizations adopted SRE initially during the early 2000s, as there were no clear or defined principles, various organizations did not even see the need for SRE due to their scale. Some organizations are already running part of SRE in the name of production support. Over time, software applications started to grow, and due to increasing demand, there was a need to manage and speed up operations and development. So Google also defined the SRE role, and the adoption of SRE increased. with the cloud gaining popularity today, almost every IT organization has an SRE division to manage operations and engineering for high-class reliability and scalability.

SRE is the bridge between development and operations. DevOps is also similar and shares some principles with SRE. However, they are two different sets of practices. In some organizations, SRE and DevOps are two separate teams, whereas in others, they share roles. The relationship between SRE and DevOps is explained further in the next chapter of this book.

SRE is a set of practices that defines software reliability, availability, and resiliency 24/7. It applies engineering principles where engineers identify and fix problems before they go into real software applications, also known as the production environment, and if any problem persists in production, then identify, troubleshoot, and resolve it. SRE involves operations and engineering, and the role of each SRE engineer is clearly defined as managing large-scale software systems. Operations have always been an integral part of software organizations, but with an increase in demand, there was a need to scale up software systems, and that, in turn, put pressure on organizations to have faster development and big operations teams to support software. Operations are sometimes also referred to as production support teams. Some organizations have SRE and production support teams, where the support team acts as L1/L2 and SRE as L3 engineers. On the other hand, some organizations have removed the production support team and formed only SRE that manages support, troubleshoots problems and provides solutions. The SRE team spent 50% time on operations and 50% of the time on engineering tasks. However, any SRE team's goal is to ensure the software system is always up and running.

Some fundamental principles and practices of SRE are as follows:

- **Observability:** The monitoring system is one of the critical functions of SRE. Unless you monitor and observe your system, you cannot identify the gaps to be closed.

- **Automation:** Eliminate manual and repetitive tasks by automating as many as possible. Engineers should focus on developing new features and tools and enhancing systems to avoid real-time failures.

- **Metrics service level objectives (SLO), service level agreements (SLA):** Set reasonable expectations for system performance to ensure that end-users and stakeholders understand how the system is supposed to perform at various levels.

- **Measure:** Always define metrics for each service to measure how the system is performing. If you cannot measure it, you cannot resolve failures.

- **Risk management:** No system is designed to perform perfectly, and no system can be 100% available all the time. So, it is important to identify potential failures and mitigate those failures with minimum impact.

- **Incident management:** Defined clear standards and processes around managing incidents for timely response and resolution of failures and end-user requests.

- **Change management:** Outline and document processes for developers and testers to release changes in development and production environments.

# Site reliability engineering in SDLC

Software development lifecycle is a set of steps or processes for software developers, software testers, requirement analysts, designers, and support engineers. SDLC originated in the 1960s to help software developers, designers, and testers follow a model to build and deliver large-scale systems. Organizations follow various SDLC models, and Waterfall is one of the well-known models that many organizations follow. However, with the emergence of the cloud and increased demand and scalability, the Agile methodology also came into the picture. In today's technology world, Agile methodology is commonly used by almost every software organization, and SDLC and SRE principles are in accord with Agile principles. SRE, following Agile practice, makes a robust SDLC model and help organizations to run smooth development and delivery systems (refer to *Figure 1.1*):

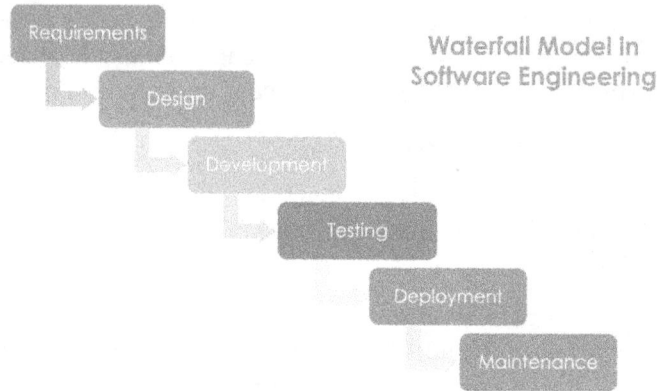

*Figure 1.1: Waterfall SDLC model*

The Waterfall SDLC model is a linear model where each phase depends on the deliverables of the previous phase. This model worked very well for organizations with small-scale and software systems that often do not change requirements. However, with an increase in demand, user requirements started to change, which in turn made software organizations deliver all new features in less time and scale up fast. Along with that, various other gaps were also identified with old SDLC models. To address these problems, Agile methodology came into the picture. There were various other models of SDLC, but with emerging technology, Agile methodology gained popularity. Agile methodology was introduced in early 1970s however it got highlighted around 2009s (refer to *Figure 1.2*):

*Figure 1.2: Agile methodology in SDLC*

Today's SDLC follow Agile methodology that is basically a project management approach emphasises on continuous collaboration, communication and continuous improvement. Agile is not only set of techniques but it is group of methodologies used to demonstrate continuous development, strong feedback cycle and continuous improvement.

As described in *Figure 1.2* above there are various phases in Agile methodology similar to Waterfall. Nevertheless, each of these phases follow sprint, where each phase is repeated every sprint till that project is completed.

Let us take a real scenario of an e-commerce software project that follow Agile. The sprint cycle followed in project is of 1 week. Team get requirements including build modules to search, filter items and payment module on e-commerce website.

- First, is planning where business analyst team define and collect requirements and create a high-level data flow for the software system.

- Design phase is where designers create wireframes and design the user interface, architects design architecture flow and outlook of that software application. At this point there are other requirements in pipeline so planning team start picking those from backlog.

- Developers then start writing code, perform unit testing, package the code and pass on to testing team.

- Quality analyst then test the packaged code and handover to release management team.

- Release management team deploy the code to production environment.

- Support team review and make sure system is up and running as expected.

Once it is delivered and users started using the features in website, new requirements from pipeline were picked up and started as soon as planning team delivered their data flow to design team. Moreover, this process repeats.

The major role of SRE comes at the end of the Agile model, is review. Some organizations call that phase as support or monitoring or maintenance or operations phase. This is the phase where SRE comes in to picture, where SRE team support and own the production software application. They review if code is behaving as expected, if there are any user complaints or tickets, they review if infrastructure is able to handle the load of user requests. Along with monitoring production environment SRE engineers develop tools, controls and capabilities to help developers release their code in production smoothly and identify any issues before it impact users. Though it seems SRE fit in the last phase of Agile, but SRE roles also falls throughout Agile process and it is sometimes hidden.

In continuation of above real time example for e-commerce website, SRE falls in the last phase. Let us take same scenario with SRE as part of SDLC:

- **Project flow description:** Once the requirement was rolled out to production environment, SRE team monitor the website for spikes in traffic, errors in websites, failures in application, also technical tickets or complaints from users that customer support team of that organizations could not solve as it needed technical expertise. For any technical error reported, SRE is the first line of defence to troubleshoot the problem and fix it.

- **Real scenario:** during monitoring of application, SRE team noticed that payment service was throwing `http 500` error intermittently. Though none of the customer reported but these are proactive monitoring alerts configured by SRE teams. SRE team is skilled to troubleshoot and identify the cause of error and fix it depend on their skill set. Some cases SRE team pass on the problem to developers to fix the failure.

Although SRE here is positioned at the last phase, many organizations involve the SRE from very beginning in SDLC, where planning of application start. SRE is the team consist of skilled engineers who has knowledge on architecture of actual software system aka production environment from infrastructure and code perspective. SRE help business analyst and designers by providing them real view of software application also known as, production environment. SRE team has data on percentage of traffic flow, scalability, fallback, load balancing, data replication and many more.

If you take same example as above. Now, involve SREs during planning, designing and testing all three phases and see how it helped the SDLC process.

In the real scenario, after testing search module, **quality analysis (QA)** team identified a bug in code where search module failed 1 time when requested. As, this is only 1 request failure QA and development ignored the error. Now, SRE is also a part of the testing review. QA, shared the results to SRE. SRE provided the data on number of users access search module in a day and also performed load and chaos testing. The testing result showed multiple failures in search module due to system was not able to handle the load. SRE provided that insight to QA, and QA, SRE, and the development team collaborated to identify the fix for this problem. Either scaling up of server is required, or the code has to be rewritten with a light query.

Consider this example, SRE is involved in the planning and designing phase. During the design phase, SRE shared insights into the actual customer load that helped the architect to include a database that only uses lightweight queries. Also, SRE engineer added a recommendation for extra capacity for servers to handle the load. Both of these two cases help businesses to identify failure before production and save time and effort (refer to *Figure 1.3*):

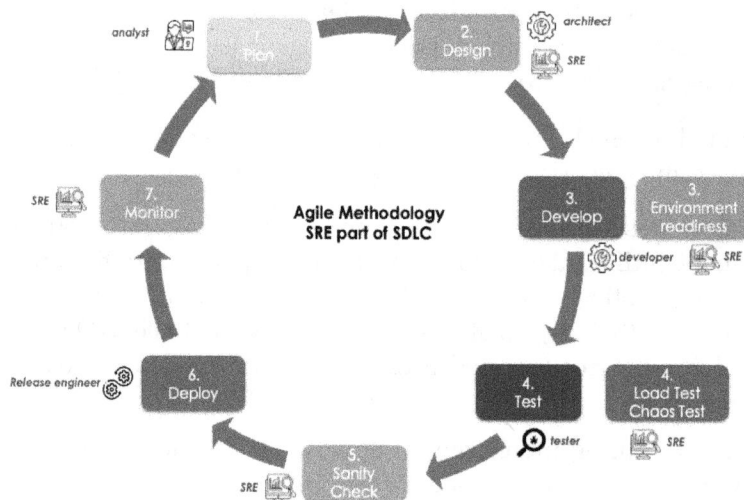

*Figure 1.3: SRE involvement in various phases of Agile*

The following is a continuation of the above example with more details. Detailed description of roles performed by different teams in each phase (refer to *Figure 1.4*):

- **Plan:** Requirement capture by analysts.

- **Design:** Data flow, architecture diagram, tech stack by business analysts, software architects, product leaders, designers, SRE and DevOps SMEs.

- **Develop:** Developers develop UI and backend. The DevOps team creates CI/CD pipelines. In the earlier diagram, the DevOps team is called the release engineering team. However, DevOps and release engineers are sometimes the same team, and it also depends on the type of project.

- **Environment readiness:** The SRE team creates a monitoring dashboard. The DevOps team prepares the development, testing, and production environments using CI/CD pipelines, which are used to install infrastructure.

- **Test:** The testing team performs regression testing and progression testing. The SRE team performs load testing and chaos testing.

- **SRE review:** The SRE and testing and development teams review a few high-impact bug fixes. The SRE team also performs a round of sanity on production.

- **Deploy:** DevOps team uses CI/CD pipelines to deploy code to production

- **Monitoring:** SRE monitoring system performance. SRE also manages incidents and technical tickets from customer service.

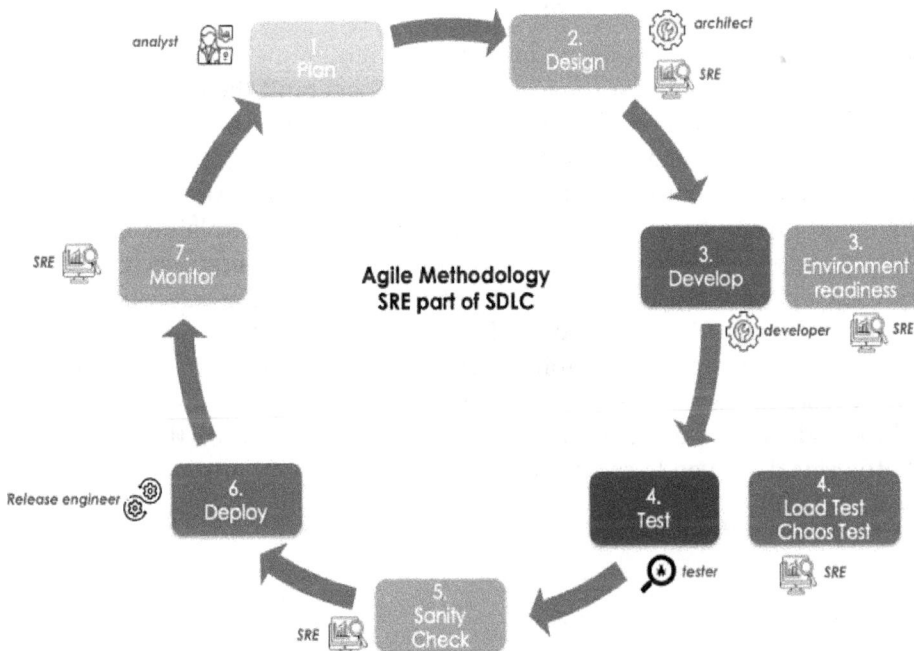

*Figure 1.4: Roles performed by various team in each phase*

# Need for site reliability engineering

So far you clearly understood what SRE is and its journey in SDLC. Also, a high-level view of SRE roles and responsibilities. In this section, you will understand the need for SRE in current software organizations and how SRE contributes to bridging the gap between development and operations. Site reliability engineering, as its name conveys, ensures the reliability of software systems. However, various engineering and operational aspects are involved in ensuring reliability, such as infrastructure management, application support, observability, availability, scalability, tools, and capabilities. We cannot deny Murphy's law that anything that can go wrong will go wrong and is also applicable to service. However, we can improve and ensure a reliable user experience.

Let us take the real scenario of an e-commerce software project without SRE but with just operations. A few considerations about this project:

- Project follows the Agile methodology.
- Tech stack hosted on public cloud, NoSQL databases, Redis, S3 Storage, Java backend, and all the latest tools.
- **Observability tools:** ELK, Grafana, App Dynamics, Splunk
- **Technology team structure:** Product management, UI designers, Agile champions, developers, quality analysts, performance testers, DevOps team, operations team, and customer service team.

Let us consider a use case in this project.

The product team finalized the new payment feature requirement. Product and architects finalized data flow and design for the feature, developers built the code, the tester tested the code, the DevOps team created a CI/CD pipeline to create a production environment and deployed code in production, and the DevOps team created alerting and monitoring dashboards, operations team monitor production environment. After a few days of the feature release in production, the customer service team got complaints from users that they could not make payments. The ticket was moved to the operations teams as part of the process. The operations team did their level 1 troubleshooting but could not identify the real cause and passed the ticket to the DevOps team. The DevOps team troubleshot and identified that this was not an infrastructure issue, but they were still not able to find the real cause, so they moved the ticket to the developer's queue. As the dev team developed the code, they were able to identify the root cause and fix the bug in the code, and this hotfix was deployed to the production environment.

This full process took around three days, and for three days, users were not able to use the application, and it eventually a loss to the software organization (refer to *Figure 1.5*):

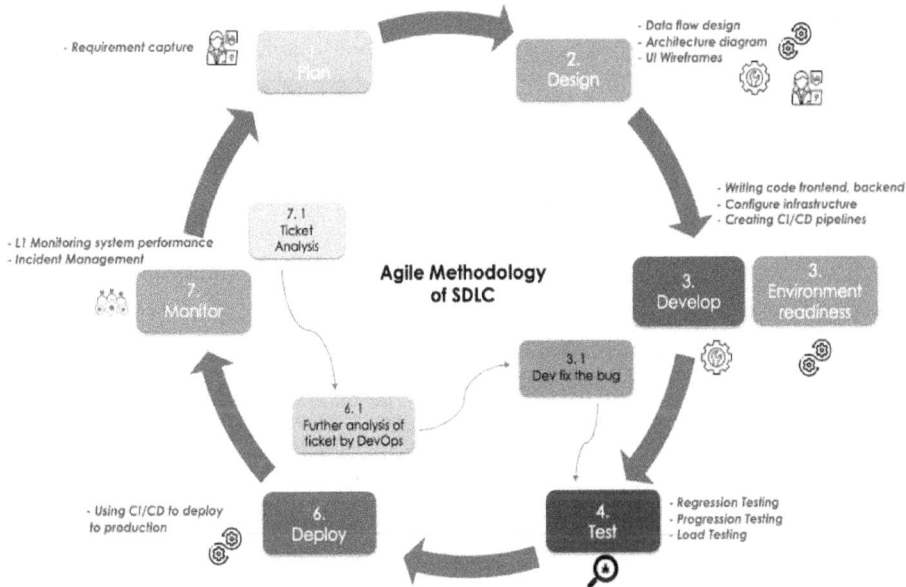

*Figure 1.5*: *SDLC phases without SRE (replaced by DevOps and L1 ops)*

Take the same use case, but now with the SRE team as part of the project. Everything remains the same, but the operations team is replaced with the SRE team. This SRE team consists of developers and operations.

Let us consider a use case.

The new payment feature requirement was finalized by product team. Product and architects finalized data flow and design for the feature; developers built the code; tester tested the code. The DevOps team created the CI/CD pipeline to create a production environment and deployed code in production. The SRE team built alerting and monitoring dashboards that also auto-heal, SRE teams built an in-house troubleshooting tool to identify and simulate issues reported in the past for this application, and the SRE team also monitored the production environment. After two days of feature release in production, the SRE team got an alert for failure requests. As the SRE team is also supporting production and building the alerting dashboard, the team was able to catch the issue even before customers reported and identified it. As soon as the SRE team got alert, they troubleshoot the error and run through their in-house tool they built and identified that similar error happened in past as well. Their tool provided the root cause and SRE collaborated with the developer of the code and got the bug fixed in system and the DevOps team deployed the hotfix. The issue got fixed within few hours and customers did not notice any major failure.

The above-explained two scenarios with and without SRE explain the importance of SRE teams in the software development lifecycle process. Without an SRE team, it took almost

3 days to identify and fix the problem, and that cost money, and the organization might lose its customers also. However, with the SRE team in the picture, the project was able to identify and fix the problem within a few hours. You can argue that DevOps and operations teams can also build the same tools and dashboards and solve the problem. Yes, this can happen, but when an organization works at a large scale and builds something like an e-commerce project, it is better to have separate teams and defined roles, else you will burn out people, and they will not be able to meet any of the requirements.

Almost every software organization have operations team that manages and support production environment, however SRE team has been formed to fill the gaps between operations and development and to speed up development and delivery of software. SRE team consist of team including developers, infrastructure engineers, system engineers and support engineers. They are multi skilled team trained to support and troubleshoot production environment and have skill set to develop code, that is why they understand both operations and development side of SLDC. Along with supporting application and infrastructure, SRE team are developers who build tools and capabilities that reduces toil, configure infrastructure, create observability dashboards, implement auto-heal tools, and help developers to identify and fix issues in code. With these skill sets SRE team can identify and fix issue before it impacts software application. SRE teams are responsible for maintaining reliability, scalability, and availability of system. Any change going in production environment can impact running application, but SRE team, with their tool kit make sure applications are always up and running and end user do not face any problem while accessing software. This, in turn, helps organizations to save application crashes, provide good service to their customers, increase customer onboarding, and increase business.

The SRE team is an investment in any software industry. Sometimes, organizations increase their IT budget to hire and form an SRE team due to the demanding skillset. But if you consider ROI, there is a good return by increasing the reliability and availability of software systems. Having said that, not all organization have budget, and the project do not always require a separate SRE team. So, organizations also extend DevOps team that perform SRE functions. This is alright for small-scale projects; however, for large-scale projects, it is better to have separate DevOps and SRE teams to define clear roles and responsibilities and also save the burnout of team members by working extra hours to meet the requirements.

# Pillars of site reliability engineering

To understand SRE in depth, one needs first to know its pillars. However, there is no *one-size-fits-all* way of achieving goals. You may use different approaches to solve problems, but the end result and goal matter the most to the end user and to the business. SRE gives confidence in achieving that goal.

The following are the four golden pillars of SRE:

- **SLO and service level indicators (SLI):** Objective and quantitative metrics that defines successful service levels. It is simple, if you cannot measure it, you cannot achieve it. SLO are the goals internal to the organization to keep the system up and running as per standards. SLI measure the reliability of service quantitively. These metrics are actual numbers to be measured, such as throughput, latency, and correctness. There is the third metric that also plays an important role, SLA. SLA is an organization's promise to its customers on reliable delivery of service that includes uptime, responsiveness, and responsibilities.

  For example, as an organization, your SLA is defined as 99.9% availability of your system for customers. Now, the SLO will be 99.999% availability. That means the internal goal for the team involved in the project is to make sure the availability of the platform is 99.999%. As you are committed to keep availability as 99.999%, even if it drops you will still be able to meet your SLA. Now comes SLI, how you actually measure the availability is defined by SLI. So when you measure uptime and throughput, and it comes to 99.999%, that means you meet your SLO and SLA.

  This metric defined the goal for any service and help tracking SRE teams. If your SLI, SLO and SLA are meeting that means right practice and processes are being followed by the software project. SLA are the top metrics for any organization to meet, without meeting SLA means organization did not deliver what it promised to its end-user, customers or clients.

  Defining and understanding these metrics can be challenging. It is important for organization's product team to define SLA and SLO in plain simple language that is easily comprehendible by engineers. More clear and achievable the SLA, SLOs be, it will be easy for engineers to define SLI. For example, you can never meet 100% SLA, as there will always be some service that can go down.

  Let us now look at an example. Take one month, SLA is 99.9% availability of application. SLO is 99.999% availability. SLI is measured by % of uptime in a month and % of throughput. There was some issue in service where a few customers experienced intermittent failure. SRE teams have configured alerting and auto-healing in place. As soon as the application saw the error, auto-heal recovered the failure by moving the service to another server, and only a handful of customers intermittently experienced failure. At the backend, developers and the SRE team collaborated on fixing the issue. So here, SLO and SLI are impacted as service is down. However, SLA is not impacted.

- **Monitoring:** Collecting metrics of the system to understand its performance is another important aspect of SRE. One of the daily tasks of SRE team is to monitor system. The quicker SRE reaction to failure is, the better be the reliability of system. Monitoring means keeping an eye on system performance by various metrics defined during initial stages of SDLC. Generally, there are proactive and reactive monitoring of system. However, proactive monitoring is preferred and also help system perform better than reactive.

Metrics are defined during design of system and with past data available. Some of the metrics to monitor are uptime (% of time the system was available and functioning as expected), error rate (% of requests that resulted an error), response time (amount of time it take for a request to complete the transaction), **mean time to recovery (MTTR**—average amount of time it take to fix system to recover), **mean time between failures (MTBF**—average amount of time between failures or outages), latency (amount of time it takes for a request to be processed by system), resource utilization (CPU and memory utilization of various services in system).

SRE teams configure various dashboards and alerting systems to measure performance by these metrics. Alerting system notifies engineers of any failure or outage in system that help them fix issue faster. However, SRE teams uses dashboard to proactively monitor system behaviour. Various automations are also build by these engineers to auto-heal or auto-recover system during failures. To ensure project or organization is meeting SLA, it is important to collect and monitor the system performance. And defining and configuring multiple metrics for each service help SRE teams to maintain SLA. There are few common metrics being called out here that are important to measure, however, every system is different and there can be multiple other metrics required to monitor the system. It is advised to configure metrics for every service in software application to help track system end to end. But multiple metrics means multiple dashboards, so SRE role become important to understand the system, prioritize the metrics on the basis of SLA, and create easy monitoring dashboards.

There are various tools available today for monitoring dashboards. A few commonly used tools across organizations are ELK, Prometheus, Grafana, Splunk, Google Analytics, and Azure Insights.

- **Emergency response:** These are a set of processes that help in responding to incidents when they occur to reduce customer impact. It is also referred to as an incident management system. Operations are an important part of SRE, sometimes referred to as front-line technical firefighters. So, managing and solving incidents is one of SRE's daily tasks. An established incident management system is critical for any organization to manage customer requests, complaints, and queries.

The incident management process helps prioritize the incidents according to impact and risk. Then, as per priority, it defines the resolution time. Along with defining the process, it is important to configure incident management by using the appropriate tool. A tool that will notify the team in real-time on any incident, help the team track the timeline workflow, and also update the requester about resolution. The goal for any project or organization is to deliver a smooth experience to end user, so solving their queries on time is a critical piece of that goal. And strong emergency response helps achieve that goal.

Incident management has 5 phases: incident identification, incident logging, incident categorization, incident prioritization, and incident response. These 5 phases help classify incidents with correct information so that they can be routed to the respective team without multiple follow-ups. Incident category and priority defined SLA for that incident. An SLA is an acceptable time for any incident to be responded to and resolved. There are multiple tools available today that help automate incident management systems.

During the initial phase of SDLC that is designing, organizations also finalize what tools to be used in order to complete the project. Tools that will help software development teams to deliver their work. For example, coding software, testing software, documentation software, repositories, incident management tool, monitoring tool etc.

- **Change management:** It is the process of planning, testing, and deploying code or configuration changes to ensure quality and minimum risk. It is a very popular saying within SRE and DevOps teams, *if nothing goes into production, nothing will break,* but we have Murphy's law: *Anything can go wrong, and it will*. Change is inevitable and also required for continuous improvement of software system. The more changes applied; more are the chances for things going wrong. And that is why change management was introduced as one of the SRE pillars.

To make reliable application, one need to know the services and infrastructure behind it, and to know the service and infrastructure one need to understand the code behind, various dependencies, and communication between services on current infrastructure. Not necessarily knowing every code but knowledge of components and flow is critical to package services as one entity. And this is where SRE play important role. As mentioned in the previos section, SRE team is diverse skill set and the goal of their role involve providing reliable service to end user. SRE is being involved in SDLC from beginning to deploying to support, that is how they gain knowledge and understanding of all aspects of software application.

Change management play important role to control *what, when, how changes can go in production*. SRE and DevOps are the team who work together to own change management process by getting involved during initial phase of change planning, then change deployment for testing, acting as gate keeper to control changes flow to production, and tracing back if any change introduce issue in application. Let us take one real organization scenario.

Take for example, an e-commerce application platform. Project got requirement to introduce cash on delivery feature in application along with other online payment features. Business analysts, product management collected requirement. Next steps, involvement of designers, SRE and software architect in deciding the flow and required infrastructure and tools. Developers started coding. As part of change management changes got deployed in lower environment and pass on the code to QA for further testing. SRE was onboarded for performance and chaos testing. QA published the testing reports and SRE team analysed the report. As part of change management that is owed by SRE team, they reviewed the code and identified a small bug in report published by QA. The bug is, 2 times failure of COD screen and with manual restart of service screen worked fine. It looked a small issue in testing environment but consider live application where 1000+ users will use application, this could result a huge failure. SRE team manages production application they understand the impact of this small issue could be huge. So, after review of testing result, the code was rejected and moved to development team to fix this failure. Again the process begin, developers fixed the code, QA tested and shared new results. SRE reviewed and approved the code. As part of CI/CD this new feature got deployed in production environment.

Aforementioned is a small example of how change management control changes to ensure quality and reliability of system. It also explained the role of SRE in change management cycle and its importance, as follows:

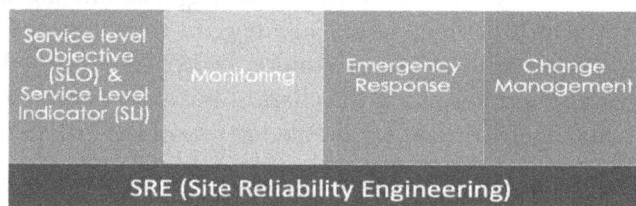

*Figure 1.6: Pillars of SRE*

# Significance of SRE in cloud-native era

Today, there is a lot of focus on cloud applications, and you see and read a lot of these terms, such as cloud computing, cloud-native era, the importance of cloud application, and many more cloud-related terms in the software world. Though all these topics have different meanings, they are all focused on the importance and need of cloud applications with the advancement of technology.

So, what does cloud-native mean? Cloud-native refers to services and software applications built to run on environments that leverage cloud computing technologies and methodologies. Today, almost every software organization uses cloud technologies to host their software application. It helps with continuous development and integration, quick and easy access to information, centralized data security, geo-location agnostic, cost-effective, and many more such benefits of using cloud technologies.

Cloud-native space has changed the way organizations look at the SDLC model. Cloud has enabled continuous development and integration of software, and this introduced the need to fix problems before they break. SRE's role has also changed across the journey, and SRE is now focused on enablement rather than fire-fighting. Everything is fast-paced, and the SRE role has also matured. With the advancement of developing methodologies, SRE is focused on empowering developers with self-service. The idea of fixing it before it breaks helps faster delivery and a reliable experience for end users.

# Empowering developers with self-service

Cloud-native space is a fast-moving, less-linear, and highly distributed model. It provides the latest tools and technologies, speeds up development, and offers quicker problem resolution. Cloud space has fundamentally redefined the traditional role of developers, operations, and SRE. And collaboration among these teams is the key to the successful delivery of any software system. That is where SRE plays an important role, where SRE brings developers and operations together. SRE's job is to use cloud space to configure tools and capabilities for development teams to improve overall developer productivity.

For example, building a self-service tool to get production performance metrics that help developers to understand how the service is behaving in production and they can code as required. This will save developers time by building standard code that do not need re-coding. In turn, this will save SRE time as they will not have to respond to multiple repetitive requests from developers. SRE methodology help business and technology to deliver quality on time. Agile approach works best with cloud space. Agile says continuous development and continuous integration and cloud provide the required platform to practice Agile.

In this new cloud-native world, SRE teams empower developers by building self-services to minimize toil. Another good example is SRE building infrastructure and tools on cloud, so developer do not worry about underlying platform and build their code cloud infra agnostic.

Along with developers, SRE also empowers business, product management teams by building various self-service dashboards to pull required data from live system. That will in turn help business in reporting the success of software system.

SRE is a new approach introduced to address problems of modern scalability-related applications. SRE methodology adopted on cloud technology helps organizations to solve problems effectively. The idea of cloud technology is that applications can be accessed from anywhere, regardless of geography. One should not worry and depend on underlying infrastructure while building software, as the cloud provides easy lift and shift capability. Many development and testing tools today are built to support applications running on the cloud. Cloud also promotes open-source software configurations. SRE practices highlight quick scaling of applications and fast resolution of failures. If software applications run on the cloud, that will help provide advanced infrastructure that can be scaled quickly. Tools supported on the cloud help the SRE team identify failures faster and offer the capability to resolve them soon.

Let us take an example of a software application running on the AWS cloud and see how the SRE role impacts system reliability in the cloud:

- SRE used AWS-provided dashboards and customized them according to project needs. This required the same effort and time as building anything from scratch.

- SRE installed open-source software as a plugin to add extra monitoring. AWS supports this open-source software and is also good at compatibility with it. This saves the organization money on purchasing new software.

- SRE can access applications irrespective of their location.

- AWS cloud provides easy configuration for adding extra servers in case of load increases. SRE can easily scale up the system whenever required.

Cloud provides in-built tools to manage micro-services through containers and multiple containers. SRE and DevOps teams save time configuring container management tools from scratch.

One such example is the AWS cloud. However, all clouds today provide these capabilities. Though this configuration can also be done on physical servers, it takes time, money, and skill set, and resolving any configuration error is also time time-consuming task (refer to *Figure 1.7*):

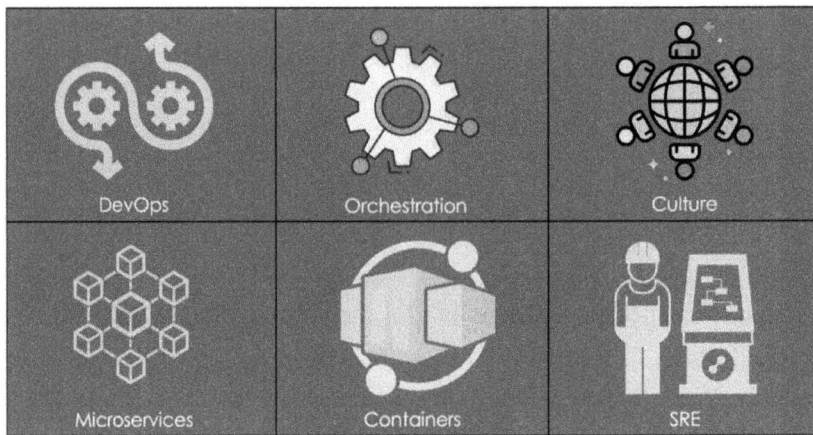

**Cloud Native**

*Figure 1.7*: *SRE positioned in cloud-native environment*

Cloud-native development is taking over the traditional monolith, deploying, releasing, and operating model. With the rise of cloud, the learning curve is also increasing. Developers, testers, and operations all have to learn cloud technology. SRE comes for the rescue as they are skilled engineers. However, SRE is also new practice, and few engineers have the skill set to bridge the gap between developers and operations. However, software organizations can build such teams by hiring people with different skill sets, including developers, system administrators, release engineers, and cloud practitioners. Train them with SRE principles and best practices and create an SRE team.

# Conclusion

This chapter provides a high-level overview of SRE and its role in the software industry. It also explains its history, the need for SRE in modern systems, and its principles.

In the next chapter, we will cover the commonalities and differences between SRE and DevOps approaches.

# CHAPTER 2
# SRE and DevOps

## Introduction

Operations as a discipline is difficult. Though there are various best practices to manage operations smoothly, and there is no one solution that fits all, organizations still take operations as a cost center. The need to solve this problem invented two newest solutions called SRE and DevOps.

This chapter explains the role of SRE and how it relates to DevOps. It will describe various common practices between SRE and DevOps and how both methodologies are different. We will cover some real examples from software organizations to help you visualize and understand these two practices. Additionally, the chapter also describes the importance of both methodologies in today's software development. As part of any software organization, we will understand how SRE and DevOps collaborate with each other and empower collaboration between other teams to deliver quality and reliability.

## Structure

The chapter covers the following topics:

- Understanding SRE and DevOps
- SRE and DevOps common practice
- Difference between SRE and DevOps

- New era SDLC model
- Real-world examples of SRE and DevOps

# Objectives

By the end of this chapter, we will understand the meaning of SRE and DevOps and how these two methodologies change the SDLC model. We will also explore the basics of SRE and DevOps, which will give us a vision of the delivery of any software system.

# Understanding SRE and DevOps

SRE is a set of principles and practices that applies aspects of software engineering to IT infrastructure and operations. There are various definitions of DevOps captured by organizations. Some of them are as follows:

- DevOps is a methodology used as a set of practices and tools that integrate and automate the work of software development and IT operations to reduce toil and deliver fast.
- DevOps is a set of practices, tools, and a culture philosophy that automates and integrates the process between software development and operations.
- DevOps is a combination of development and operations. It is a methodology that aims to integrate development and operations.
- DevOps is a union of people, processes, and technologies to continually provide value to the customers.
- DevOps is a practice that defines continuous development and integration to speed up the delivery and ensure higher quality.

These definitions have been accepted by all IT organizations that use SRE and DevOps. In the previous chapter, you learned about SRE. As you understand the aspects of SRE, it will help you understand DevOps in detail. However, as is already mentioned, there is no *one-size-fits-all*. The definition of DevOps also changes depending on the type of software project, the domain of the IT industry, and business requirements.

SRE as a practice was introduced by *Google* in 2008 to address the scaling problem of web-scaling. Soon after Google, many organizations that faced similar challenges also started adopting SRE. Though DevOps as an approach came before SRE, it was clear that DevOps alone cannot guarantee an excellent user experience.

Let us go back to history lane and understand why SRE was introduced. In the early 2000s when, Google faced significant challenges in maintaining the reliability of the rapidly growing system. With the increase in users, the company's infrastructure had also grown to thousands of servers across multiple locations (data centers), and managing this huge infrastructure required a new approach. *Ben Treynor Sloss* is the person behind inventing the

SRE practice at Google. His vision was simple, apply engineering principles to operations, emphasize automation, proactive root cause analysis and its application and continuous improvement. SRE's basic principle is to build only the % of functionality system that you can easily manage and have enough resources to scale up to foster increased user load.

When DevOps was introduced, the idea behind it was continuous integration and continuous development to foster the need for growing user demand. Their engineering teams automated the process and built tools that allow the tight collaboration of the software development team and operations teams, so the software delivery is faster. For example, software developers share updates on upcoming feature development with the operations team in advance. In turn, operations teams make sure the infrastructure is ready before the software features are ready to be rolled on to users.

Though DevOps was introduced to solve the problem of faster delivery, it did not solve the challenge of software failures due to an unmanageable growing infrastructure. And that is why SRE was introduced to manage reliability. SRE and DevOps in tandem are two sides of one coin that help organizations achieve the goals of quality, reliability, and faster delivery.

When SRE and DevOps teams work in harmony, they complement each other and help achieve the same goal of delivering modern applications. The preceding definitions of DevOps differ when it comes to how to achieve that goal. However, when they all talk about collaboration, automation, faster delivery, and quality, the underlying goal for each one is the same. That means deploying the code smoothly and at velocity in order for the business to meet the end-user requirements.

DevOps methodology builds a culture of collaboration from the very beginning. It focuses on teams coming together to build and deploy code to development and production environments and maintain it.

The core principles of DevOps are:

- **Silos breakdown**: The DevOps approach focuses on bringing development and operations together and ensuring strong collaboration. Collaboration in the form of transparent and regular communication helps the teams empower each other. Here, both teams, dev and ops, are aware of each other's timelines, processes, and data flow.

- **Automation**: The DevOps team automates the process of code integration and deployment. They build various pipelines using automation tools and automate various repetitive manual tasks. This increases accuracy, removes toil, and saves the time of developers.

- **Continuous integration and continuous deployment (CI/CD)**: It is one of the key practices in DevOps, where the DevOps team focuses on building pipelines so that developers can use those automated pipelines to build and integrate multiple codes and deploy them automatically.

- **Feedback loop**: Collaboration is the key to DevOps, and feedback also comes as part of that collaboration. Continuous feedback from developers, testers, SRE, and businesses on the efficacy of their automated tools and pipelines helps DevOps to identify gaps and issues and quickly resolve them.

- **Measuring**: DevOps team measures the outcome by defining various metrics. These metrics help the team achieve success.

The following figure represents the various stages of DevOps and how each stage is related:

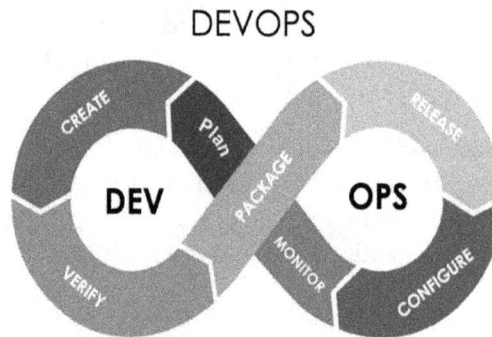

**Figure 2.1**: *Representation of stages in DevOps*

# SRE and DevOps common practice

SRE and DevOps both methodologies define collaboration between development and operations to break silos. Though both use distinctive and creative strategies to address different problems, the underlying aim is the same: to deliver quality at velocity, in order to cater to the fast-paced requirements of end-users.

Many organizations today have adopted SRE and DevOps as their main strategies for building modern software applications. In the previous section, you learned what SRE and DevOps are. Now, the question that arises is, *when these functions are similar then why do we need both*, and *how are both functions different from each other*?

SRE focuses on designing and implementing highly scalable and resilient systems, and it also emphasizes operations. That means SRE will help speed up operations, remove toil from operational functions, and support developers.

DevOps focuses on collaboration between developers and the operations team through communication and automated tools. That means DevOps, like the SRE approach, also defines how to support developers in coding faster while ensuring quality and deploying the code to production.

To better understand the need for DevOps along with SRE, let us take an example of an e-commerce project running on cloud-native, with some latest tools and technologies.

The following is the structure of the project:

- **Teams**: Business analysts, designers, development, Agile champions, product management team, testers, operations, system administration, and customer support.

- **Technology stack**: Java for backend, React for UI, high-performing servers on the cloud, NoSQL database, S3 storage, Redis in memory, monitoring, and logging tools.

- **SDLC flow between teams**: Business analysts get requirements, architects from the development team, and designers finalize the design. Developers will then write the code, testers test the code, and the code is deployed to production. The operations team then monitors and supports the live applications for any technical failures.

The project follows an Agile approach for SDLC. This project does not have DevOps and SRE teams. However, it has a traditional system admin for operations teams.

Let us look at the scenario.

The requirement for a new payment platform was captured by this e-commerce organization's analysts as the existing platform is slow, and users often experience failure while making payments.

This is how the organization implemented its SDLC model to code and deliver this new feature:

1. The business analyst collects the requirements from user researchers and creates a requirement document with all the details for technology teams.

2. Architects from the existing development team, business analysts, designers, and system admins collaborated and designed a data flow and architecture of this new payment platform. This document includes technical specifications of tools, data flow, and service communication, and separate UI wireframes were also prepared.

3. The system administrator started configuring and installing infrastructure and any new tool required to run this feature.

4. In parallel, developers got a high-level requirement analysis, and they started designing a development model, identifying people in the team with the required skill set, and preparing their machines to start coding.

5. The document was handed over to **Agile champions** (**ACs**), ones who track the changes and create features for the development team, and developers. There were multiple services and various modules to be written as part of this new feature.

6. ACs defined tasks for each developer and the sprint cycle as part of the Agile methodology. They also tracked development progress.

7. The development team is also responsible for building and integrating their code and deploying it to the development environment. To remove manual work, the dev team also automate some of the tasks.

8. As the dev finished the coding of a few modules, the code was deployed to the testing environment by the developers.

9. The testing team already created a test suite and started testing the code. They test and identify bugs and keep reporting the bugs to ACs.

10. ACs then identify dev capacity and assign defects to the dev plate for fixing.

11. This process of coding, testing, and defect fixing continues till all the modules are fully tested and the feature is bug-free. However, the timelines were set by the product team in advance.

12. Once the code is ready, it is deployed to the production environment by developers.

13. The operations team monitors the system for its performance.

The new era software development lifecycle model with SRE and DevOps. It represents the replacement of system administration and operational tasks by SRE and DevOps. System admin and operations are part of SRE and DevOps.

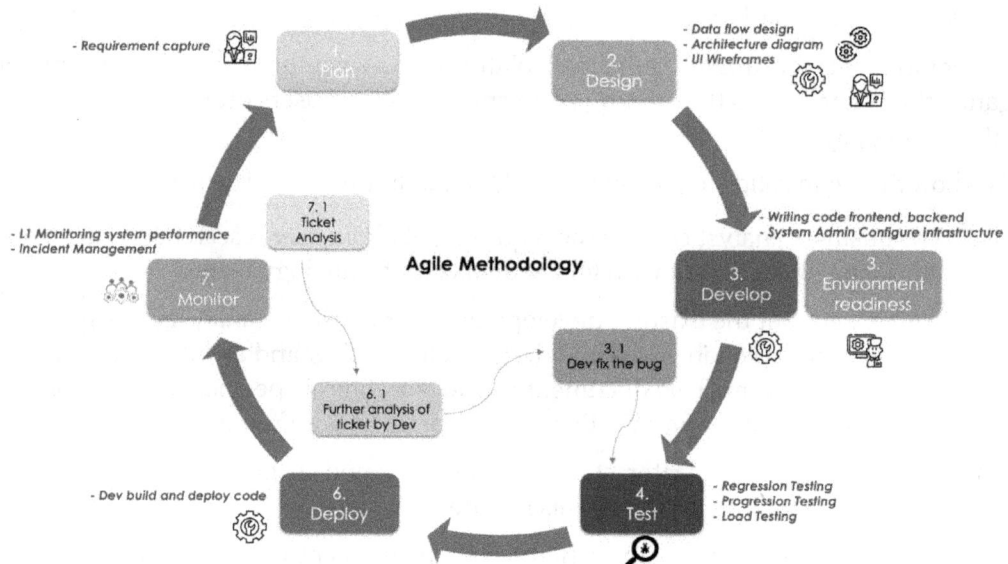

*Figure 2.2: Representation of SDLC: DevOps and SRE replaced by system admin and operation*

The preceding example is a scenario where the Agile approach is followed, and a new feature is ready in one month. As we know, nothing is perfect in the technology world, so let us assume there were multiple defects identified by testers in the last sprint cycle and one of the automations for building code started failing and not running as expected. This will impact the delivery timelines; hence, to meet timelines, developers might compromise with the quality standard and might deploy bad code in the production manually.

This problem can be solved by onboarding SRE and DevOps teams in their SDLC journey. The new team has business analysts, designers, developers, testers, DevOps, SRE, Agile champions, product management, and customer service.

Let us see what the flow of SDLC looks like with SRE and DevOps also part of this project:

1.  Business analysts collect the requirements from user researchers and create a requirement document with all the details for technology teams.

2.  Architects from the existing development team, business analysts, designers, DevOps SMEs, and SRE SMEs collaborated and designed a data flow and architecture of this new payment platform. This document includes technical specifications of tools, data flow, and service communication. Separate UI wireframes were also prepared. The document, this time, is more detailed and architecturally strong as it includes historical insights from the SRE team of the old payment model.

3.  The DevOps team is already using an automation tool for creating CI/CD pipelines. They re-used their tool and started creating pipelines so that the developers could use these automated pipelines to build and deploy their code. The DevOps team also automates the pipeline to integrate testing with the same pipeline.

4.  The DevOps team also created pipelines using tools to configure infrastructure as per requirement for SRE teams.

5.  In parallel, the SRE team started creating and monitoring dashboards and alerting tools and preparing the existing production environment to get this new feature released. For example, increasing CPU and memory of underlying infra to deploy this payment module.

6.  In parallel, developers have a high-level requirement analysis, and they start designing the development model, identifying people in the team with the required skill set, and preparing their machines to start coding.

7.  The document was handed over to ACs and developers. There were multiple services and various modules to be written as part of this new feature.

8.  ACs defined tasks for each developer and defined the sprint cycle as part of Agile methodology. They also track development progress.

9.  The development team is only responsible for writing the code and using the pipeline built by DevOps to build, deploy code and test. This saves them a lot of time and the dev can focus only on development.

10. As the dev finished coding a few modules, the code was deployed to the testing environment automatically with just one click.

11. The testing team already created a test suite, and they started testing the code. They test and identify bugs and keep reporting bugs to the ACs.

12. ACs then identify the dev capacity and assign defects to the dev plate for fixing.

13. The DevOps team creates a channel between dev and SRE, where their tools pull defect reports and share continuous change reports from AC to SRE. SRE reviews changes and suggests solutions if required. For example, one bug was an intermittent

failure in a testing environment, but any intermittent failure in production multiplies as there is more traffic of requests, which can impact customers.

14. This process of coding, testing, and defect fixing is continuous till all the modules are fully tested and the feature is bug-free. However, timelines were set by the product team in advance.

15. Once the code is ready, it is deployed to the production environment by the DevOps team after SRE approval.

16. The SRE team starts monitoring through dashboards and automated alerting. When a bug is identified, SRE teams are skilled at routing traffic to a working instance to avoid customer impact, and in parallel, they troubleshoot the issue.

Let us see how the problem in the previous flow is solved by the SRE and DevOps team. The testing team identified multiple bugs in the last cycle. The developers' team is focused on writing and fixing bugs. They have enough capacity in this design as the DevOps team is taking care of all automation. As things are automated, there are fewer chances of bugs in the system. Even if any automation fails, teams are working in parallel. Dev and DevOps teams have separate roles and fix different issues. As the bug was fixed on time and delivered to production, SRE teams monitor that flow, and if they still identify the bug, SRE teams have the option to disable the new feature and move all customers to the old payment platform. By doing this, though, customers will not be able to access new payment platforms, but they can still shop on e-commerce applications without failure.

The following figure represents the SDLC process with SRE and DevOps, including the root cause analysis phase, which is part of the SRE function:

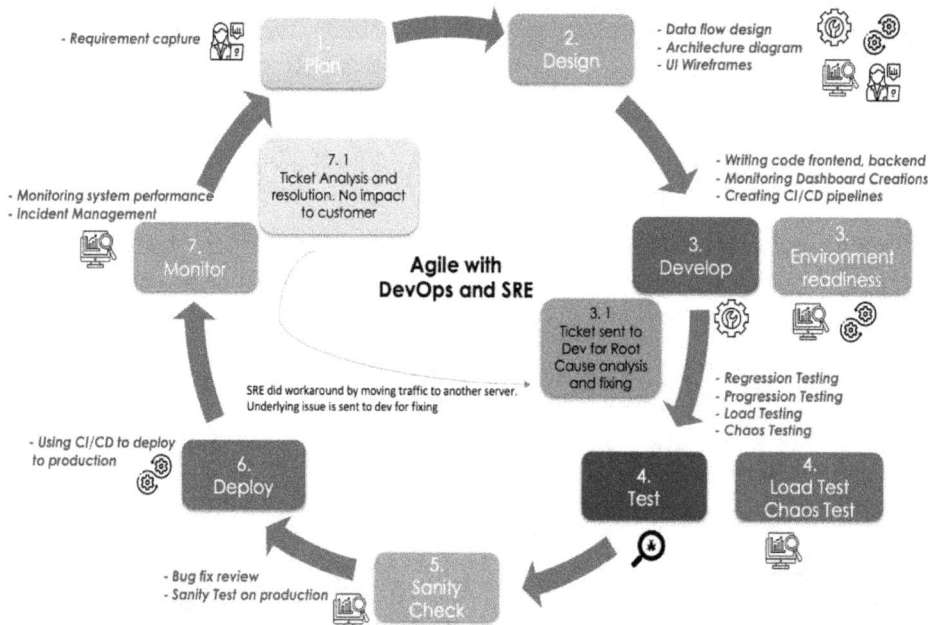

*Figure 2.3: Representation of onboarding SRE and DevOps to effectively deliver quality on time*

This example explains the importance of SRE and DevOps teams for any software project to deliver quality. DevOps creates CI/CD pipelines to help developers focus on writing the code. DevOps creates a transparent communication channel between developers and SRE through their tools. The automated pipelines also share reports to SRE before changes get released to production. This helps SRE gate-keep changes and ensure quality. SRE helps design code from a production perspective. It also defines the change management process (change management is a process of defining and implementing changes without fail). DevOps team automates this change management process through pipelines. That is how both teams work in harmony towards one goal: to deliver a quality and bug-free system with speed.

SRE and DevOps have various similarities. Some of the common practices between both are:

# Structured approach

DevOps and SRE both define processes with a structured approach to monitor production. Both ensure the effectiveness of operational management. A structured approach in software development means a clear definition of each task in every phase of development, defined roles, clear processes and standards, workflows, and data-flow diagrams. DevOps follows a structured approach such as clear CI/CD standards, a change management process, clear process of collaboration between dev and ops/SRE.

Similarly, SRE follows a defined incident management process, clear change management, gate controls process, and defined roles between automation and operations model.

# Automation

It is one of the key principles for both DevOps and SRE to automate as much as they can to reduce toil and save time, effort, and human error. Both teams focus on automating their day-to-day manual tasks with one goal, to empower the dev to focus on building quality code with velocity. DevOps automates CI/CD pipelines for dev to automatically build and deploy code. They automate these pipelines to deploy infra and code in production for the SRE/ops team to focus on monitoring rather than configuring the production environment.

SRE daily automation includes automating monitoring and alerting via the help of tools. SRE also automate an incident management system; the automated system resolves and notifies issues to SRE automatically. SRE teams also build tools that help dev to mimic production scenarios in a development environment.

# Quality control

Quality is one of the key metrics for businesses to measure system performance, and DevOps and SRE inculcate this metric in their **key performance indicators** (**KPIs**). Both functions focus on the quality of code getting deployed in production, which overlaps with automation. They automate tasks that put control at multiple steps, remove human intervention during deployment, and save time.

DevOps ensures quality by creating CI/CD to avoid any manual code commit and release. Multiple code reviews before it is integrated into the main code. Automated infrastructure configuration keeps consistent versions across.

SRE creates a strong quality control process, that defines what, when, and how changes will go into production. SRE defines a change management process to ensure DevOps implement controls in their pipeline that stop any faulty code from going into production. SRE reviews bugs with dev and testers before production as part of the quality check.

# Measuring

Organizations need to create metrics at every level to measure how SDLC performs, which in turn impacts the software performance. SRE and DevOps both approach practice measurement. Each of these functions has its KPIs defined that help them create metrics to measure how their model is performing, as that has a direct impact on software performance.

DevOps metrics are the time taken to build, fix bugs, deploy the code, frequency of development, lead time for changes, and change failure rate.

Some of the key SRE metrics are system availability, change failure rate in production, mean time to resolve the issue and mean time between failures.

These metrics help teams and businesses to track performance and improve if required. It also gives lead time early in SDLC to improve. Today, organizations regularly measure their system and each team's performance ensuring delivery on time.

# Change management

It is one of the components that bring SRE and DevOps together. Change management processes are tightly coupled with DevOps continuous integration and deployment approach.

SRE team defines the process for change, such as the timeline for change to be deployed, what changes are allowed in the system, multiple approval workflows before the change goes into production, the impact of change, fallback or rollback option available with each change. The DevOps team collects these processes, and guidelines and integrates them into the pipeline.

For example, the CD pipeline first validates change by comparing existing production vs change configuration. For any change that impacts production as per SRE guidelines, the pipeline will fail and not process the change further. Another example is DevOps integrating the approval process in the pipeline, where the leader has to review and approve the change; without the approval, the pipeline will not proceed further.

# Difference between SRE and DevOps

So far, you have learned the similarities between SRE and DevOps. In this section, we will cover how these two approaches are different from each other. As no *one-size-fits-all*, adopting SRE and DevOps approaches in SDLC is solely the organization's decision. These new methodologies help with quality and faster delivery, and many organizations are also adopting them for better performance of applications. SRE and DevOps were introduced to address different problems in the SDLC model. Though a lot of enhancements have been made to both approaches over many years, the goal remains the same. Some organizations onboard both the SRE and DevOps teams, and some organizations have only one, and that one team performs both functions, shared with dev teams.

DevOps is an approach to managing the software development process that collaborates between developers and the operations team. The DevOps team focuses on CI and CD of code and infra. They use the latest tools to create pipelines and automate CI/CD. This automation aims to save dev time by manually integrating the code. As there can be multiple developers working on a project, and each development can have a different timeline to complete, so integration and testing become difficult without automation. Automation also removes human intervention, so there are fewer chances of configuration errors. DevOps also uses automation to configure infrastructure. With just one click, the pipeline can scale up multiple similar config infra if required.

DevOps aims to improve communication between dev, testers, and ops/SRE teams through automation. As different teams involved in SDLC work together, they become aware of the entire project lifecycle timelines, which helps teams work effectively. Before the DevOps function, organizations used to work in silos where developers were not aware of the production system, and ops were not aware of the underlying code and timelines of development. That, in turn, created issues such as more time to identify and fix issues, a lot of time spent on manual tasks, and manual work leading to errors that compromised the quality of the system. DevOps was introduced to address these issues by opening a collaboration channel between teams.

SRE was invented to focus on designing and implementing highly scalable and reliable systems. The SRE team is responsible for monitoring the systems, automating, self-healing, alerting, and improving systems. These responsibilities can also be called the advanced role of the old operation model, which organizations sometimes refer to as L1 support. SRE teams are engineers who build tools to automate and reduce toil. SREs practice designing and implementing systems that can scale automatically, on-demand, and that can failover automatically.

For example, DevOps used CI/CD to create infrastructure. SRE developed tools that help infrastructure auto-heal in case of any failure to minimize end-user impact. The focus of SRE is operations, where they build tools to monitor the system to ensure 100% availability, and other operational aspects such as incident management, quality control, and audit control.

To better understand the role of both teams, let us consider a real scenario of an e-commerce project. The requirement of building a new payment feature and integrating the UPI option. The following is the structure:

- Team: analysts, architects, designers, developers, testers, product management, ACs, SRE, DevOps, customer service
- Latest tech stack on public cloud

Scenario:

- A team of analyst gather requirements and passes on the detailed information to architects and designers.
- Architects, designers, and SRE collaborated to design the architecture and data flow for this feature.
- The design was shared with all teams involved along with DevOps.
- DevOps team added new pipelines to integrate and deploy the code for this new feature.
- DevOps team also added a pipeline to scale up infra to support this new feature.
- Developers started to write code by using CI/CD for continuous development and deployment.
- The testing team started testing as part of CI/CD.
- The testing team identified bugs and then moved them to dev.
- ACs reviewed these bugs with SRE in case this can impact production with respect to load.
- Developers fix the bug, and the code gets deployed.
- In parallel SRE team also added new dashboards for this feature.
- After the code is deployed to production, SRE monitors the system through dashboards and alerting.
- SRE follows incident management to take any technical queries from customer service.
- SRE spent 50% of their time monitoring the production system and getting the report of system performance, including bugs, if any, problems and failures.
- The same SRE engineer will spend 50% of the time as a developer with the development team. As an engineer already has real-time scenarios of failures in production, he/she will take that feedback, collaborate with other developers, and start building solutions to solve these production issues.

As per the definition of SRE from Google, engineering practice should be incorporated into operations. SRE as the team was identified by Google, where a dedicated team of engineers who directly work on production applications (also called an operations team) should have access to collaborate with developers and enough tools to build automation that helps reduce errors in live software, providing seamless user experience. Google says SRE engineer should spend only 50% of their time on operational activities, and the remaining 50% should be spent on developing. In this model, engineers spending time in operations get exposed to live software and its problems. So that the remaining 50% of the engineer's time can be used to develop solutions to those problems. Unlike DevOps, where the development and operations teams work very closely, they are still two separate teams.

Each organization is different and has modified SRE and DevOps roles as per their requirement. Other than Google, many of the organizations have adopted the SRE and DevOps approach. Let us take a real scenario of how other organizations adopted SRE and DevOps. This organization is in the transition phase of adopting the SRE model, which is still not a mature model. A big financial technology organization SRE model is:

- The technology team structure is the same. Here are the teams: analysts, design, development, testing, product, DevOps, and SRE teams.

- This organization has separate SRE and DevOps teams.

- The role of SRE here is 70% operations and 30% engineering.

- As the organization is still in the nascent phase of adopting SRE. SRE engineers invest 2 months on operations tasks. As part of operations, the daily role is to support applications, support infrastructure, monitor production systems, identify false alerting, create new alerting, create dashboards, identify areas of automation, identify bugs in systems and log those bugs, identify areas of system design improvements to improve the overall performance of the system. After working for 2 months in operations, the same SRE engineer moves to a development role. The daily tasks in the development role are automating the manual tasks (identified during operations), building tools to support SRE and development teams, fixing some of the bugs, and collaborating with developers to re-design systems wherever required.

- The DevOps team in this organization creates CI/CD pipelines to help developers build and deploy their code to multiple environments without many interventions. DevOps engineers also collaborate with SRE and developers for change and release management, ensuring correct and quality changes are merged into the main code. They act as a bridge between development and SRE concerning continuous development and deployment.

The following is a summary of the difference between SRE and DevOps from different aspects:

SRE and DevOps Differences

| Parameter | DevOps | SRE |
|---|---|---|
| Definition | An approach to manage software development process that collaborates between development and operations team. | An approach to design system that is highly reliable, scalable, and resilient. |
| Focus | It focuses is more on the development side of SDLC. Where it defines how to speed up and improve quality of development process. | It focuses on the operation side of SDLC. Where it defines how to improve operations by automations, standards, and process, ensuring quality and availability. |
| Approach | Cross-functional by opening collaboration channel between development teams. Use automation tool to implement collaboration. | Enabling strong observability through dashboards and automations. Empower development teams to deliver quality code. |
| Goal | Improve communications between software development groups to work together effectively and break silos. | To ensure scalability and reliability of system for minimum customer impact through various automations and practices. |
| Tools | CI/CD tools —Jenkins, Ansible, Chef, Terraform<br><br>Container management software — Kubernets<br><br>Source code software —Git, Jira<br><br>Collaboration tools—Slack, Microsoft teams<br><br>Cloud is common with SRE | Monitoring tools—ELK, Prometheus, Splunk, App Dynamics, Grafana<br><br>Ticket management tools—Service now, Jira, pager duty<br><br>Collaboration tools - (same as DevOps).<br><br>Automation tools—Shell, Python, Java, Jenkins. Cloud |

The following figure represents the similarities and differences of SRE and DevOps:

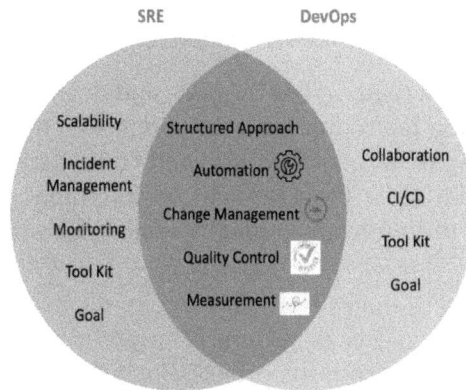

*Figure 2.4: SRE and DevOps*

# New era SDLC model

Over a period, software organizations have adopted various SDLC models to develop faster, quality, and reliable systems to give a smooth experience to end-users. SRE and DevOps both were introduced to the software industry around the '90s and the early 2000s. Since then, both of these approaches also matured as per the market demand. In the previous chapter, you learned the importance of SRE in the SDLC model and how the SRE team helps achieve business goals. There were a few examples demonstrated earlier that also explained the importance of DevOps and gave you a basic understanding of its role in SDLC.

SRE and DevOps working harmoniously with development teams is the recipe for a successful software system. It depends on the type of software project, software requirement, business need, type of organization, budget assigned, and many other such factors for any organization to decide if they need both SRE and DevOps as part of their SDCL or one of them or even none of these approaches. And that is ok if the organization can achieve the goal even without both functions. SRE and DevOps are the approaches for modern applications and are proven methodologies for successful software projects.

Earlier SDLC models did not find the need to invent or use any of these SRE/DevOps approaches. However, with the increase in demand, the requirements for technological advancements in business also changed. Now, organizations need to deliver faster and to deliver fast; they need to code fast and, in turn, must improve the SDLC process. There were various gaps and problems identified in earlier SDLC models that blocked the pace of development. To understand the importance of SRE and DevOps in today's SDLC, let us understand the problems faced by organizations in earlier development lifecycle models.

The very known and tested SDLC model in Waterfall was used by many organizations in the early 90's. The Waterfall is a linear model where the start of each phase depends on the success of the previous phase. The problem with the Waterfall model is each team works in a silo. They are not aware of the timeline and progress of other phases. This blurs the vision of teams, and they face difficulties in visualizing the final product.

For example, the development team writes the code and does unit testing, and they cannot send their code to the testing team unless all the services in the application are built and integrated. Once the testing team gets the packaged code, they start testing and identify bugs. But they cannot send a few bugs back to development till the full application is tested. So, the dev and the testing team sit ideally while others are working.

Let us take another example.

The timeline of Waterfall projects is around 6 months to 1 year, and requirement gathering happens only at the start of the project. So, if the customer or client wants new requirements to be added to the application, the Waterfall model does not allow that. Any few requirements identified mid-way must wait for the last phase of the Waterfall to complete. With fast-paced technology, organizations started seeing blockers in the Waterfall model. There was manual and repetitive work, the team was not able to code faster, and it was a waste of time and effort.

The following is a representation of the Waterfall model, which is linear, as explained. Each phase is input to the next phase, but teams in each phase work in silos, and there is no collaboration between phases.

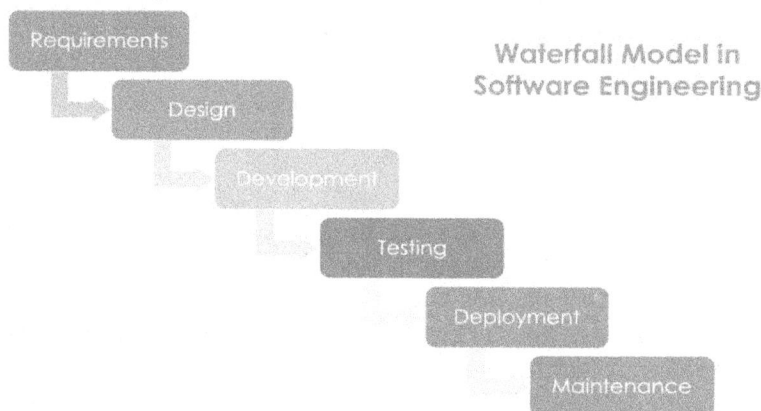

*Figure 2.5: Waterfall model in software development lifecycle*

To solve these problems, Agile methodology was invented. It is a set of best practices that ensure continuous development and continuous delivery with a small sprint cycle. Where development teams get requirements as a part of multiple small features, they take one or two weeks to write the code for features and deliver it to the testing team. So, coding and delivery happened in a small chunk of features. This gives lead time to the development team to react faster if anything goes wrong or if new requirements are published. Agile also promotes micro-service architecture, where small independent services are built, tested, and deployed without impacting the full application.

Agile methodology worked best to address gaps in the Waterfall model, and software teams were able to pace up the development. However, as technology grows, customers also mature and advance in technology usage. This leads to more usage of software applications and increased traffic. With increased customer load on applications, organizations had to ensure the scalability of the system. So, they need a strong operations team to manage the production environment. The Agile approach faced some gaps where developers and operations teams were working in silos, as dev and ops were not communicating, and teams were not aware of each other practices and approaches followed. Though they were a part of the same project, both teams had different approaches and different tools. They might have the same use case, but different tools were used to solve the use case. That is a waste of time, effort, and money. Along with that, developers write code without any perspective of production. For example, the dev does not know how the system behaves with high traffic, and they never implemented auto-run of service if any service fails.

The following is a representation of the Agile approach. It shows how SDLC has grown from Waterfall to Agile. The Agile approach is where teams in all these phases give input to the next phase, like a Waterfall, but there is a closed loop between the first and last phases. The difference between Agile and Waterfall is that the review phase gives input to the plan phase in a repetitive manner. However, as explained, there are still teams that do not collaborate directly with each other, and to solve this problem, the DevOps methodology was introduced as follows:

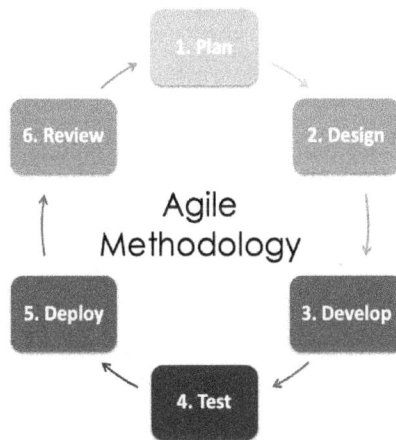

*Figure 2.6: Agile methodology in SDLC*

To solve the problem in the Agile approach, DevOps was introduced. The underlying approach for DevOps is a collaboration between dev and ops using automation tools. DevOps, along with Agile, addressed a lot of gaps in SDLC. Adopting DevOps helps dev and ops to collaborate regularly. It gives visibility of timelines, approaches, tools used, and, if required, re-using the tools. This increased the speed of development as ops were included during development, and they could share their ideas and strategies during the early development phase. It also ensures quality as developers are now focused on writing code. Building and deploying ownership moved to DevOps. The DevOps team was automated through pipelines that removed manual intervention.

The following is a representation of the Agile approach with DevOps methodology in software development:

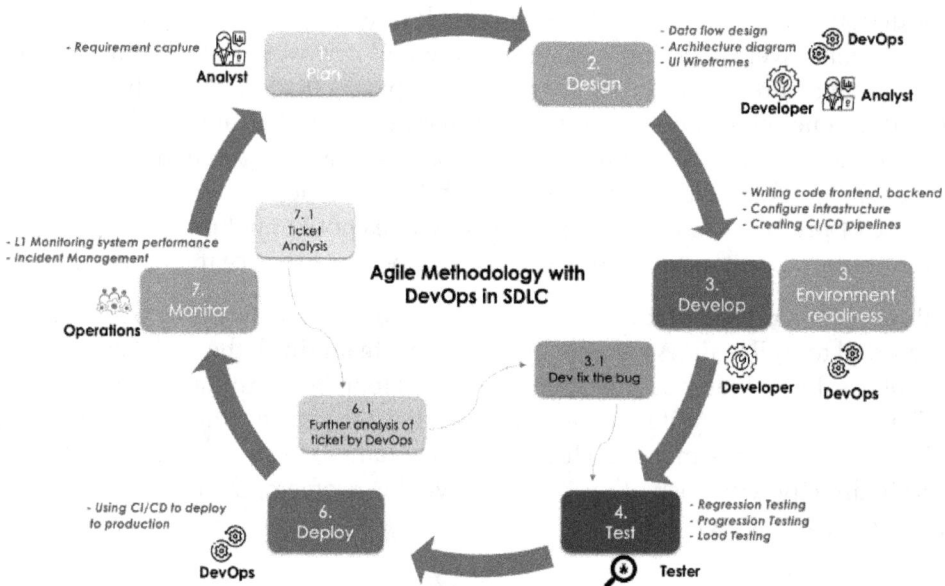

*Figure 2.7: Agile methodology with DevOps in SDLC*

DevOps with Agile is one of the best approaches to follow for a successful software project. However, with the accessibility of the internet and mobile phones, there was a continuous increase in demand to scale up software applications and ensure availability 24/7. The operations team is the soul of any software application when it comes to live and production environments. Organizations also needed to scale up operations teams to meet high demand. SRE was introduced to address this problem. The goal of SRE is to design and implement scalable systems and ensure reliability. Earlier, the ops team was more focused on L1 and L2 support. However, SRE is a team of engineers who develop tools, implement self-services, and auto-heal functionality in production systems along with operations. SRE engineers also build interactive dashboards and automated alerting systems to proactively identify any problem in the system before the customers notice it. As they are skilled engineers, they have the knowledge to resolve code and infra issues in a production environment.

SRE and DevOps following the Agile SDLC approach are the recipe for success for any software project. However, onboarding multiple teams with different skill sets can be expensive, so organizations must decide depending on their requirement. These new approaches help software development teams to work effectively and focus on the end goal. Organizations can also change the roles and responsibilities of DevOps and SRE teams as per their requirements, but the underlying aim should be followed. SRE and DevOps overlap in various phases of SDLC, but the role of each team is different. Organizations are adopting both functions to effectively release their product in the market.

The following is a representation of SDLC where Agile and SRE are both part of the software development:

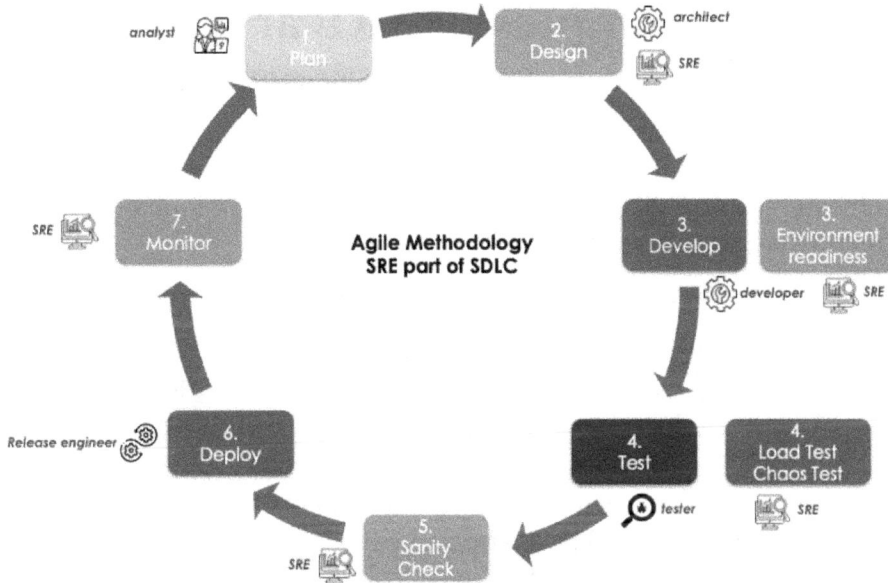

*Figure 2.8: Agile methodology with SRE in SDLC*

The following is a representation of Agile, DevOps, and SRE, all three in SDLC:

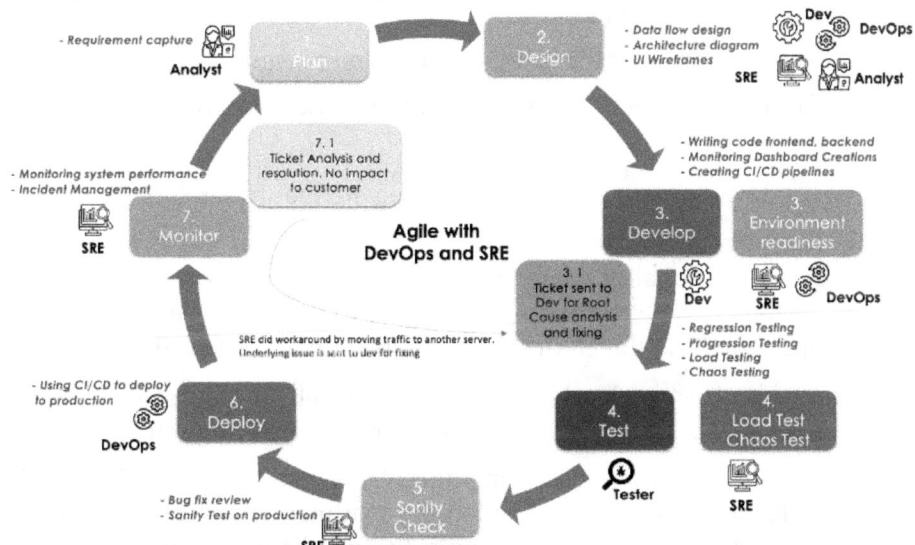

*Figure 2.9: Agile methodology with SRE and DevOps in SDLC*

The aforementioned figure explains the combination of DevOps and SRE working together in an Agile approach to software development.

All five aforementioned figures show the evolution of the software development approach from Waterfall to Agile to DevOps to SRE.

# Real-world examples of SRE and DevOps

Let us go through some real-world examples of how SRE and DevOps help software development projects and what their role is, as follows:

- **Project**: A financial technology organization decided to migrate its old banking software to a new platform hosted on cloud technology and an application that can run on the mobile devices of its customers.

- **Structure of project**: The structure of the project is as follows:
  - Business allotted budget for this new project.
  - Technology teams got onboarded, i.e., analysts, developers, designers, testers, product management, SRE, DevOps, and customer service.
  - A high-level tech stack was planned, such as AWS cloud was selected, databases were planned (NoSQL and RDBMS both), Java as a backend language, React and Java Script as front-end language, GitHub as source code repository, application monitoring tools, Infrastructure monitoring tools, and other open-source tools required to complete the application were planned.
  - The timeline for the project was planned for one year. Along with that, milestones were decided, where the first batch of software applications will be rolled out in 5 months.
  - The methodology for SDLC was decided as Agile.
  - Business and technology leadership planned the roadmap and onboarded all the resources.

- **Software development flow**: The following are the steps required:
  1. Business analysts capture the requirements of projects. Such as high-level functionality where a software application should have UI to log in, customers can see their account details, transfer money, invest through the app, purchase shares, and get real-time account analysis.
  2. Architects and subject matter experts from all the teams collaborate to design data flow diagrams and architecture flow (including infra design).
  3. Steps 1 and 2 are also sometimes called the planning phase. All leaders collaborate to design and plan the roadmap and the high-level design of the software project, along with the timelines, number of teams needed

to be onboarded, skills required to complete the project, hiring process, purchasing infrastructure, and all the other planning.

4. From this step, the actual development starts:

   a. The UI designers started building wireframes, and in parallel, the development team started writing the code.

   b. The product management and ACs designed the development roadmap. As part of the Agile practice, the project was broken down into multiple small services; each service was broken down into modules. Then, these modules were assigned as tasks to each developer.

   c. Developers were given 2 weeks to complete one module development.

5. The DevOps team started creating the CI/CD pipelines using automation tools. They Prepared to configure environments through CI/CD, such as installing software, databases, and other tools. They also created pipelines to automatically pull code from GitHub (as soon as developers commit their code) and build and deploy the code to development, testing, and the production environment.

6. SRE teams start creating the skeleton of monitoring dashboards. As soon as modules and services are complete, the SRE team collaborates with the dev through the pipeline and adds monitoring modules to their dashboards.

7. Steps 4 to 6 happen in parallel. These steps sometimes overlap, or there is a gap of one or two weeks.

8. After DevOps configures their pipelines, the code automatically gets deployed to the testing environment and testers start their testing.

9. The process of coding and testing happens in continuous mode. Dev does not wait for all services code to complete. As it is micro-service architecture and services are independent of each other, testing and coding happen in parallel.

10. Once DevOps installs production infrastructure. The DevOps and SRE teams collaborate to validate the environment by doing a sanity check.

11. Steps 9-10 happen in parallel.

12. As the full application is tested, environments are validated. With the help of CI/CD, the DevOps team deploys the code to the production environment after the SRE review.

13. SRE now monitors the production environment. If there is any failure in the system, the SRE team resolves the failure. If a bug in code is identified, the SRE team reports to the dev team to fix the code and deploy the fix in production.

14. The first version of the application was released in 5 months as part of the first milestone.

SDLC is an ongoing process. As part of these operations, the SRE team monitors the application and identifies a few bugs in the code. Some customers reported complaints through customer service. Customer service logged the complaints in a ticket. The ticket was moved to the SRE queue for further analysis. This process is called **incident management**. As part of the SRE responsibilities, the incident management process was outlined, where the priority of tickets, SLA to respond to tickets, workflow of tickets, and response channel were planned.

Continuing the same project scenario, let us take another case. One of the bugs in the system was that the customer was not able to generate statements for more than six months.

The following is the breakdown of the events:

1.  The SRE team analyzed the bug and identified a service that is failing for memory. So, SRE scaled up the database, but that did not solve the issue.

2.  SRE then moved the ticket to the dev team queue. Dev was not able to replicate the scenario as they do not have enough data in their dev environment. To replicate, the dev wanted similar data in the development environment.

3.  The development team took 1 day to finally resolve the bug and fix it in production.

4.  It was a loss of 1 day to the business.

5.  Financial technology companies are conservative about data, and as per policy, sensitive data such as customer card numbers cannot be stored locally.

6.  SRE proactively addressed this gap and decided to build a tool for dev teams to mimic production data and create sample data.

7.  A few days later, another similar bug was identified in the application. So, the dev used the tool built by SRE to create the sample data and replicate the scenario within a few hours, and the fix went into production on time.

The problem statement in the aforementioned scenario is that the monthly statement customer journey is not working, decreasing the overall availability of the system to 99.888% from 99.999%. Also, it increased the MTTR and decreased MTBF. After SRE addressed the problem in the above scenario, MTTR was decreased (as teams were able to quickly fix the problem and recover systems). That, in turn, increased the overall availability of the system. SRE involvement also solved decreased MTBF determines the frequency of failures or time between two failures. This helps understand software reliability. More time between failures means the system is more reliable). To solve MTBF, SRE and development teams collaborate and identify the root cause of the problem. As the SRE tool helped replicate the scenario in a testing environment, software development teams could pinpoint the root cause and fix the problem faster. A faster fix in the system increased MTBF and improved overall reliability.

Let us explore every phase of SDLC via diagrammatic representation. The following figure is a detailed version of the steps mentioned aforementioned:

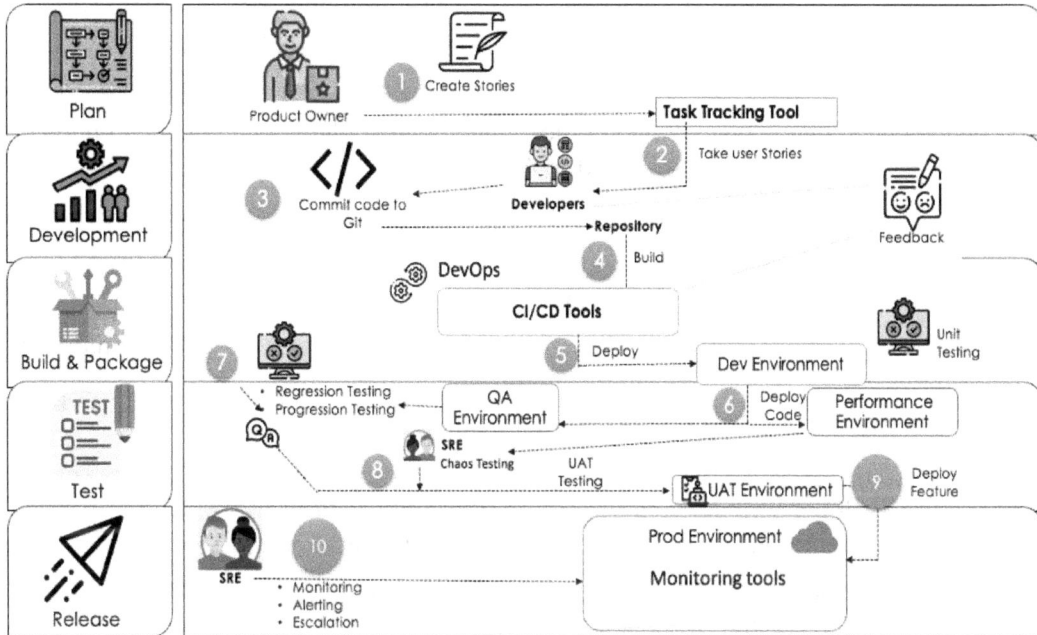

*Figure 2.10: SDLC flow for a software project*

The preceding figure is a software development lifecycle after business requirements. In the earlier examples, you have seen the plan as the first phase of SDLC, where the analysts capture requirements from businesses and share the recorded requirements with the software team for designing the data flow and architecture. The aforementioned figure is the sub-flow in SDLC where the actual coding and deployment happens.

The following steps are a brief description of this sub-flow:

1. This is the first swim lane in the figure, referred to as the planning phase.

    a. After product owners or Agile champions get the design and requirements from the business, they break the design into multiple features (a feature is a service/function that provides business value).

    b. Features are divided into user stories (user stories are a way of describing that service/function in plain language. It defines tasks for developers).

    c. All the user stories get stored in a task-tracking tool (Jira is one such tool).

2. Developers are assigned to these user stories by the product owners.

3. Developers start writing code on their machine (referred to as local code). Then once it completes, they commit their code to the source repository (*GitHub* is one such repository tool).

4. The DevOps team creates the CI/CD pipeline and gives the pipeline to the dev teams (*Jenkins* is one such tool).

5.  The dev team uses the CI/CD pipeline for building and packaging the code and the same pipeline to deploy the code to the development environment.

6.  At this step, the dev team performs multiple actions of testing and deploying the code.

    a.  The dev team performs unit testing and deploys code to the testing environment, also referred to as the QA environment.

    b.  The dev team also deploys the same code to the performance environment.

7.  The QA team (testing team) starts their testing. There are different types of testing regression, progression, performance, etc.

8.  This step is again multiple tasks as after multiple testing, code gets merged, and it gets deployed to the UAT environment.

    a.  The SRE team did chaos and performance testing.

    b.  After the QA and SRE complete their testing, the final packaging of code is done, and it is deployed in the UAT environment (user acceptance environment- pre-production env to mimic production).

9.  After the UAT testing is complete, the code gets deployed to production via CI/CD pipelines created by DevOps.

10. SRE monitors system performance, takes care of any issues in the system, and escalates to respective teams if required.

This process repeats depending on the sprint cycle timelines.

There are multiple such scenarios where the SRE and DevOps teams help address and resolve issues. These approaches were introduced to empower development and operations. Though they do not go and fix bugs in the code, they help developers act fast to avoid impact on the application. Today, software organizations are moving at a very high pace. Every day, some or the other technology is getting introduced in some part of the world. Everyone is working towards the goal of using technology to solve the problems of end-users. The role of both SRE and DevOps is also changing depending on the type of requirements.

# Conclusion

In this chapter, we discussed the SRE and DevOps functions. Both these functions are changing the SDLC model for modern software applications. The adoption of these methodologies and Agile is a proven recipe for success. Moreover, we covered some real examples from industries on SDLC with various phases.

In the next chapter, we will explore SRE and how we can build effective solutions using its principles. We will also discuss in detail the various ways to achieve successful software building with the help of some scenarios derived from various industries on how they solved challenges around building reliability in their software system to give best-in-class user experiences.

# CHAPTER 3
# Build Effective Solutions with SRE

## Introduction

In the previous chapters, we discussed SRE and its importance in today's IT world.

In this chapter, we will understand how to deliver efficient software solutions using the SRE methodology. We will also get a detailed description of multiple facets of SRE and their specific techniques for a successful software development project. Additionally, this chapter will also walk you through real-time scenarios where the SRE approach helped software organizations achieve their goals. Indeed, in a recent survey, 75% of organizations using SRE have reported improved service reliability.

## Structure

In this chapter, we will cover the following topics:

- Building scalable, reliable, and available system
- Capacity planning and cost management
- Importance of testing
- Using monitoring and observability tools
- Build strong incident management process
- Automate to reduce toil

- CAMS model as an SRE essential
- Agnostic approach
- No measurement no improvement

# Objectives

By the end of this chapter, you will be able to understand how to build effective software systems by using SRE principles. The chapter also highlights the importance of collaboration between all cross-functional engineering teams, which will help you visualize software development as a whole. Moreover, we will understand how these SRE principles help advance software development. Along with the theory, the chapter explains some examples to relate the actual use of the SRE approach.

# Building scalable, reliable, and available systems

Every organization today aims to build a software solution that can scale on demand, be always available to the end-users, and be reliable. These are the key factors in the design and development of software systems, as these factors decide its future. Any unavailable software that cannot fulfill user requests can never sustain itself in today's competitive world. These seem simple factors, but they are not easy to implement. It requires detailed architectural design and development to achieve them. Let us understand the meaning of all the factors in detail.

Before we examine the factors of a reliable system in depth, let us discuss the following summary of the key differences between traditional scaling and modern SRE-driven scaling methods.

Difference between traditional and modern scaling is as follows:

| | Scaling speed | Resource utilization | Response time |
|---|---|---|---|
| **Traditional scaling** | Manual and slow | Inefficient and non-balanced allocation | Delayed |
| **Modern scaling** | Automated and real-time | Optimized by autoscaling | Immediate |

*Table 3.1: Difference between traditional and modern scaling*

# Scalability

It refers to designing solutions that continue to function efficiently with a growing number of end users. That is a system that can handle any number of user requests. It handles the increased user requests by scaling itself. Scaling in software engineering means a system increases its performance on demand.

Scalability does not always mean increasing the performance on demand. It also means that the system can scale down when not in use or when the end-user requests to slow down. The scaling up and scaling down capability of a system defines its scalability. Scaling up helps software meet customer's demands and load. Meanwhile, scaling down helps organizations save extra costs by cutting down infrastructure resources not in use.

A system is composed of services and components. Each service or component's scaling has to be handled separately to scale the system as a whole. Today, scalability is one of the key features to be considered as part of any software product delivery. Since this is for a production environment that is a real-time application, the SRE team comes into the picture. Scalability is one of the objectives and key results for SRE teams, and it is also one of their primary goals. They use tools and automations to implement automated scalability in the system. To scale infrastructure, the underlying service code should also be able to scale up along with the infrastructure. Before SRE and DevOps were established, the system admin teams in IT organizations used to scale up infrastructure (servers, databases, etc.) as per the demand. However, the scale-up was not real-time. As part of the scaling system, admin teams get requirements from operations and clone existing services as per the requirements. Since cloning and creating a new instance of a service takes time, organizations were unable to scale up in real-time. The system admin teams started automating the scaling process to overcome this challenge. For example, creating automation that will copy the current configurations of service and application servers, create a new server, and install the service on this new server. However, someone must run this automation once they get a request from the operations teams. They used to receive tickets on the basis of traffic from customers or end-users. The automation of creating a new server is referred to as scaling; even with automation, scaling was not real-time. This full process was time-consuming and led to a decline in user usage of the system.

In the previous chapter, we discussed the reason for SRE's introduction. This section will address how SRE solves the problem of system performance. The SRE team replaced old-fashioned operations and system admin roles. Let us understand how SRE teams implement scalability.

After software organizations adopted cloud technology, they also changed the software design from monolith architecture to microservice architecture, as cloud technology complements the microservice architecture. As mentioned earlier, for any system to scale up, the underlying code must also scale up to support the entire system's scaling. SRE teams use tools to automate the process of scaling. Automation uses triggers on a threshold.

As soon as traffic exceeds the threshold limit, the automation gets triggered, enabling another instance, which in turn adds a new server to handle the incoming traffic load. This is called schedule-based scaling (depending on the traffic pattern, it allows you to scale up or down). Let us understand this in depth to compare it with the traditional model.

For example, consider a banking software system using ten application servers across geographies. The traffic threshold defined is 80%. It has microservices running on all ten servers.

In the **software development lifecycle (SDLC)** model, the following are the implementation steps that SRE follows as part of production readiness:

- Creating a metric dashboard to calculate traffic.

- Configuring alerts on the metric dashboard.

- Automating manual tasks using automation tools, for example, Ansible. As part of automation, the team created playbooks defining trigger points, various template creations, etc. Automation tools: you can write playbooks to define what infrastructure to create, what configuration to use, when to create, how to create, etc.

The following is a scenario based on the aforementioned example:

On a sale day, customer traffic hit 80%. That triggers automation through the metric. Automation already had all the required configurations, and it just added one more instance to the server. It also installed all the required services on that new server along with configuration. That scaled up the system, and the system was able to handle customer load. These playbooks were written by SRE teams (or the DevOps team in some cases) as part of system configuration. Playbooks consist of definitions of each service and infrastructure, along with all dependencies and a master script that triggers these paybooks based on requirements. The automation is also built to scale down if customer traffic goes down to a certain limit. So, as the tool received the trigger, it scaled down one of the servers.

# Patterns used in scalability

The following are some patterns used in scalability:

- **Horizontal scaling**: The cloning of existing services or applications can be easily distributed across all the running instances. In simple language, it is adding more machines or nodes to the current system.

  Let us take an example of horizontal scaling of different components in a system, such as a service and database. The following figure represents the horizontal scaling of DB and application nodes:

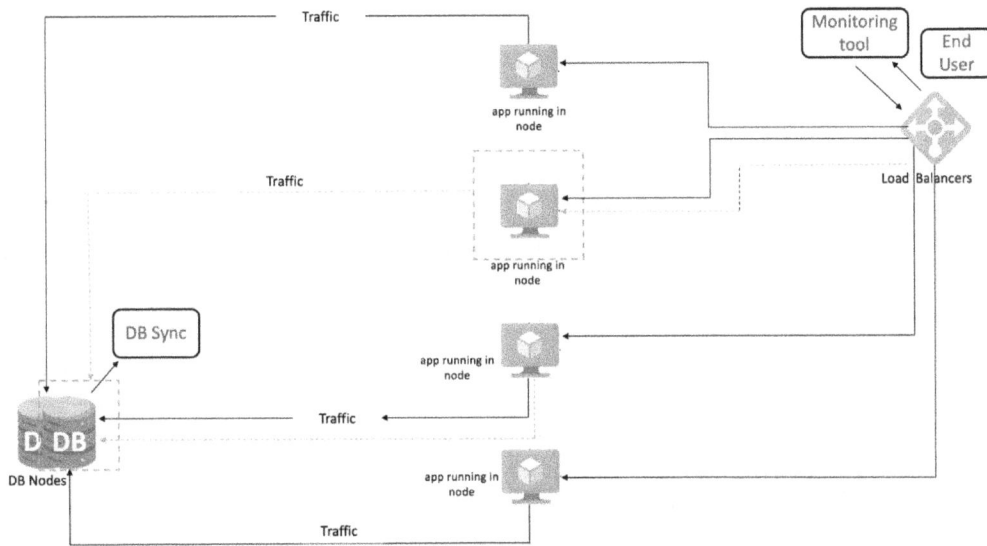

***Figure 3.1:*** *Application node and DB node horizontal scaling*

The preceding figure consists of services or applications running in four nodes (also called application servers). There is a load balancer service to balance the load, a database server with two nodes, and a monitoring tool that monitors the system. The figure is a representation after scaling up (dotted lines represent scaled-up infrastructure).

The sequential steps for scaling up are as follows:

1. The load balancer receives the request from end users. It measures the traffic and sends the data to the monitoring tool.

2. As the traffic requests go beyond 80%, the load balancer sends a request to the monitoring tool about high traffic load, and the monitoring tool internally triggers the automation tool.

3. Along with high customer requests, the system also noticed high read-write requests to the database. The high read-write requests triggered the Automation tool via load balancer and monitoring. Then automation tool further triggers the database to scale up the DB instance.

4. These playbooks or scripts clone the existing database node and create another node.

5. It also then clones the existing application server. Install the application in a new server and add this new node to the system.

6. As soon as new nodes are added, the load balancer identifies them via IP address and starts sending requests to the new application node.

7. This new application node then identifies database nodes and sends a request to the new nodes. One of the old application nodes also identifies a new DB node, and to balance the load on the system, it also moves its traffic to new DB nodes (load balancing algorithms are configured during the initial phase of system designing. And the DevOps team writes the infrastructure code and takes care of the load balancing configuration).

- **Vertical scaling**: This refers to adding more power/resources to an existing system without adding any new machines or nodes. Adding a CPU or memory to the existing machine is one such example of vertical scaling.

  Let us take the example of scenarios where vertical scaling works. SRE gets an alert via the monitoring tools on one of the failing services in an application, and the error displays out-of-memory logs for the failing service. SRE has configured auto scale-up of underlying memory on receiving out-of-memory alerts. The automation tool triggered the memory configuration and increased the memory of the existing node or application server on which the application was running. This is also called CPU-based scaling.

  There are multiple scenarios, and a decision needs to be taken accordingly to choose between vertical and horizontal scaling. A few cases are discussed as follows:

  o **Horizontal**: Used to distribute load evenly. Suppose resources are already running at their maximum capacity. Also used if maintenance is required by one of the nodes.

  o **Vertical**: Used when resources are running out of memory and existing resources have capacity available.

To make the system scalable, some of the best practices to be used are as follows:

- **Measuring**: There are various tools available to measure these metrics. However, performing chaos and load testing of the system helps identify the baseline and threshold of the system.

  Here are some metrics to monitor the scalability of the system:

  o Number of concurrent users a system can handle at a given point in time.

  o Maximum RAM and CPU of each component the system can handle.

  o Maximum volume of data that the system can handle without failure.

  o A number of new resources can be added with a high load.

- **Proactive automation**: Create responsive scaling rules. Adding any new resource or capacity can take time. So, SRE teams should always keep n+1 capacity in the buffer. As soon as there is a spike in traffic, your scaling configuration can instantly scale up resources.

- **Create separate scaling configurations of different components**: Each component in the system has different scale-up requirements. SRE teams should write separate configurations for each component so that they can be scaled up individually.

To understand better, let us take a brief case study of a well-known *Netflix* on leveraging modern SRE practices to improve the scalability and reliability of the system.

Netflix has some major challenges, such as scalability, accommodating millions of users, reliability, uninterrupted service and minimal downtime, and performance, high-quality video. To solve scalability, Netflix leverages horizontal scaling using AWS auto-scaling to dynamically add/remove instances based on traffic demand, ensuring seamless streaming.

# Reliability

In theory, it means the percentage of failure-free systems for a specified period of time. It is one of the measures of system quality. Achieving 100% software reliability is hard, due to the complexity of today's software systems. However, there are software (tools) available to help organizations achieve at least 99.9999% of reliability.

The name of SRE itself is site reliability engineering. Reliability is one of the most important factors of SRE methodology. It defines the extent to which a software system is reliable, i.e., performs as per requirement, on request.

Let us see reliability and scalability through one lens as a part of the system. Scalability is defined by how efficiently a system can perform and handle the increasing demand of end-users without compromising the quality. Reliability defines the extent to which any system can maintain its functionality and service level without errors. Together, they define software performance. For example, a software application that does not fail and is functioning as per requirement, and customers are able to use the application without any problem of failure, is reliable. Scalability of the system is when the software application is able to run without any lag, not getting hung even when multiple users are using the application. In the previous section, we learned about the scalability of the system. Now, let us see how we add reliability to the system.

Reliability is not a one-stop shop that can be added to software; it is a process. The software should be designed with reliability from the beginning. That means that while designing the software, you must include techniques such as fault tolerance, redundancy, error handling, and rigorous testing to identify errors. With time, software requirements changed, and that led organizations to adopt modern software development approaches such as Agile, DevOps, and SRE. The software's architecture was changed from monolith to micro-service, which helped the reliability of the system but also increased complexity. With increased complexity, the reliability of the system became more critical to deliver and manage. So, new approaches were introduced for development and operations to help build reliable systems.

# Delivery of a reliable system

The approach that should be implemented in the SDLC process to ensure reliability is as follows:

- **Design reviews**: It involves examining proposed design changes or new designs to ensure it does not impact the existing system. Also, examining the new design covers all aspects of system failure recovery. Design reviews are part of the initial phase of SDLC, and to have these reviews covered from all aspects, you should involve development architects, product managers, SRE, DevOps, and testing **subject matter experts** (**SMEs**). The involvement of SMEs from different aspects of SDLC brings diverse ideas and enables you to inspect any system design from multiple directions. For example, a software architect defines the data flow and identifies the underlying code dependencies on infrastructure, product managers define the business flow and give inputs on use cases for the business requirements to help architects build data flow, SRE gives perspective on production flow, DevOps helps define the implementation of the infrastructure required to run any application, and testers help define the feasibility of test cases. The initial discussion on review generally involves multiple brainstorming sessions where these SME go through the design in detail and identify if any of the flow can cause failure and how to handle that failure in the system. The key to design review is to involve SMEs from all SDLC teams, to have multiple perspectives, to improve quality, and to make required changes in the software at the initial stage.

- **Code reviews for quality**: Similar to design reviews, code reviews are one of the important key factors in ensuring the reliability of the system. Though code reviews are mostly considered software development's best practice approach, they indirectly impact the reliability of a system. The better the code quality is, the lesser the chances of software defects. The less defects mean that the system is error-free and stable. Code review is one of the processes that helps improve code quality. There are different processes organizations follow in SDLC to improve code quality, such as advanced tools to catch any syntax or semantics errors in code, implement best practices while writing code, and review of these best practices to ensure the approaches are being followed. Code review should be included in the development process, where developers write their code, commit code in the central repository, for example, GitHub, then create a pull request. This pull request should be approved by SMEs after reviewing the code. Once approved, the code gets merged into the main branch (this is the code repository that is the source of truth, and all the latest code is merged to the main repository) along with other code. This process should be part of any code version control software. GitHub is one of the examples and is often used in software organizations.

- **Testing**: It involves testing the software system thoroughly before releasing code to production or the live environment. Testing is one of the key factors in software development. Software quality depends a lot on the testing process. There are various types of testing that can be implemented in the SDLC process. After code is developed by developers, testers or quality analysts run multiple test cases to cover the system from all aspects and identify any bug or defect in the system. If any defect is identified during the testing process, the code is sent back to the developer for fixing. Different types of testing that you should include in your SDLC are as follows:

- o Unit testing (breaking code into smaller parts such as modules and testing each small part).

- o Regression testing (testing to ensure new code does not break old functionality).

- o Progression testing (testing each new code for any new defects).

- o Load testing (testing with increased load on the system, such as an increased number of user requests hitting software).

- o Chaos testing (deliberate ingestion of failure into the system in a test environment to assess how the system responds to failure and then fixes accordingly).

All this testing helps run multiple test cases on software systems and access system reliability and ability to respond to failures. Testing helps identify bugs in the system before it is released to the production environment and gives developers the opportunity to fix the issue. Testing also includes infrastructure testing, such as Chaos testing. DevOps and SRE, generally perform chaos testing to catch infrastructure issues.

- **Self-healing**: It involves the ability of the system to detect and remediate issues without human intervention. Self-healing is one of the important factors in increasing the reliability of the system. When the system identifies issues and fixes them automatically, it means there is very minimal impact on end-users, or end-users might not even notice this failure, or in the next attempt, their request might be successful. To ensure reliability in the system, you should implement self-healing capabilities within the code and as part of observability. Implementing self-healing in code is adding retries in code wherever possible. However, self-healing capabilities are added on top of software applications by SRE teams. Some of the self-healing examples are as follows:

  - o **Infrastructure self-healing**: Automatically identifying infrastructure issues, such as if the system encounters high CPU or high memory, system will automatically increase the memory or add another instance/server to the infrastructure. Another example: if one service is down, move that service to another available node automatically. This is a **preventive approach**, where we are preventing the issue before the end-user sees any failure.

  - o **Code self-healing**: This means automatically identifying known code issues and implementing the solutions automatically to resolve the code errors. For example, if one service fails to call the dependent service at the first instance, then the service should be able to call multiple times to that dependent service, referred to as retries in code. If all retries are exhausted, then the service should be automatically restarted. This is also called the **reactive approach**. In this approach, the end-user might experience intermittent failure, but they will still be able to use the software.

# Ways to measure the reliability of a system

Following are some of the metrics you can use to measure how reliable your system is.

- **Mean time between failures (MTBF)**: We use this metric to calculate the mean time between failures. If there are multiple failures in the system over a week, it will become difficult to identify the difference between the time of the first failure and the next failure. The more time between failures, the more your system is reliable and stable, and there are not many failures. But if there is very little time between failures, that means your system is not reliable.

- **Mean time to recover (MTTR)**: We use this metric to calculate how much time your application takes to recover from any failure. The shorter the time, the more reliable it will be. Self-healing also helps reduce MTTR.

- **Rate of occurrence of failure (ROCOF)**: This metric is used to calculate the number of failures in a system. To measure the reliability, you can take the record of behavior of the software in certain timeframe.

# Availability

It lets us know for how much time the system was available to be accessed by end users. The difference between reliability and availability is that availability measures the ability of the system to be operated if needed. Reliability means the ability of the system to perform efficiently without failure. The system can be available, but some of the components can fail, which will impact reliability. If the full system is inaccessible, that impacts the availability of the system. However, sometimes availability and scalability are used interchangeably.

Availability is one of the key factors in building a robust software system. If the systems are not available, then other factors, such as scalability or reliability, are out of the picture. Today, organizations use various infrastructures to ensure the 24*7 availability of their software across the globe.

The following are some of the ways to implement availability:

- **Building distributed systems**: As software applications are growing, they are using a micro-service architecture. It is important that they are deployed on distributed infrastructure. That means you should create multiple servers in different locations as per your end-user's needs. So that even if one server faces any issue, your application can still run on other available servers.

- **Implement replication**: To maintain consistency in the system, use replication so that if one server is unavailable, you can easily move the load to the other without any data loss. **Example**: Keep multiple database instances where data is replicated in all instances. If one DB instance goes down, other DB nodes can fulfill the requests.

- **Geographic distribution**: Having a multiple and distributed architecture is not sufficient sometimes. For applications that have users all over the world, geographic distribution is also required. That means building software systems in different locations of the world. This could be having physical data centers at different locations and then using cloud applications on those data centers. Implement logic in your infrastructure such that if the user makes any request to the application, the request should go to the nearest data center for response to the end-user.

- **Regular maintenance and updates**: Regular maintenance and upgrades are crucial for achieving high availability. By keeping the system up-to-date with recent **operating system** (**OS**) upgrades, patches, security enhancements, other bug fixes, and vulnerabilities, we can mitigate the risk of failures. This increases the availability of the system. It involves regular infrastructure and software inspections and reviews them proactively.

One of the main metrics to measure availability is a **percentage** (%) of the system's uptime with respect to the total system time (uptime and downtime). Availability is also dependent on underlying reliability and scalability metrics.

Building a robust system that is highly available, reliable, and scalable is not a straightforward task, and it involves a lot of planning and design review. You cannot implement any of these features without understanding your system as a whole. That is why it is important to include the right approach in the initial phases of SDLC. Regularly measuring your system across these three factors ensures high performance of the system and eliminates risks of failures.

# Capacity planning and cost management

To build any system software or hardware, planning plays a key role. If your planning is good that means you have solved half of your battles as part of any system development journey. However, it is not that easy. Planning requires brainstorming and covering various aspects, and it is a source of truth for an organization to start any project. There is planning involved in SDLC in each phase. The initial planning phase is to create a roadmap of a software system that defines and kick-starts software development. However, capacity planning is one of the most crucial factors of SDLC.

Capacity planning is the process of determining the capacity of hardware and software to meet application requirements. This is capacity planning specific to software development; however, when it comes to SRE and overall SDLC, it involves the process of determining the hardware, software, time, and effort of each engineer involved to meet system needs. Today, most organizations follow Agile. Agile teams need to be able to respond quickly to the changing needs of customers. To do so, the SDLC team needs to have a good understanding of capacity from engineers, hardware, and software perspective.

Let us understand capacity planning in detail. There are three types of capacity in SDLC:

- **Software and hardware capacity**: This involves the process of defining the configuration of hardware and software required to meet application needs, such as the number of servers, CPU, Memory, what software to use, etc.

- **Workforce capacity**: This involves the process of determining how many hours of effort are required from each team involved in the project to meet the requirements, along with various skill sets.

- **Product capacity**: This involves forecasting demands for products and anticipating customers' needs to ensure businesses have the resources to meet them, such as changing customers' needs to have particular features in your software. The product should be built in a way that it can add new features in demand in less time. To support future needs, organizations should reserve the workforce's capacity and infrastructure. Along with that, the product should be agnostic of demand. That means the software application should be built keeping in mind that technology can change in the future, but the underlying code should be able to lift and shift to meet demand.

Organizations divide capacity into two broader categories: long-term and short-term capacity planning. Let us look at them in detail as follows:

- **Long-term capacity planning**: This involves high-level planning to identify areas where the system may need changes in the future and how the team needs to grow to meet the needs. Product capacity falls under long-term planning.

- **Short-term capacity planning**: This involves defining short milestones and identifying the capacity of both the system and teams. Software or hardware and workforce capacity are a part of short-term planning. It is important to do short term capacity planning in each phase of SDLC. The Agile model helps teams implement short-term capacity planning depending on the **planning interval** (**PI**) cycle.

Typically, PIs are 8 to 12 weeks long. That means SDLC teams do planning at the start of each PI. So, the organization has to plan capacity accordingly.

Capacity planning and cost management go hand-in-hand. When SDLC teams plan for capacity, one of the important factors is cost. All capacity drills down to the cost of running a project vs profit gained. For example, to have the right workforce, the organization needs to hire people with the right skill set; that is a cost to the organization. Then servers and software have to be purchased to support the SDLC; that is also a cost to the organization.

Cost management is very critical and should be done at the planning stage. Organizations have separate technology teams that assess the cost of running a technology project, where they assess cost from all aspects such as workforce, tools required, infrastructure required, virtual or physical office locations, laptops or computers required, etc. You should also assess if open-source software can be used to complete the project to save some money.

Let us see the different types of capacity planning models out there. Though these strategies are more suitable for manufacturing organizations, you can follow them for software development as well:

- **Lag strategy**: It involves waiting until the actual demand increases before adding further capacity. In this strategy, you plan the capacity required to complete and support the project and keep a little buffer budget. This strategy also reserves the cost for future demand. However, workforce and infrastructure capacity are limited to what is required to complete the project. With increased demand, organizations pull the buffer budget and then plan for the new capacity required to meet the increased demand. This strategy minimizes the cost of the project, but when demand increases, there is a lag in fulfilling customer's needs since even though there is no extra cost involved, replanning is needed to align the right capacity, which takes time.

  The lag strategy works well for projects where increased demand delivery has a fixed timeline and does not fluctuate significantly. For example, consider banking software. The bank identified that with their latest investment scheme, there is increased demand from customers for investment functions. Existing and new customers are also onboarding to the bank due to the new scheme. The bank defined a fixed timeline to scale up the system to meet the demand. They can use the lag strategy as there is a fixed timeline as baking customers have multiple options to invest, such as physically visiting the bank's branch, by customer care support, etc. Unlike e-commerce applications where customers are volatile, they switch between various similar e-commerce applications if one app does not perform well.

- **Lead strategy**: It involves the planning strategy that focuses on proactive management of resources (human and infrastructure). In this strategy, organizations anticipate customer demand from historical data and research and make sure that the necessary resources are in place to meet demand. During the initial planning phase, SDLC teams define the capacity required to deliver the project. Also, extra capacity is reserved for the future. In lead strategy, extra members are onboarded in the workforce, and extra capacity is added to hardware and software from the beginning. However, as this involves anticipation of future trends, there can be chances that the organization does not see the increase in demand as anticipated, and resources (adding workforce and infrastructure) are not utilized, potentially leading to a waste of money.

  Project where customer's demand changes significantly follow lead strategy. Such as retail applications. There are others external factors also that play a role in defining future trends such as economic conditions, competition, industry trends, etc.

- **Match strategy**: This involves focusing on the right amount of capacity that matches demand. It is a combination of lag and lead strategy capacity planning.

This strategy defines analyzing current and future demands to determine how much capacity is required to complete, deliver and maintain the project and accordingly adjust their SDLC process. Organizations reserve some budget (cost) for technology projects. They review demand in various phases of SDLC. If an organization sees trends in customer needs halfway through SDLC, they add workforce and infrastructure capacity beforehand. Though it is also anticipation, these are short-term future trends that help organizations scale up as per demand.

Some of the best approaches and best practices for cost management that help in capacity planning are as follows:

- **Capacity reserve**: Organizations should always keep a buffer for capacity to meet future demands. If that buffer remains unused, it can be utilized on other projects.

- **Development strategy**:
  - Build software applications, keeping future technology in mind, that are easy to scale up horizontally and vertically. Underlying code should be built in frameworks that can be easily extended and integrated with other frameworks if demand increases.
  - With the increase in cloud technology, software code should be cloud-agnostic. That means, if in the future demand increases and you are not able to meet the needs of customers on the current cloud, you can lift and shift your application to another cloud.

- **Cost management:**
  - Detailed design of software plan. Depending on the software design and delivery requirement, plan where you can use open-source software that is free to use.
  - Scale down infrastructure when not in use to save the extra subscription cost. Or if any servers' tools are not in use after a while (on SDLC), then reuse those servers for another project in the organization.
  - Consider virtual locations for workforces to avoid the extra cost of an official location.

- **Workforce management**: This involves reusing engineering skill sets. For example, SRE teams have a highly diverse skill set. Depending on the requirement of the role, engineers can be moved to different tasks within SRE. 50% of the time, the SRE team is involved in operations, and 50% of the time, SRE engineers can be used for development to share the load of developers. Similarly, when customer load increases and SRE teams need an extra hand to support the applications, then developers can be moved to SRE teams to support the application.

- **Observability**: To plan capacity and reserve cost, forecasting is important. Along with that, it is critical that the system has correct alerting in place that notifies

SDLC teams to scale up or scale down their infrastructure. Over a period of time, these alerts can be used as data points (historical trends) to analyze future trends.

# Importance of testing

Testing is an integral part of SDLC. Even in traditional approaches, testing has been given great importance when it comes to software development and delivery. With changes in technology and an increase in demand, new approaches in testing have been implemented within processes and within tools or software used throughout SDLC. Testing is a process of identifying bugs, errors, and defects in software supplication before the application is launched in the market for end-users. And that is the reason testing and SRE are tightly coupled. The more detailed and thorough testing performed on the system, the more stable the software system will be, and that, in turn, helps SRE to focus on other aspects of production rather than circumvent errors.

In this section, you will understand different types of testing and understand how testing helps build ancient systems.

The following are the different types of testing:

- **Unit testing**: It is the first and very low level of testing performed to identify errors on smaller units or modules. This testing is mostly performed by individual developers on their modules. After the developer completes the code, they perform testing on their code. Once it is passed, the code will be moved to a central repository. Unit tests are easy to automate. Today, many development tools come with an in-built unit test case that can be easily customized as per application. Unit test cases are functional in nature but are limited to smaller modules.

- **Functional testing**: It focuses on the business requirements, which are also called functional requirements. This testing includes verifying the output of an action and does not check the intermediate states of the system when performing that action. For example, if service A is supposed to send data to service B and all data is sent as expected, then functional testing will approve that service. Now, if that service took, let us say, 1 hour to send that data, this type of intermediate testing will not be taken care of. There is another type of testing that should be used.

  Functional testing is one of the critical tests in SDLC as it tests the functionality of each service. There are two types of functional testing:

  o **Regression testing**: This is a type of testing conducted after every new code is merged with existing code. This is to ensure no bugs have been introduced by the new code that can break the existing code's functionality.

  o **Progression testing**: This is the type of testing conducted on a new code to check if it has any bugs.

- **User testing**: This involves simulating user behavior in the complete application environment. This testing is conducted mostly from a user's perspective and how the user accesses the software. It verifies various user flows for any errors. Though this testing involves more on the user interface, in turn, the user interface communicates the backend code. So, if any user flow fails, that will also help analyze the issue at the backend functionality. Unit testing is also interlinked with functional testing.

- **Performance testing**: This involves evaluating systems' performance under a particular workload. This testing ensures system performance and reliability during high workload. Today, there are various automation tools available that can help inject a high number of requests into the system. Also helping testers determine bottlenecks, stability during peak traffic, performance requirements, etc.

- **Chaos testing**: This involves the deliberate injection of failures in a controlled manner to test the stability of the system and its ability to respond during failures. This is an effective testing approach to minimize downtime and outages before they occur.

- **Smoke testing**: This involves testing to check the basic functionality of the system in its entirety. It is also referred to as **shakedown testing**. Smoke testing is performed where test cases are executed end-to-end to test if the system's basic functionality is working. This testing is mostly performed on a pre-production environment before going live to test everything one last time. This ensures that the system is ready to be launched in the market and is ready to perform basic functionality.

The following figure represents the various phases of testing and the teams responsible for these tests in the **software development lifecycle (SDLC)** model, such as unit testing, regression testing, progression testing, chaos testing, and smoke testing:

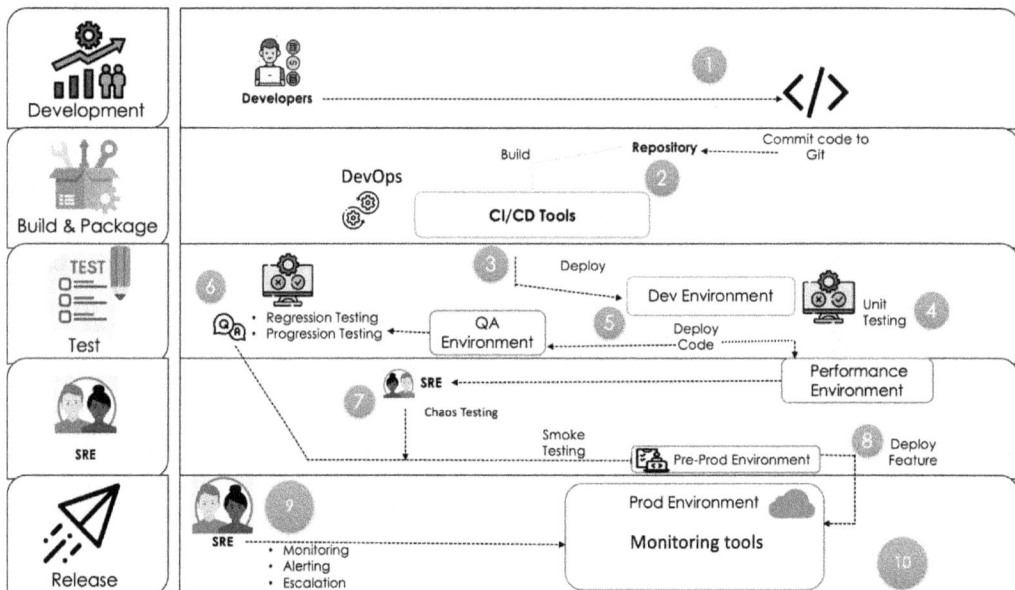

*Figure 3.2*: Overview of various phases of testing

Different types of testing define how efficient a software system is. Testing helps SDLC teams to identify errors and bugs in the system before launching the final application. Testing is directly related to the reliability, stability, and availability of the system. As explained in the previous figure, different types of testing are performed through different phases of SDLC. It also depends on the type of project. Some organizations combine a few testing approaches in one phase.

# Importance of testing

The following are some of the reasons why testing is essential:

- **Quality of product**: All types of testing explained previously, if performed as per the process, help determine various types of bugs present in the system, if any. Unit testing helps identify bugs in smaller modules. In some cases that are not caught during unit testing, functional testing helps identify errors in functionality, performance testing helps identify system scalability during load, chaos testing helps identify how the system of service will behave if infrastructure fails, and then smoke testing does end-to-end overall system testing. Once a software application goes through all these types of testing, the issues identified during these tests go back to the development team. The development team fixes these errors and then does a re-testing of the fixed code. This cycle repeats till the system becomes error-free. Testing certifies that the product is ready to be used and stable enough to handle end-user requests.

- **Security**: It is another crucial reason that makes testing important in SDLC. Today, organizations implement security testing during the initial phases, such as unit testing and functional testing at times. Testing helps identify security vulnerabilities present in code and any sensitive data used in code. It also ensures the security of infrastructure, not just code. Security testing for infrastructure ensures that the latest versions of operating systems are being used, all firewalls are configured, and other infrastructure vulnerabilities are taken care of. It makes the system secure and helps prevent data breaches.

- **Cost-saving**: Testing helps identify errors in the system in the early phases. The sooner the issues are identified, the more teams can fix them in a timely. This saves the extra cost of hiring developers to fix these issues in later phases. There are various types of bugs that can be identified during different tests that help the team to fix issues on time, such as security vulnerabilities (these issues cost huge money to any organization if identified in a live environment), capacity of infrastructure, functional issues, etc. Organizations keep a budget for engineering projects. The budget also includes costs that might be incurred during the fixing of the issues, but if there are issues identified after the system goes live, then extra cost is required to fix those issues. That is how testing helps save this extra money.

- **Performance of system**: Testing helps identify how the system will perform during high loads and failures. With technological advancement and an increase in demand, system performance has become one of the key factors for any software application. Testing helps SRE to prepare and be ready for the production environment as per the testing results.

- **Customer satisfaction**: Testing helps catch errors before production. This helps developers, SRE and DevOps teams to fix issues on time. A system without issues or fewer issues increases customer satisfaction, the goal of any software project.

Let us take one of the examples from a real industry scenario where not following a good testing strategy can impact the software's reliability. In 2017, there was a major outage on S3 storage across major AWS services, impacting thousands of businesses worldwide using AWS S3. The root cause was a typo in an S3 scaling command that inadvertently removed larger sets of servers, impacting the S3 outage. The reason behind the typo is the lack of testing the infra code in the lower environment before running it in the production system. If a team could have tested the command in a lower environment first, they could have easily caught the typo. The example explains the importance of testing and correct planning in designing test cases. It is not just software code testing; infrastructure code testing is equally important to maintain the reliability of the system.

# Real-world examples of different phases of testing

This example explains the scenario of different types of testing (explained previously) in one project. Software development followed best practices, completed the development, and is now entering the testing phase. Just before the first version of the software is given to the testing team, developers run unit tests on their individual services and functions. Unit testing is the first testing phase. After development is completed, the code is packaged by **continuous integration and continuous deployment (CI/CD)** (this is one of the DevOps principles, which means code development and deployment should be continuous to speed up the development process) pipelines and gets deployed to the testing environment. Then, testers/**quality analysts (QA)** start testing the code. There are multiple types of functional testing that QA covers. For this example, consider progression testing and then regression testing after QA's tested code gets deployed to the pre-production environment, where SRE performs chaos and performance testing. Once these tests are completed, the code is finally ready for the production environment.

Organizations should ensure testing is included in every phase of SDLC. You should use tools that come with in-built testing to help developers enhance development and focus on writing quality code. The testing team should use automated test cases to ensure broader coverage of code and infrastructure. This ensures the stability of the system and, in turn, increases customer satisfaction.

# Using monitoring and observability tools

Organizations today are moving towards distributed architectures to provide software services. Highly distributed environments require advanced observability and monitoring.

To build sound observability and monitoring, you need tools or software that provide this capability. Mostly, SRE or operations teams are responsible for implementing observability and monitoring software applications. SRE teams have skilled members who have knowledge of various tools, automation, and knowledge about production environments.

Monitoring and observability include catching issues in production or live applications proactively and reactively. This helps SRE teams act and resolve these issues accordingly. Monitoring comes in the last phase of SDLC. When the software reaches the last phase, it has already been tested thoroughly to remove errors and problems in a live application. However, no system is 100% error-free. There are a lot of external factors involved in causing errors when software is launched. So, to catch issues in live applications, monitoring, and observability are two approaches used by SRE teams. They help SRE to identify issues and fix them before customers notice.

**Monitoring** means the process of watching and analyzing the data captured through various metrics. And then providing certain results on the basis of that data. For example: watching specific system metrics such as CPU, memory, HTTP 500 errors, request/ response ratio, etc., and watching the log for errors and warnings. Then, collecting these metrics' data and analyzing and determining the impact on application. Example: high CPU is alarming, so the SRE team can investigate the reason for the high CPU and what actions need to be taken to resolve it.

**Observability** means the process of watching, collecting, and analyzing the data captured not only via metrics but also through the detailed logs of each service. Observability can also be considered as an advancement to monitoring, where SRE teams implement observability in a system that will continuously watch the system's state automatically, proactively auto-heal sometimes, and for any anomaly that cannot be auto-healed, it provides data to SRE teams, which will help them investigate the root cause of the issue.

Both monitoring and observability go hand-in-hand. They use dashboards and logging to collect the data. SRE teams analyze the data using both of these approaches. This helps SDLC teams to fix errors and make the system more stable and reliable. However, there is a difference between the two approaches.

Let us consider the following example:

- Consider an online travel booking software project. The project is in its last stage and is planned to go live in two months.
- The SRE team identified suitable monitoring tools that can be used to measure the application and provided the list to technology leadership. Once the monitoring tool is finalized by leadership, SRE teams build various dashboards to capture system metrics, such as CPU, memory, request/response time, uptime, or every service.
- SRE bookmarked these dashboards so that the team can monitor them regularly.
- SRE teams build various alerts on logging (application logs are captured by the logging tool). This will notify the SRE team as soon as something goes wrong or

exceeds the threshold. These alerts have a detailed stack trace that helps teams identify the root cause. Sometimes, these alerts are auto-healed, such as when services go down; the service automatically restarts and resolves the error.

These examples explain the difference and importance of both monitoring and observability in SRE's world.

Some of the common tools for monitoring and observability are:

Prometheus, Grafana, Dynatrace, New Relic, Datadog, Dynatrace, VMware Aria Operations, Application Insights by *Microsoft*.

There are various other tools available in the market: open source and subscription. It depends on the type of project and organization needed and is solely the organization's decision to use a tool that is most suitable and easy to customize as per their requirements. All these tools have multiple uses, such as infrastructure monitoring, application monitoring, and also as observability. For example, Prometheus and Grafana: if the input data source for Prometheus is containers, then Prometheus and Grafana (UI dashboard) can be used as infrastructure monitoring. If the input data source is application logs, then Prometheus and Grafana can be used as an application monitoring tool. Prometheus and Grafana can publish data in the form of alerts, which can be integrated with any messaging tool used in the organization.

It is not straightforward to decide what tool to use. During the SDLC planning phase, subject matter experts should decide on the tool to be used to monitor the software. Some of the best practices in deciding tools are as follows:

- Define metrics of your software system performance. Select the tool that can pull data for those metrics.

- Design an integration plan identifying how to integrate the tool with your software architecture. Is there easy compatibility between the tool and your application?

- Identify the cost of purchasing the tool and integrating it. Assess what skillset is required to use that tool and whether you need to hire people with a special skillset.

- Open-source or subscription-based tool to be used.

- The tool's ability to scale up easily along with the software application to meet the requirement.

- No tool will be perfect to meet the requirement. So, gather if the tool provides customization and how easy it is to customize and build your own automation on top of that tool.

Let us understand in detail with a real industry scenario how SRE teams build monitoring and observability. In continuation of the previous example of an online travel booking software project:

- Tools like **Elasticsearch, Logstash, Kibana (ELK)** for logging, Prometheus and Grafana for the dashboard, Slack as a messaging tool, ServiceNow as an incident management tool, and PagerDuty for incident reporting.

- The SRE team collaborates with the development team to get metrics introduced in code. Both teams define thresholds for each of the metrics.

- After metric collection, the SRE team builds queries in Prometheus and integrates them with Grafana for dashboards. Grafana dashboards display data from Prometheus. Here, input data to Prometheus is metrics exposed in code by developers.

- Various dashboards are built to capture all services involved.

- SRE teams also configured alerting in Grafana. And Grafana is integrated with Slack. As soon as any metric goes beyond the threshold, Grafana sends an alert to the Slack channel and notifies the SRE or operation team about the anomaly.

- SRE teams also configured alerting in Kibana. ELK stack helps capture logs from code, and Kibana displays it (the DevOps team helps with ELK integration). Alerting in Kibana is also integrated with Slack.

- As an alert is generated, the Slack channel gets a message, and SRE teams get to know the error in the system.

- The flow of alerting is as follows:

  o Alerts set up in Kibana is HTTP 500 for all services in online travel booking software.

  o Suddenly, the search service in the software started throwing HTTP 500 alerts.

  o Slack channel receives a message of HTTP 500 error. The SRE team clicked on the message.

  o That alert message navigates SRE to Kibana logs with the stack trace.

  o At the same time, the slack channel received a high memory alert on the database server.

  o This infrastructure alert was configured to fire as an incident, too. So, the incident gets created in ServiceNow.

  o ServiceNow is integrated with PagerDuty. PagerDuty notifies the engineer on duty via phone SMS.

  o Within a few minutes, the SRE engineer was able to identify the root cause as a full stack trace was available. HTTP 500 error stack trace also highlighted the high memory alert in the database. So, the same stack trace highlighted both errors.

  o SRE teams scaled up another database instance to handle a high memory load (you can also automate this process).

  o Scaling happened within a minute, and alerts were fixed.

The following figure diagrammatically represents the flow of alerts from the monitoring tool to the incident management tool and to the operations team:

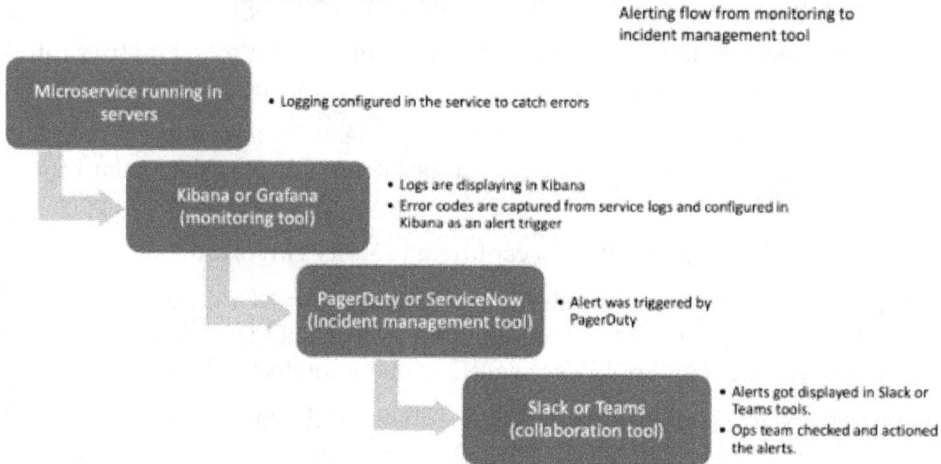

*Figure 3.3: Alert stages in operations*

Advanced and next generation approaches to monitoring and observability are automation, co-relation, and artificial intelligence. Today, with distributed architecture, the stability and reliability of systems have become critical. Every organization is moving towards building online applications for their products. With increased competition in the market, customer satisfaction is one of the key metrics to measure software performance. To deliver and run stable software, you need advanced observability, and AI is the next-generation approach. AI does not mean only automating SRE tasks; it means automation that first identifies errors, takes appropriate decisions, and resolves them before that error breaks any functionality in the system.

There are multiple tools available in the market that help you observe your system, however, co-relating errors and resolving them automatically need human intelligence (subject matter expertise).

For example, three errors were seen across two services, and these alerts were generated due to one reason. However today, SRE teams have the expertise to look at the stack trace and co-relate all three errors. Now, if you must advance your software, you must build a **machine learning** (**ML**) algorithm that will learn from these errors and decide how to resolve them. SRE's job should be to capture data points from production applications and build such ML algorithms that can auto-heal errors, even before end users notice them.

# Build strong incident management process

The previous section explains the importance of observability in the system. Incident management is tightly coupled with observability and is one of the critical factors contributing to the stability of any software system. Incident management is a process used by the development and SRE teams to respond to an unplanned event or service interruption and restore the service. **Incident (INC)** management is an integral part of operations. It helps in tracking and managing tickets received from end users. This is a platform for your customers to connect to your organization for queries or complaints. SRE teams are the first point of contact for all technical queries. Hence, having a process to track such queries from customers becomes critical.

An incident is defined as a disruption to any service in software that affects users. So, anything that interrupts business continuity is referred to as an incident.

Organizations follow best practices and do several tests before rolling out software to production. However, software applications still see failures and service disruptions. There are multiple factors for such disruptions; for example, your application pulls some data from a third-party application, which is down, in turn, impacts your application. That is where the operations team comes into the picture, managing the disruptions in production environments. Let us assume there is no incident management process in the organization. Software applications see some service disruptions that impact the customers, rendering them unable to use some services in software. Customers will reach out to the organization's customer service and raise their complaints. Customer service will report this complaint to the technology team (SRE) either via email or messages. As there is no process to track these complaints, customer service does not have a clear picture of whether the SRE team is working on that ticket. They will always have to communicate via email or messages. This is a non-transparent, time-consuming process, and there are chances that the members will forget to action the complaints if the customer's complaints increase.

To avoid these issues, a process has been introduced to track incidents. Today, we have various tools that help implement the INC management process. The service desk, SRE, and dev teams can access the tool. The service desk logs user complaints or queries in the tool as an incident. If they cannot solve the user's request or complaint, they assign the INC to SRE teams. As soon as the SRE team gets this INC to their queue, they get a notification. Since the tool is a central place to update all INCs, teams can see the latest status and comments on INCs. If the SRE team adds their investigation comments to the INC, the service desk can also view them and respond to the customers accordingly. This is a basic INC management flow. However, there are various phases in the incident management process. To create a process, the following points are to be considered:

- **Incident logging**: This involves the how, what, when, and where to log any incident. During the initial phase of SDLC, organizations should also decide on the tool to be used for incident management. That tool will be used as a central repository that will log all incidents. Once you have the tool configured, decide on how to log incidents. There are various automation available in tools that create an incident automatically on a user's phone call request via chatbots. Also, the service desk team can manually create an incident. Organizations should clearly define the template for logging incidents. Anyone who is creating an incident will have to follow the template while capturing the details of any query. Today, tools have built-in templates in the INC process. The service desk fills the template to create any incident. The template defines what information is to be collected, the type of query, the impact on the customer, etc.

- **Incident creation**: This involves creating incidents after capturing details. Incident logging and creation are interlinked. Tools are used to capture details, fill templates, and create incidents.

- **Incident categorization**: This involves defining categories of incidents. Organizations should clearly identify all categories of incidents and the template (what incident should fall in which category). In general, there are three categories of incidents high, medium, and low. The category of an incident depends on the type of the incident (is it a customer complaint or internal error), the source of the incident (application, infrastructure, UI, etc.), and its impact. Depending on these factors, you can define the category of an incident.

- **Incident prioritization**: This involves ranking the incident. The ranking is done on the basis of business impact, % of the impact, and incident category. Category and priority are both interrelated to each other, i.e., both of these processes go hand-in-hand. They help define the timeline of the incident and give a clear picture to the operations team on resolving the ticket. There are three or four types of priorities, P1, P2, P3, and P4. Each priority has a timeline called **service level agreement** (**SLA**) to resolve these incidents. For example, an incident for service intermittent failure throwing **page not found** error for one page can be categorized as medium (assume that the page is not critical functionality of software). Once a category is defined, the incident is prioritized as P2 (it has a timeline to resolve in twelve hours). The service desk logs this INC with category and priority. Then, they assign this INC to the SRE team. They know the details and priority, and they will solve the ticket accordingly. This will avoid a lot of back and forth between teams and also with the customers. Today, there are tools that help define the category and priority of INCs, such as ServiceNow ITSM, Jira Service Management, PagerDuty, SolarWinds Service Desk, BigPanda.

- **Incident accepting**: This involves acknowledging an incident as soon as it is created. Depending on category and priority, each INC has an SLA on acknowledging and accepting the incident. This helps other members of the team to know that a particular INC is currently being worked on by an engineer.

- **Incident resolution**: This involves resolving the ticket as per the timeline. Not all tickets and INCs can be of the same priority, and so with priority, the timeline for solving is also defined. Such as, P1 is to be solved within four hours, and P2 timelines are to be solved in eight hours. It depends on the organization's processes and standards on how they prioritize their incidents. SRE teams build automation in the incident management tool where they get regular alerts on new incidents in their queue upon an incident approaching their resolution timeline. This keeps the incident management process transparent and easy to use.

- **Incident closure**: This involves closing the incident, adding the required details, and sending the incident to the requestor queue to update on closure. Incident resolution and closure are interlinked. As soon as the incident is resolved, the team should close it; once the incident is closed, the requestor will get updated automatically.

- **Incident root cause**: This is the last step of the process, where respective teams identify the root cause of the incident and store details in the central database. Once an incident is closed, teams create another stage for the incident, but that stage is internal to the organization and not for external customers. This internal stage is called the root cause analysis stage. The incident is then assigned to the team who is responsible for finding the root cause of the issue. This stage is not built for customers. This stage is also referred to as problem management. Though this is the incident management stage, however, in some organizations, problem management is a separate process that works in collaboration with incident management. The key difference between the incident, and the problem is incident management circumventing the immediate issue. And problem management is fixing the root cause.

The following are the stages in the incident management process:

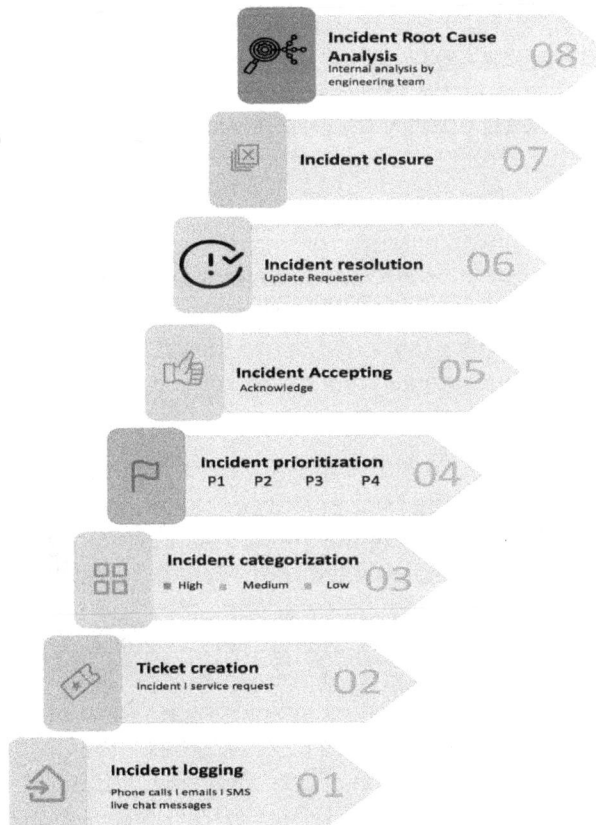

*Figure 3.4: Incident stages in operations*

It is important that during the initial phase of SDLC, the organization define the incident management process. There should be a clear definition of the stages of incidents. Then, only operations teams will be able to act on queries faster and resolve them in time. The quicker incidents are resolved, the better will be the customer satisfaction. This defines the stability of the system.

Some of the best practices for building intense incident management process are as follows:

- Use advanced tools that provide automation of incident management, such as automatically linking any new incident with similar past incidents to help teams in quick resolutions.

- Implement alerting on the incident tool. As soon as any new incident comes to the queue, teams are notified so that they do not miss any incident.

- Build automation to acknowledge incidents automatically. This is one of the roles of SRE to automate acknowledging on INC so that there is no confusion within a team in shift and helps avoid repetitive work.

- Daily stand-up for operations teams to discuss the status of INC. If your software application is huge, with 24*7 customers across the globe, then it means there will be multiple queries you might receive from end-users and other stakeholders who use your application. Even if you have automated the INC management tool, sometimes it can be difficult to keep track of all INCs. So, it is advised to have daily stand-ups and discuss priority INC. For example, online travel booking. They can get queries from customers, travel agents, third-party payment companies, etc.

- Define a clear correlation between application errors and incidents. When you receive a query from a customer on service disruption, there is a high chance that SRE teams might have also received an alerting error. As a best practice, SRE teams should list down some high-impact alerts, such as service down, and link those alerts to incidents. As incidents are the first task for any operations team, such internal incidents, if created automatically, will help SRE teams act on errors before they create any major impact.

Let us look at a real-world example of how incident management enables SRE and operations teams to act on time and circumvent problems. Take the example of an online travel booking software. While booking the flight, customers using the software suddenly saw an error on the web page display **page not found**. When the error popped up on the web page, an internal automated ticket was generated and logged into the operations teams' queue. Also, a customer service representative got a call from customers. The same ticket was updated by the customer service representative with the information provided by the customers. The incident management tool automatically added the category as high and priority as p1 (the tool has an in-built algorithm to decide on the type of errors). As part of automated incident management, the ticket was automatically assigned to an operations team member. Since the ticket has high priority, it was quickly picked by operational engineers, application support, or SRE team members. They started troubleshooting the error and initiated the circumvention of the problem as per runbooks. During circumvention, the application support engineer moved user traffic to another server. As a result, the customers started getting responses on the web page, and they were able to book the travel ticket. This whole process took less than five minutes. While traffic was moved to another server, application support and SRE engineers investigated the issue, found the problem, and worked on a solution to fix it permanently. After fixing the issue, engineers updated the ticket with the required **root cause analysis** (**RCA**) details and closed the ticket or incident.

# Automate to reduce toil

Automation is the key for all organizations, irrespective of domain. Software, manufacturing, medical all types of organizations seek automation to reduce toil and repetitive work. You see automation in day-to-day life also, for example, software in washing machines that operate automatically, refrigerator software that operates automatically, car software, etc. Software organizations focus a lot on automation. Automation is a key enabler for SRE, helping them to streamline operations and achieve their goals.

The following is a snippet of the code that automatically self-heals the service:

```
import os
import time
def check_service():
    status = os.system("systemctl is-active --quiet myservie")
    return status == 0
while True:
    if not chek_servie():
        print("Service is down! Restarting...")
        os.system("systemctl restart myservice")
    time.sleep(60)
```

## Importance of automation to SRE

There are various benefits of automation. Some of them are automating repetitive manual tasks (called **toil**), which saves time and effort and prevents human errors; automating alerts, which helps quick turnaround for error resolution by making it self-healing; and automating to improve the system's performance.

## Ways to automate

SREs are skilled engineers who work in a production environment and automate manual tasks. Automation can be done by tools, where SRE engineers use and customize these tools as per their requirements. The SRE team also builds its own automation from scratch by writing code. Manual, repetitive tasks that are tactical and do not need human intelligence are referred to as toil. SRE's key responsibility is to eliminate toil.

The following are the areas of automation opportunities:

- **Manual repetitive**: Tasks such as running a job daily to pull reports. Such tasks can be easily automated. Automating manual tasks saves the time and effort of SRE engineers; they can use their time for other important tasks. Manual tasks are also prone to human errors, so automation removes these errors.

- **Automated alerting and monitoring**: SRE teams should automate alerting where any high-impact alert will notify the required team. Automating resolution of certain errors such as traffic-increased system auto scale-up, if traffic reduces system auto-scale down. This increases the scalability and performance of the system.

- **Automated incident management**: SRE teams should implement automation around incident management where any incident that comes to their queue is automatically acknowledged. It is automatically linked to alerts that are fired in the system, co-relates errors, and notifies respective teams.

- **Automating other tasks:** Such as security vulnerability scanning, log scanning, access management, and continuous health checks. This type of automation helps enhance security.

Various ways automation helps in building stable and reliable systems:

- **Automation**: Automation of manual tasks saves time and this helps SRE and DevOps teams focus on other daily tasks. This, in turn, helps save the cost of hiring an extra workforce.

- **Scalability**: Automation built by the SRE and DevOps team allows them to scale up and scale down the system automatically, when required, without any manual trigger.

- **Reliability**: Auto-healing and auto-restart of the service resolved the errors before the customer noticed them.

- **Availability**: Auto moving or diverting of customer traffic to available servers, in case one server has issues, helps maintain the availability of the system.

As mentioned earlier, one approach does not suit all. There are tools available that help teams build automation. The following are some common processes to consider when eliminating toil:

- Identify automation opportunities areas, such as automated incident management, auto alerting, self-healing, and auto-scaleup. These are some known tasks that should be automated. Automation must be an ongoing activity, where the team keeps on identifying opportunities to automate and reduce toil.

- Identify metrics and follow a metric-based approach to decide whether the task needs to be automated. For example, a manual task is required to be done only two times a year, and it takes only 30 minutes. Automating this task will require one month of man-hours; hence, it is not advisable to automate since the cost of automation is higher than that of the manual task.

- Once all the open manual tasks are identified, categorize them and then decide on tools to be used for automation if required.

- While selecting tools, list down your requirements, match the functionality of the tool that it offers, and check if customization is available for the tool.

- Cost of the tool; questions like whether it is open-source or subscription-based, whether it is a one-time purchase or a yearly subscription, are important to assess. If the cost of purchasing the tool is higher than that of hiring engineers who can automate by writing their own code, then go for hiring engineers.

- There are no one or two tools that can be used directly to automate. However, first, identify the automation category, then select the tool. For example, for monitoring, you have Prometheus and Grafana. While selecting the monitoring tool, also check if it provides automation customization. ServiceNow is chosen for incident management; it also provides automation for notifying incidents automatically. The Ansible tool is selected for configuration management to configure infrastructure. It also provides auto infrastructure creation. These are some examples of tools that come with in-built automation.

- Feedback loop implements regular feedback sessions with various SDLC teams including SRE, DevOps, developers, testers, and businesses. Feedback sessions help identify the manual tasks that can be automated to improve operations.

The previous topic of incident management is also one of the examples of automation saving time for SRE and offering application support. Automating incident creation, acknowledgment, assigning right priority and category helped saved 80% time of the engineers and enabled them to work on the circumvention of the problem, thereby ensuring minimal customer impact.

# CAMS model is an SRE essential

Before going in-depth into each phase of **Culture, Automation, Measurement, and Sharing (CAMS)**, let us understand the invention of CAMS. Before DevOps and SRE were invented, many software organizations were running in complete isolation, as there was no collaboration between cross-functional teams. All the engineering teams were responsible for their own tasks. Such an environment creates silos (a silo is a team or a resource working in a vertical that is more or less cut from other verticals in an organization), blame games, and impacts the development and delivery of products.

In previous chapters, we understood the importance of SRE and DevOps and how they break silos and help increase productivity. The CAMS model is also derived from the approaches followed by new methodologies (Agile, DevOps, and SRE). The framework that addresses the silo challenge, if summarized, is CAMS.

# Culture

In literal definition, it is defined as a group of people who practice the same routine in their day-to-day lives. That means they follow the same norms and standards daily. Similarly, in software organizations today, engineering teams practice their own culture. This culture defines standards, processes, and vision, which are the same across teams. This helps them achieve the organization's goals.

Let us assume that innovation and stability are the vision of any organization. Then, one culture within SDLC teams means development teams build their code while keeping innovation in mind, such as using the latest languages, Python, Ruby, Java, etc. Developers also follow best practices while building their code to ensure stability. SRE and DevOps teams empower developers by creating automation that helps developers focus on their innovation, creating strong monitoring to bring stability to the product. Such collaboration is referred to as culture. Though the internal processes might differ between teams, their objectives and vision remain the same.

Some factors define the culture of any organization. You can build the culture by defining the following factors:

- **Vision**: This should be a top-down approach. An organization shares the top vision, and all projects should follow that vision. It is the responsibility of top leadership and management to clearly define the vision of the company. All projects or teams should create their internal standards, keeping the company's vision in mind. For example, for an online travel booking company, the vision is to become the world's leading online travel company.

- **Objectives and key results (OKR)**: This involves defining goals and results on how to measure and assess whether they are achieved. Once the vision is defined, organizations should define high-level goals for all the teams to follow. Then, all the engineering teams should use these goals and identify the milestones to achieve them. This is also a top-down approach. For example, the objective is to improve the performance of the application. The key results will be the metrics to measure the performance. To achieve this goal, teams should define milestones.

- **Standards and processes**: This involves following the same standards and processes across engineering teams, such as defect or bug management process, incident management process, testing process, deployment process, etc. These standards should be defined enterprise-wise, and all teams should follow these processes. Teams can internally create their own smaller processes, but the standards and key goals should be the same. For example, developers, testers, SRE, and DevOps all follow the Agile approach, where they build, test, and deliver the system on the basis of **program increment (PI)**. All teams follow this PI model for their tasks; developers' complete development in one PI, and the SRE team also builds observability in the same PI. That will have teams follow the same culture.

- **Tools and software**: This involves using the same tools and software for development and delivery. For example, developers use the JIRA software to log defects and tasks, and SRE teams also use the JIRA tool for defects and task logging. Re-using tools helps the team collaborate more.

# Automation

Automation eliminates toil by automating manual, repetitive, and routine tasks. Automation saves time, effort, and cost for the organization. Automation should be the enterprise's goal, and teams should define their OKR and **key performance indicators** (**KPIs**) that include automation. Automation improves productivity by increasing collaboration between teams.

**Example of automation**: The DevOps team creates a CI/CD pipeline to integrate and deploy the code. This pipeline is used by developers, testers, and SRE teams. As there is one pipeline used by all teams, it creates an open communication platform between them.

There are various manual tasks that the engineering teams might have to do, and sometimes these are repetitive across teams. Let us say one team created a tool that automates a manual task, the same tool can be re-used by other teams. They both can use and add advancements to this automation. As you have learned the importance of automation in the previous section, it is one of the key approaches for CAMS, DevOps, and SRE teams.

# Measurement

It defines measuring your milestones and goals to achieve vision. Measurement is one of the driving factors for the CAMS model as it helps measure performance and improvement. Measurement, in general, is a key factor for all organizations to improve. If you do not measure the performance of your product, you will not be able to evaluate it.

Measurement plays an important role in operations, and it is one of the essential practices for SRE and DevOps teams. It also helps in collaboration. Let us first understand what measurement is. It is basically asking questions on how well we performed. Engineering teams should define their goals at the beginning of SDLC, that is, before development. They should create regular achievable milestones, and with each milestone, an assessment needs to be done to monitor the progress. If only a part of the milestone is achieved, we need to check what the roadblocks are and how to overcome these roadblocks. As part of assessing the performance for the milestone, you should implement a feedback or retrospective process within and with cross-functional teams. In the process of feedback, individual teams share their ideas that help them explore opportunities for further improvement; that is how measurement helps collaboration.

In the next section, you will observe a detailed explanation of measurement and its importance.

The following are some of the metrics SRE should implement, considering there is an operational milestone one month after releasing a new feature in the application:

- % of failures seen in applications for that month.
- MTTR for various failures.
- MTBF between various failures.
- % of manual tasks automated.

All these questions will ultimately help the SRE team assess how well their operations did. Did their automation help improve the system's performance? Did alerting and monitoring help speed up recovery? Did self-healing help increase stability? How was the collaboration with the development team in identifying bugs and fixes? How well did SRE teams deliver for a month?

# Sharing

This is the last factor in the CAMS model, and also the most important but often neglected. Sharing is not any technology that can be built or automated in system, it is human preferences. Building a culture of sharing in organizations is one of the most difficult tasks. Sharing help teams to collaborate smoothly, increase productivity of individuals and the project.

There are two factors to sharing, and they are explained as follows:

- **Openness**: It means the ability to extend and improve. This term is also used in technical aspects, where openness in the distributed system means its ability to extend and improve its hardware and software components. Similarly, this practice has to be followed within team members, where each team member is willing to help others. As an SRE leader, one can implement some of these processes within the team so as to help them to inculcate the practice. The following are some of these processes that can be implemented to build a culture of openness in the team:

    o Creating a process of regular knowledge transfer sessions within team.

    o Regular mentorship sessions, where senior members mentor junior members, and the leader takes the feedback.

    o Retrospective sessions to understand challenges better.

    o Regular acknowledgments and accolades.

- **Transparent**: This means the leader and teams should be transparent on the progress of the project along with team member's progress. Transparency allows the team to move towards a common goal. Some transparency can be achieved through technology and implementing processes. Some of the processes you can implement as a SRE leader are as follows:

    o Using a central repository or tool to track the performance of projects, where the full team can see and track.

- o A central tool to track the daily tasks of each team member so that it gives transparency between the teams.

- o Daily meeting with the team to understand the status of their task. In case anyone is stuck or is facing any challenge, others can help that person.

- o Sessions with other teams to discuss challenges within SRE and those between cross-functional teams. This allows engineering teams to collaborate effectively and work towards a common goal.

CAMS model is a summary of various factors you learned in the chapter as an SRE essential. The uniqueness of the CAMS model is the sharing factor, which involves the human side, since to make SRE successful, you need human resources. In order to achieve their goals, organizations should consider the human factor along with implementing technology.

# Agnostic approach

An agnostic approach in technology is one that is interoperable across the system without any prejudices towards using specific technology, model, or methodology. In software engineering teams, it means developing software products without being tied to any specific framework or platform technology.

Today, with increased demand and competition, organizations have to build their software applications quickly. Requirements change frequently; new technology also gets introduced in the market, and new tools are launched faster now, putting pressure on software companies to deliver quickly while also maintaining the quality of the product. In order to address fast-paced development, the Agile approach was introduced. It helps the SDLC team to divide their task into smaller sprints and deliver quality products promptly. Then came the DevOps team, followed by SRE. All these methodologies share some practices and principles with one vision: to deliver quality, stable products on time. This sounds easy, however, completing SDLC for delivering a product is not straightforward and is also a time-consuming task. Organizations do a lot of planning before they start developing any software. It involves tasks like deciding on technology, architecture, framework, workforce, skillsets, timelines, etc. They also have to keep up with the fast-changing demand. To address this challenge, the agnostic approach was introduced.

Let us take an example to understand the agnostic approach in detail. Consider a software organization planning to build a product for online delivery of product.

The following SDLC steps are to be undertaken:

- Planning phase to decide application architecture, framework, underlying language, infrastructure, cloud provider, workforce, tools to help teams in development, and the operational model.

- Tool stack, Java, React, micro-service architecture, AWS cloud, NoSQL database, Kubernetes for containerization, ELK for logging, Grafana and Splunk for monitoring, Jenkins for CI/CD, testing automation tool.

- The development team starts writing code. DevOps team creates CI/CD pipeline. SRE teams develop monitoring dashboards.

- Code gets deployed to the testing environment, and the testing team starts testing. SRE team performs chaos testing.

- Once testing is completed, bugs are identified and fixed. Then, the SRE teams do smoke testing.

- After all the testing, the code gets deployed to the production environment. SRE teams start monitoring.

- After a month, the business decided to move away from AWS Cloud and start using Google Cloud. There could be multiple reasons for this business decision. Now, engineering teams have to re-start their planning.

- Engineering teams already consider future changes and design architecture that does not depend on the underlying infrastructure.

- Java and React both languages are both cloud agnostic, and applications can easily be moved to the Google Cloud. However, underlying configurations have to be changed. Developers build applications to keep the code and variables or configuration separate, which makes it easy to move the applications to any infrastructure.

This is a small example of how the agnostic approach works in software development. This approach has its own pros and cons, though this is also considered as one of the factors for building stable and reliable system. However, it depends on the type of project, duration of project, teams involved, framework, and future anticipation.

There can be various ways in which a software company follows an agnostic approach. To highlight, mentioned below are some of the examples are given as follows:

- Choose a coding language and framework that does not depend on a particular infrastructure and can be run on any type of operating system and server.

- Designing system architecture in a way that it can be used with any database and cloud provider.

- Write code so that it is easily extensible if required, to run on new infrastructure.

- Design logging framework for software such that any logging tool can be used.

- Build your metrics in code so that the SRE teams can use any monitoring tool to configure dashboards.

- The application framework should not depend on any one of the CI/CD tools. Backend and frontend languages can be made flexible. If, in the future, there is a requirement to change the frontend coding language, then the backend application should be agnostic of the frontend, which means the backend application can be changed without impacting the frontend application.

These examples do not fit all; each organization is different and has different requirements, and organizations have to choose their approach according to their requirement. There are pros and cons of using an agnostic approach, and the next section will help you understand both.

The following are some of the pros of using an agnostic approach:

- It can save an organization money over time. If, in the future, a software product is required to be moved to another cloud or infrastructure, you save cost by not having to build it from scratch.

- Flexibility to choose your own tools, where you can even switch between the tools.

- Easy scalability of application and infrastructure. Since your application is not dependent on one infrastructure, if scaling is required beyond capacity, you can easily move your application to other servers or infrastructure with scaled-up capacity.

- It gives organizations more freedom and control. As you are not dependent on one cloud infrastructure, you get the liberty to customize and configure the application as per your requirements.

- It can be a lower long-term investment. If your company anticipates a future rise in demand, then investing in an agnostic approach can help save costs long-term.

The following are some cons of using agnostic approach:

- It may have high upfront cost of building the software. To choose your own infrastructure, you might need to build everything from scratch. Unlike a subscription-based cloud infrastructure where initial configuration is taken care of by the cloud provider, here you might have to take the complete responsibility of building and managing.

- It also requires unique skill sets. Organizations will need to hire people who have the required skills and knowledge to build a framework that is agnostic in nature. This can be expensive.

- Application might not take advantage of everything. Sometimes organizations build their applications as cloud agnostic, so they do not use all features provided by the cloud platform.

Considering the pros and cons, companies should decide the best approach for them. Some of the factors to consider while deciding whether the agnostic approach is for you or not, are as follows:

- If organizations want flexibility and freedom and anticipate future changes in their domain, it is better to use an agnostic approach. It will help the team to lift and shift the software to a new platform as per the requirement.

- For software applications that have frequent customer onboards and offboards, chances are high that they might need to choose a different technology to compete in the market.

- For software applications that are small products, there are chances that they might be merged with some big players in the market. In such cases if application is agnostic of platform, it provides easy merging.

- If organization has enough budget allocated for software development, they can consider investing into building an agnostic approach.

# No measurement no improvement

The above phrase is right in all aspects, not just through the SRE lens. Whether it is software, manufacturing, or medical, any institution or organization wants to be productive and needs improvement. Measuring or assessing your performance is one of the easiest ways to identify when and how to improve. In previous sections, we learned briefly about measurement as one of the essentials in the SRE world. In this section, we will learn the importance of measurement in SRE in detail.

Measure is the quantification of attributes of an object or events, which can be compared to other objects and events. That means, it helps in determining how large or small a quantity is as compared to another. Measure in the case of SRE is defining metrics. The SRE team has the responsibility of managing the production environment and getting involved in other operational activities. They monitor live applications, i.e., production, and get involved in assessing the performance of the production environment. The best way to measure the performance of software systems is by defining metrics at different phases of SDLC.

The goal for all software organizations is to build a system that is scalable, reliable, and available. All engineering teams involved work towards the same goal. No software application is 100% bug-free or 100% scalable and reliable, but engineering teams regularly seek improvement in software systems and work towards achieving this goal. As SRE teams work more closely with the production environment, they get access to the real-time performance of software, and they work towards implementing solutions. And SRE teams should define various metrics to measure all aspects of an application. These metrics help the team understand if a particular milestone is achieved, and they also help assess whether the software system is performing as expected.

The following are some of the common and powerful metrics that the SRE teams should use:

- **MTTR**: It explains how much time your system takes to recover from any failure. Analysis of this metric data helps teams to understand various aspects of the system, such as follows:

  o How did the system actually recover?

  o Was the system auto-recovered, or was it manually recovered by engineers? This question helps the team to evaluate the observability.

o   Was there any alert generated for SRE teams to notify? This question helps teams to evaluate alerting.

o   What tools were used to investigate the failure, and what tools helped in recovery? This question access automation capability.

o   What was the root cause of the error? This helps evaluate code quality and infrastructure quality.

o   Were the failures seen in the testing environment? This helps evaluate testing models and gaps. If the failure was not caught in the testing stage, or if it was caught in the testing stage, then we need to figure out why the faulty code got promoted to production. The failure, in turn, also raises the question for change in management and SRE teams on how effective the code quality check process is.

By just one metric data, all the previous questions will help all teams (SRE, developers, DevOps) to understand what the gaps in their system are, if any.

- **MTBF**: It explains how much gap two failures in a system were there in between. Meaning how frequent failures are seen in the software system. This metric's data helps answer the following questions:

    o   What was the root cause of the failures? This helps understand code quality and check if it is a code issue.

    o   Are two failures the same? Once the root cause is identified, it helps assess the quality of code or infrastructure. And if it is the same failure, then we look at why there are repetitive failures in the system.

    o   Are failures different? This again helps us understand code and infrastructure quality.

    o   Was there any change in the system that caused the failure? This helps assess the change management system and assess the CI/CD pipeline that deploys code.

    o   Was there any alert for failures? This again helps assess alerting.

- **Uptime of system**: It explains the % availability of the system. This metric is also dependent on various factors, such as:

    o   If the uptime of the system was not 99%, then what caused system downtime? The root cause analysis of this question helps evaluate code and infrastructure quality.

    o   Even with sound alerting and monitoring, what processes are followed by development teams to measure code quality, and what other processes are to be followed to ensure the quality of the code.

    o   Are there any external factors that impacted system uptime? This helps assess how much your system depends on other systems and helps find areas for improvements, such as the unavailability of another system that created downtime for you.

- **Latency of system**: It explains the amount of time taken for a request to be processed by the system. The data from this metric helps assess the performance of the system. If latency is high, then we try to figure out where the problem is; is it in the underlying code, a network problem, a server issue, or a database issue?

- **Resource utilization**: It explains the % of available resources that are being used. However, we first need to understand the configuration of the system. Configurational details will help create metrics that measure the performance of the system. The following are some of the data that you should collect to create the right metrics such as:

  o   The CPU and memory are configured for your infrastructure.

  o   The threshold is configured on CPU and memory utilization, with auto-scaling on threshold breach.

  o   The reason for high memory

  o   The reason for high CPU.

Some of the other metrics that can be used to measure the performance of the system are as follows:

  o   **Load balancing**: The distribution of requests across multiple servers so that no single server is overwhelmed, and the system is performant.

  o   **Error rate**: % of requests failing.

  o   **Response time**: The amount of time it takes for a request to be completed by your system.

In all these metrics, you will have to answer questions and find detailed analysis. In this process of answering and analyzing, teams will have opportunities to identify gaps in the system that need to be fixed. Hence, measuring is important for any system to perform. If you do not know how your system is performing, you will not be able to identify areas of improvement. For any problem in the system that lowers the performance, root cause analysis is the key. Only after the teams collaborate and perform a root cause analysis will they be able to point to the direction of the gap and work on the solution(s).

To summarize the solutions learned in this chapter, take an example of an online booking travel software. The example will explain how the previously mentioned best practices are interlinked and help the team build reliability in the system. Let us continue the previous example where while booking a flight, customers using the software suddenly saw an error on the web page, displaying **page not found**.

Different solution categories that help in this scenario are explained as follows:

- **Incident management**: Due to automated incident management, as soon as an error occurs, the incident is logged automatically and assigned to the respective team. Also, as part of the root-cause analysis in incident management, the team was able to identify the root cause and pinpoint the error, and enhance some metrics too, such as response time to user and check on the memory of service.

- **Automation**: Automated incident management that creates and assigns tickets automatically also defines the priority and category.

- **Monitoring**: Due to the monitoring dashboard built by SRE teams, they were able to capture the error within a few seconds. Though there were incidents logged, due to monitoring and alerting application support, teams were quickly able to co-relate the alerts and the created incident.

- **Measuring**: The team has integrated metrics in the dashboard itself to calculate failure requests or the total user requests. As it was integrated into the dashboard, support teams were able to assess the impact on a number of users facing the problem and take the required action promptly.

# Conclusion

Building an effective solution is a journey that involves a lot of planning. Planning is the key to any effective system. The better processes and standards you have, the better your system will perform.

In this chapter, we discussed various factors that play an important role in building an effective solution and how SRE teams today are following these factors. Additionally, we discussed collaboration and ways in which collaboration helps achieve success.

In the next chapter, we will be introduced to anti-patterns and the impact of anti-patterns on software development. We will also understand how anti-patterns the reason for recurring problems in the software development lifecycle are.

## Join our Discord space

Join our Discord workspace for latest updates, offers, tech happenings around the world, new releases, and sessions with the authors:

https://discord.bpbonline.com

# CHAPTER 4

# Understanding Anti-patterns

## Introduction

In this chapter, we will understand anti-patterns and their impact on SDLC. We will discuss some common anti-patterns that act contrary to best practices in software development. This chapter will also cover some of the recurring problems in software engineering that interfere with the progress of SRE and impact the final product.

## Structure

We will cover the following topics in this chapter:

- Pattern and anti-pattern in software engineering
- Common anti-pattern in SRE

## Objectives

By the end of this chapter, we will understand the recurring problems in SDLC that impact SRE and product delivery. This chapter will frame the baseline for the next chapter on how to find solutions for recurring problems. You will understand what patterns and anti-patterns are and how these anti-patterns are introduced into the system. To understand the pitfalls in SRE, it is necessary to understand how anti-patterns in software engineering impact development and SRE. After going through this chapter, you will understand and be able to co-relate these anti-patterns between SRE and developers.

# Pattern and anti-pattern in software engineering

The pattern in software design is an effective and reusable solution that can be applied to common problems in software engineering. Anti-patterns are the opposite of patterns. They are some of the common problems that might not be intentionally introduced by teams but fail the design as a whole. In simple terms, patterns are known to design solutions or best practices used in software engineering to solve recurring issues, and these patterns can be applied to multiple issues. Anti-patterns are those designs that look correct in the beginning as part of an effective solution but create bad consequences later.

In this section, you will understand the various anti-patterns in software engineering and their cause.

For example, a simple pattern uses code that can be reused across services to solve a common problem. An anti-pattern is applying a quick fix in code to solve the problem, but later, with a new service introduction, the quick fix fails both services.

Let us discuss some of the common anti-patterns that you should avoid as a software developer.

# Spaghetti code

As the name suggests, spaghetti code is a mess of code that lacks structure. It is derived by using old code and adding new code on top, applying quick fixes without any planning and structure. That eventually makes it difficult to manage even by the source code. Or when multiple developers work on a piece of code for months or years, copy-paste multiple times without defining the structure, leading to unmanageable and erroneous code.

Though this practice is not used by most developers and engineering teams today, unknowingly, some part of the spaghetti code is sometimes introduced in the system and becomes an anti-pattern.

Let us discuss some of the examples of the cause of this anti-pattern, as follows:

- Legacy code moved to any migration project. Developers insert their code in legacy code, making it complicated to manage.

- Lots of features are required by businesses to build in code, but the delivery timeline is one year. Leading to a lot of code writing but not delivering to production, causing a messy code without actual user testing. When it gets released to users, it becomes difficult to investigate the issues in the code, if any.

- Short timelines to build and deliver a feature in code. The leading code quality is compromised when developers do not follow the best practices and compromise with coding standards to meet timelines. Leading to a messy code.

- Applying quick fixes to the huge code to meet the timelines.

The aforementioned are some examples where developers write messy code that leads to anti-patterns in a system that impacts the product. Spaghetti code is usually a result of a lack of planning and not following standards and processes.

# Golden hammer

This anti-pattern involves excessive dependency and overreliance on one tool to solve multiple problems. It is a little different, as sometimes, if used accordingly, it can be considered a best practice or pattern. However, in some cases, it can lead to an anti-pattern where no one-size-fits-all philosophy works. In other words, it is a result of a mismatch between a problem and a solution.

The golden hammer occurs when the development teams do not plan properly and use one tool or existing tool to solve multiple problems. In some cases, this approach works when an organization is using any enterprise suite that can fulfill multiple requirements; however, sometimes developers do not explore much on the solution of a problem or requirements, and they reuse the existing tool or code available. However, that can lead to issues such as non-performant systems, non-reliability, and not meeting the requirements of end users.

Let us discuss the following examples as causes of the golden hammer:

- An organization is committed to one vendor and is using the vendor's tool. So, for any new requirements, without exploring other solutions, they try to fit in the requirements within the existing tools, doing some minimal customization.

- Due to a lack of time, development teams do not explore other solutions and, with minimal effort and planning, reuse the existing tool to deliver a solution.

- Lack of skill set. When SDLC teams do not have the right skill set for a new requirement. And organizations, do not spend on hiring or training developers. So developers still build the code with their existing knowledge, but that can lead to an anti-pattern as the system might not fulfill the requirement.

In general, SDLC teams have strong planning before deciding on any new requirements, however, golden hammer anti-patterns are introduced unknowingly due to some of the aforementioned reasons.

Let us understand *Golden Hammer* through a real industry scenario. The healthcare technology planned to add new functionality and enhance their software. To meet user's demands, organizations migrated their software to cloud-based solutions. In the initial 2 years, the healthcare software platform performed very well. However, gradually, users started complaining about the performance of the software. The software started crashing frequently; the QA team also highlighted various issues in the software during the testing phase. The SRE team analyzed the complaints and multiple issues in the system. After collaboration with the software development team, it was identified by teams that the cloud solution on which the software is running cannot manage the users' load. Also, the recent functionality of reporting based on big data technology is consuming 50% of the memory of the cloud infrastructure. Dependency on one cloud solution is the reason for the low performance of healthcare software. Once the organization realized the root cause of the problem, they migrated their reporting feature to the cloud provider, a pioneer in big data technology. Though it was an extra cost to the organization, in the long run, it improved the reliability and performance of the software.

The idea is to not rely on only one solution for all problems. Sometimes, organizations choose one solution for all their requirements, but that is informed planning and decision-making based on certain criteria such as the requirement aligning well, being short on budget, and having time limitations.

# Boat anchor

This anti-pattern happens when the developer leaves a piece of code in the codebase that (a piece of code) might be used later. Leaving unwanted or future codes in the code base is not a best practice in the software development model. If the piece of code is not required in the near future, let us say for another 3-4 months, this extra code can create bugs with existing code, developers have to manage the code unnecessarily, and while debugging, developers have to go through extra debugging, compiling and building can also be slowed down, it can break build also if undefined code is lying in the codebase.

Let us discuss some of the reasons why and how a boat anchor anti-pattern is introduced in the system, as follows:

- The developer got a new requirement, and they started writing code and added it to the codebase, but later, the requirement was canceled. So, developers not removing the piece of code can create issues in the future.

- The developers got an early requirement to build new functionality that is required to be delivered six months later. They had bandwidth available, so they built the code and added it to the codebase. Now, the piece of code that is not required today is running in the live system. This can create issues, such as if any bug is introduced, then debugging and fixing is an extra effort. The live system can see defects due to this unwanted code.

- The developers got a requirement to deliver the functionality in 3 months. They added the feature in the code but made this feature as a toggle enabled (new code/functionality, developed in a way that will work depending on this toggle/config implemented, and this toggle, when disabled or enabled, will decide whether the code will work or not), thinking that after 3 months, they would enable the toggle for this code to start working in production. However, by mistake, one of the developers enabled the toggle before the timeline, causing unwanted delivery of the requirement.

The developer mostly unknowingly does the boat anchor, and when they do not visualize holistically. From the developer's perspective, they are building a code required to be delivered a few months from their current time as they have time and bandwidth, but they do not visualize the risk of this code lying in the production environment.

# Dead code

Dead code is any section of code that gets executed, but the output of the code is not used by any other program. That means the code that has been lying there for a long but is not required. This anti-pattern is also the derivative of the boat anchor anti-pattern. As its name says, the code that was used in the past as legacy code, however, is dead now, and no one is aware of the functionality of the code, and the code is just lying there in the code base. Similar to boat anchor, dead code can also break current functionality.

Let us discuss some of the use cases where dead code anti-pattern can be introduced, as follows:

- A piece of code became obsolete or not required. However, developers never removed that code from the codebase. Now, every time the codebase is compiled, obsolete code also has to be compiled. Some new developers introduced a code that encountered an issue due to the old/obsolete code, as the developer was not aware of the old code. It is an anti-pattern, as it impacts code and is time-consuming to debug.

- A piece of code is not used anymore but is still sitting in the code base, as this code is coupled with other codes, and the unwanted code is still required to run other code unless it is decoupled. Now, developers do not have enough confidence or time to decouple the code that is not in use and remove it. Then, it became an anti-pattern, where the unwanted code is getting compiled every time with the code base, which is, again, time-consuming to debug.

Dead code anti-patterns are heavy. These codes do nothing but increase build time, decrease the performance of code compilation, and be time-consuming to debug.

Boat anchor and dead code are similar but different. Let us understand the difference between the two through real industry scenarios. A financial technology organization migrated its legacy software to a cloud-based platform. New cloud-based software builds various new functionality along with existing features. After a few months, the software started seeing issues in performance; two such issues were frequent failures of search functionality and intermittent failure of the buy stocks functionality. The reason for the search functionality failing is the introduction of one of the new features, AI-driven search functionality. This new AI-driven search was supposed to go live in six months; however, developers built the feature in advance and deployed the code in production (as one of the best practice features/functionalities are built with toggles, which means any piece of code is driven by toggle and as per need the toggle can be enabled or disabled). Though the code was disabled, one of the AI-driven search scenarios was not tested fully in the testing environment, which impacted normal search functionality. This is an example of a boat anchor. Code that is required for the future was deployed in production without full prod testing and that impacted software. The second issue of the buy stocks functionality failing is due to being out of memory. As it is, a legacy code migrated to the cloud. One of the old codes in stock functionality, which is not required, was also migrated. Developers ignored that old code, assuming that code was harmless, but every time the service buy stocks is used, the service triggers a **Java Virtual Machine (JVM)** runtime engine that helps the Java program to execute). This JVM failed without memory as the run time engine did not get enough memory to execute the code. The underlying problem is that old code was compiled every time buy stocks were used. This old code consumes all the memory of JVM. This is an example of how dead code can impact software performance.

# God object

God object is when any object or class is too good, such as when one object is responsible for too many things. That means one object is responsible for multiple functionalities in the code. Now, this also can be anti-pattern, as an issue with just one object can bring down multiple other functionalities, and this is against the best practice of object-oriented design. Sometimes, developers design code where one object is treated like a master class that takes care of the responsibility of other objects, too. Though developers can break down this god object into multiple normal objects, they keep using one object, leading to an anti-pattern.

Let us discuss the following examples and causes of the God object anti-pattern:

- Developers were getting similar requirements to build in code. They saw that there is one object that can be extended and used by just adding new parameters. This practice continued in the project. Now, after a few years, this one object has become a God object that is taken care of by multiple functionalities. For example, a payment project where one object is a customer ID that is responsible for fetching name, transaction, address, history spend, future enrolment, offers, etc. Now, if the customer id is impacted, that will impact all these parameters. However, transactions, history spent, and ennoblement can be broken down and assigned to another object.

- Developers started using one object as the master, which is responsible for multiple functionalities. Developers are not confident in breaking down this object, as this will require a change in design and effort. So, they ignore this anti-pattern and keep on using one object as a master. Though developers can argue that it is easy for them to manage the code, this can slow down the performance. One object has to work on lots of data that is not even required.

The other set of best practice principles is **single responsibility, open/closed, Liskov substitution, interface segregation, and dependency inversion (SOLID)** principles in programming. SOLID is five essential guidelines that enhance software design, making code more maintainable and scalable. Here, S of SOLID refers to the single responsibility principle. As per this principle, the class should have a single purpose or single responsibility. One function of a class is easy to maintain the code, easy to change the code if requirements change in the future, and easy to debug. However, this does not mean that all classes should have a single responsibility. There should be a balance between classes that hold multiple responsibilities and single responsibility. Following the single responsibility principle can help solve the problem of God object.

God's objects are against the best practices of software development and should not be used. The planning team should review the code regularly to identify such anti-patterns. By using one object for required functionality, too much responsibility is added to one object that can break the functionality and, again, can impact broader functionality.

# Copy and paste programming

As the name implies, it is copying other codes and pasting them into the source code as the functionality of the two codes matches. Copy and paste is never a good practice in software development. Two code bases are always different, even if they solve the same requirement. The dependencies, language, infrastructure, underlying libraries, etc., all can differ between two similar code bases, and copy-pasting one code into another can introduce bugs.

Let us discuss how this anti-pattern is introduced in the system, as follows:

- Developers working on two projects or developers move to new projects that have the same functionality. They copy the piece of code from one of the codes to another one. Though they tested the code locally, it broke in production due to the non-availability of libraries. This will make it an anti-pattern, as this impacts working applications.

- Due to the lack of time, developers found one piece of code outside and copied it into their existing code base. The code worked, but later, when another developer worked on the code base, they introduced new dependencies that were not compatible due to the old, copied code. Here, developers are aware, but still, they copy and paste to save their time and effort.

There cannot be any supporting argument for copy-pasting code, as this is always done knowingly and is against the best practice of software development. Organizations had to build standards and processes to bring this into practice for developers not to copy-paste code.

The aforementioned explanations are some of the patterns and anti-patterns that impact SRE positively and negatively, respectively. All the anti-patterns in software development impact applications, eventually impacting SRE and its process. Anti-patterns in a code slow down progress in development, introduce bugs, impact application performance, and compromise code quality. As SRE is coupled between development and reliability, it becomes more difficult for SRE to manage the availability and reliability of the system due to such issues.

# Common anti-patterns in SRE

SRE plays a crucial role in the availability, reliability, and performance of any software system. In the previous chapters, you learned the importance of SRE for a smooth application experience. In the previous section, you learned that anti-patterns in software engineering are the pitfall for development, but they also impact SRE if these pitfalls are not caught on time. These anti-patterns create issues in production that impact the reliability and availability of the system. SRE also has its pitfalls that impact the availability and reliability of the system and are called anti-patterns. In this section, you will understand the high level of the types of anti-patterns in SRE, and the next chapter will go in-depth to explain these anti-patterns.

Anti-pattern solutions are a way to catch issues in the system at the last step before it is ready to go live. So, if development fails to review and correct their anti-pattern, SRE should be able to catch them. This section will explain how to identify and avoid those anti-patterns in SRE.

The following are some of the common anti-patterns in SRE:

# Misconfigured alerts

Alerts are one of the key components of observability. They help the SRE and ops team to catch issues before end users notice them. That is why it is critical to configure correct alerts. Misconfigured alerts can lead to inaccurate or irrelevant information notifications to the ops team, leading to critical service disruption or outage. The system that depends on alerting can be impacted hugely due to such misconfigured alerts. Now, the question is why the SRE teams will configure wrong alerts, so they might not knowingly configure the wrong alert but unknowingly introduce this anti-pattern to the system.

Let us discuss some of the misconfigured alerts and the causes of how alerts can be misconfigured, as follows:

- In a project where alert setting up is manual, SRE got the requirement from the development team on a new service going to be deployed in production. SRE, by mistake, set up alerts on an old service that has a similar name. SRE did not validate the alert config, or the project does not have an automated validation process for alerting. After the service went live, production failed, but due to misconfiguration, SRE and ops did not notice it, creating an outage.

- Alerts are configured right on some services. Later, these services are decommissioned. However, the alerts were not removed, creating noise. Noise is an unwanted alert notification not required but populate the system unnecessarily, which can lead to missing original alert notifications.

- SRE has a requirement to set up some customized alerts as the automated system is not capable of creating and adding these customizations. SRE created correct alerts but, by mistake, gave the wrong channel, email, or contact to notify the alert. Now, the service has an outage, but as the notification channel was not correct, it went unnoticed.

- Creating unwanted alerts just to notify the team. At the start of the project, SRE created a few alerts as notifications and no action-required alerts. However, over a few years, the application grew, and SRE did not clean up those notification alerts. That can overwhelm and exhaust SRE to respond to every alert and can lead to missing actual alerts. This type of noise in alerting is also referred to as alert fatigue.

# Incorrect ticketing

Alerting and ticketing go hand in hand for the ops team. Depending on the SRE process, sometimes a few critical alerts are configured to create incidents along with other outages and disruption-creating incidents. Incorrect ticketing or incidents are not configuring the correct category in tickets.

Let us discuss the following incorrect ticketing criteria:

- Setting up incidents on low-priority alerts or issues that can be resolved automatically. This can overwhelm and exhaust SRE by shifting their focus from responding to other critical alerts.

- Creating actionable tickets for routine work that can be easily automated. Such as routine patching and upgrades where automated validation can be integrated. Making such tickets manual and actionable can again overwhelm SRE.

Incorrect ticketing is a practice that should be avoided, as over a period of time, this can lead to anti-patterns for the SRE process.

# No automated remediation

Automation is the heart of SRE and should be implemented in all required areas to avoid human errors. Not automating the remediations of known errors/issues leads to manual resolution and SRE burnout. This is a pitfall that leads to human error and exhausting SRE or ops teams. Some of the examples of this anti-pattern are:

- Regular alerts such as high CPU and mem. The team is manually scaling up. Such activities can be automated.

- Service intermittent failure, where the team manually validates each alert failure. Such alerts should be automated.

Manually resolving any alert is time-consuming and error-prone. It is an anti-pattern that is the roadblock to SRE.

# No change management process

The system will never break if no change is introduced to the system. But you cannot advance your application without any changes. In any growing organization, change is inevitable, and any change, small or big, comes with a risk of breaking the system. If changes are not properly planned or validated, they can break the system. Manual changes in the system are also anti-pattern. Change can be infrastructure or application; both types of changes, if not correctly planned and validated, can bring an outage to an existing system. Moreover, SRE will have to spend their time investigating and fixing the issue.

Let us discuss some examples of the changes that can impact SRE, as follows:

- The change was requested by developers to add one table to the database. By mistake, the developer mentioned the change as creating a new user and table. As there was no proper validation process for change, the change got executed (the executor ran the force create command) and re-created the existing user that changed the password, and that failed multiple services with an authentication error.

- Two changes were requested to upgrade the OS in two regions at the same time. As there was no validation of changes, it impacted both regions for an application that is the total outage.

Change management is a separate process that should be automated for validation with the right approvers. If changes break the system, SRE will have to spend hours to resolve such issues.

# Unrealistic expectations or chasing nines

Fife-nine or 99.99999% is the percentage of time a service is accessible to a user in a given period, probably in a year. This is one of the percentages that software organization uses to measure software availability. Though organizations aim for 100% availability of software, this is an unrealistic goal as no software can always be up all the time. Various factors outside software code cannot control the uptime, such as maintenance, upgrades, natural disasters, etc. This is one of the anti-patterns that impact reliability. That means you are quoting 100% of the availability and reliability of your system, which is unrealistic.

As mentioned in the previous chapters, no system is perfect, and there will be outages. Overquoting reliability as 100% is a false expectation to end users and the teams involved in building and supporting. To maintain 100% reliability, you need a fully automated system, no issues, and highly skilled teams, which is impractical and unsustainable.

# Pinpointing or no blameless post-mortem

SRE aims to ensure the system's reliability and availability. With recurring issues in the system, SRE learns and trains its automation to fix issues before they are noticed by end users. For issues occurring in the system, if SRE teams started investing time in finding the team who impacted or introduced the system, that wastes SRE's time and effort; rather, this time can be used to investigate and remediate. One of the best practices for the SRE culture is blameless post-mortems, and not doing the same creates an anti-pattern for SRE. Here, SRE does not focus on the cause of issues, which can mislead the investigation and impact the solution for the issue.

The preceding few anti-patterns are some of the common anti-patterns in the SRE world that impact the SRE's day-to-day job and, in turn, impact the reliability of the system. There are various best practices for SRE to follow, however, depending on the type of project and software system, not all these practices can be incorporated in the system. However, all anti-patterns should still be avoided to focus SRE on innovation and building a reliable system.

Anti-patterns are like traps that might compromise the system's stability. Sometimes, the team knowingly introduces an anti-pattern, or other times; it is a ripple effect of one process break. These pitfalls not only impact the system's availability but also add extra cost to the project.

# Conclusion

In this chapter, we understood what anti-patterns are and how anti-patterns impact the system. This chapter also explained different anti-patterns in software engineering that impact SRE and eventually impact system reliability. This chapter is a baseline for the next chapter, which will provide detailed descriptions of anti-patterns and how these anti-patterns can be avoided.

In the next chapter, we will help you understand more about the solutions to all the problems that you read in this chapter, such as anti-patterns that impact the reliability of software.

## Join our Discord space

Join our Discord workspace for latest updates, offers, tech happenings around the world, new releases, and sessions with the authors:

https://discord.bpbonline.com

# CHAPTER 5
# Types of Anti-patterns

## Introduction

Patterns and anti-patterns are both part of the **software development lifecycle (SDLC)**. It is seen in planning, software development, and the **site reliability engineering (SRE)** approach. It is essential to identify anti-patterns so that appropriate actions can be taken to solve and avoid these issues or gaps. The previous chapter helped us understand anti-patterns and why they are bad for any software development organization.

In this chapter, we will discuss the different types of anti-patterns and how to recognize them. The chapter will also explain the solutions to these anti-patterns. Additionally, we will understand the various ways to overcome challenges for efficient SRE practice. The chapter explains on the hidden roadblocks to SRE practices. And how it impacts overall system performance and resiliency.

## Structure

The chapter covers the following topics:

- Types of anti-patterns
- Anti-patterns in system reliability and scalability
- Hidden roadblocks to the SRE path

- Real time scenarios of anti-patterns and solutions
- Key takeaways

# Objectives

By the end of this chapter, you will understand anti-patterns in SRE in detail and how to overcome those anti-patterns to build and deliver effective solutions through SRE practices. You will also learn some of the hidden anti-patterns and challenges and how to identify those hidden gaps in the SRE process. This chapter aims to help you understand the correct identification of pitfalls and the solution. This chapter will help you implement some of these solutions and best practices in the real-world SRE model for quality and reliable product delivery. No solution fits all, but it can help you create solutions. Though the chapter will explain anti-patterns across different phases of the SDLC journey, it is presented from the lens of SRE.

The SRE team is responsible for maintaining the system's reliability; they are owners of the production/live system. So, any anti-pattern or bad practice as part of SDLC will ultimately impact the live system, affecting the SRE journey.

# Types of anti-patterns

Anti-patterns are some of the mistakes and unseen gaps that lead to roadblocks in SRE best practices and methodology. It is essential to identify and address the gaps. Also, find solutions to overcome and avoid such anti-patterns in the future. Before moving ahead to understand more about anti-patters, let us re-visit the SDLC model and SRE's position in SDLC.

The following diagram explains the SRE landscape in SDLC:

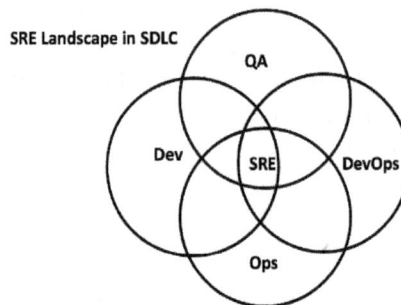

*Figure 5.1: Position of SRE in SDLC*

Let us move forward and briefly review some of SRE's best practices. There are multiple other best practices derived from the standard practices as follows:

- Analysis of changes holistically. This needs a robust change management process.

- Eliminate redundancy by automating redundant tasks. This will save time and effort and remove human error.

- Expanding skill sets is part of a strong culture and communication. This can be followed only if the right technology and processes are used within SRE.

- Learn from failure. This means you need a good knowledge base tool, strong defect management, strong incident management, and a defined process.

- Define clear service level objectives.

This is the process of SRE planning as shown in the following figure:

**Best Practice for SRE**

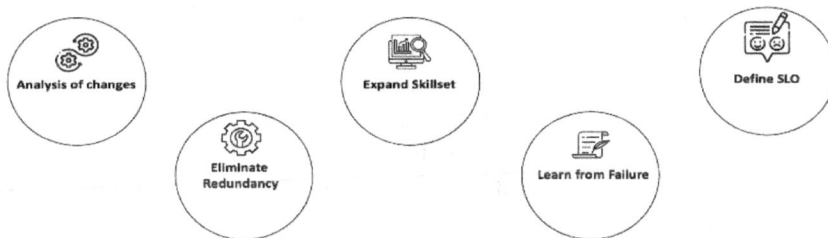

*Figure 5.2: Best practice for SRE*

Anti-patterns are sometimes attractive, accessible, happy paths but eventually create roadblocks. So, in simple language, you can call it a short-term quick fix that impacts your system in the long term.

Anti-patterns are not problems of just today's modern software development model; it is also common in legacy systems. Some organizations are still using their legacy systems, and there can be multiple reasons for using the legacy system in the era of cloud and AI, such as the system works well enough, it is small software so easy to maintain, updating the system is challenging, so no one wanted to do that, insufficient funding, limited compatibility with new systems, etc.

The anti-patterns in legacy systems are:

- Software systems are tightly tied to operating systems. That impacts its capability to port or migrate to the new model.

- Monolith architecture is a software application where all components are integrated into a single unit. It might be good for smaller software but can become an anti-pattern for large systems where it can be difficult to scale and manage large systems.

- Sequential flow (lack of request-response in service communication), where an update in one service requires to hold full software application.

- Old business processes.

For some organizations, using legacy systems is a requirement, and it is no harmful to use legacy systems. If organizations can identify some of the anti-patterns and solve these, it can help them build performant systems with legacy applications, too.

Let us discuss some of the anti-patterns in the SRE journey at different phases as follows:

# Anti-patterns in service design

Service design is one of the initial phases of SDLC, and design is the backbone of any software application. The more time spent in planning and designing any application, it helps build a reliable system. Addressing some anti-patterns during the design phase can help you avoid many roadblocks in the SDLC journey.

Let us discuss the following anti-patterns in service designs and how we can identify them:

- **One service has multiple dependencies**: One service where multiple other service depend for input or output data. However, it does not seem like a roadblock, and it is ok by design to have a service that can be treated as a master service where multiple other services depend. However, this can be turned into an anti-pattern when your system grows. When the system grows, various other services are onboarded to the existing application, and that one service still has a server master role; that can become a bottleneck if some bug occurs in that service. One service will lead to disruption to multiple other services. Sometimes, during the initial design, developers or designers need to visualize expandability, which leads to a roadblock. To avoid such anti-patterns, developers should design services in a way that can be broken down in the future if required.

  To identify this anti-pattern, you must first list the repetitive issues; out of those issues, identify the services failing frequently and the root cause of failure. Suppose the frequent shortcomings are in the master service. In that case, it is your first step towards identifying such a service and taking appropriate action, for example, dividing the service into two to share the load. One of the solutions to this problem is using microservice architecture, where services are broken into smaller independent purpose-specific services.

- **Single data source**: All services depend on input data from one data source that acts as a source of truth. This anti-pattern does not have any pitfalls or roadblocks. However, any problem in data sources can be a bottleneck for all services and applications. Let us assume there is one database that feeds data to all services, and depending on that data, all application services perform their functions. Now, issues in one data set can also block further application processing.

  To identify that a single data source can be an anti-pattern, first list down the issues creating roadblocks or outages in the application, and if issues are reoccurring due to data sources, then you need to either redesign application data flow or correct wrong data.

Another way to identify this anti-pattern is a periodic review of application design. If your application consists of multiple services and is on the path of growing concerning data and new services, then you should consider eliminating a single data source. Either break down into two or three data sources or remove the dependency of one data source.

- **API versioning**: It means maintaining different versions of your APIs. Mostly, all software organizations follow best practices and version their code. However, versioning APIs should not be overused. Sometimes, as per requirements versioning API is required but versioning should be limited. In ideal scenario even if the underlying service changes, the API should never break and return the result with all service versions. There can be a debate on whether APIs should be versioned, and here are the reasons for limit the versioning of APIs. For large software with microservice architecture that has multiple services with multiple APIs, these APIs are interfaces built to pull or push data from underlying services. Versioning API can create a cumbersome source code. If you create different versions of API as per the underlying service version, every time during deployment same version of API and service has to be deployed. If changes are needed to the API, they should be overwritten rather than maintained versions.

API versioning is considered an anti-pattern because it makes source code challenging to manage and deploy, requiring developers to invest unwanted effort and time, which is not the best practice. However, to note versioning APIs is not always wrong. Creating various versions of single APIs and versioning all APIs can be an anti-pattern for the reason mentioned above. Versioning APIs can be useful in following scenarios:

  - In a project where same APIs must return different data as per requirement. In such cases maintaining different versions of API can be a best practice.

  - If a software application has compatibility issues with one version of API, so its ok to keep different versions of API but a temporary solution until the underlying issues are fixed.

  - If a software application has grown large overtime and it already has multiple versions of multiple APIs, then the solution is to use some tool to maintain and manage those versions.

You should always incorporate best practices while designing services. As mentioned, this is the initial and critical phase in SDLC. Even after following best practices, you may see anti-patterns that impact the delivery and reliability of software. These anti-patterns in service design can be the root cause of compromised reliability. Above highlighted are some common anti-patterns that affect the system's overall performance and reliability. One of the best practices is to regularly review your service and overall product to identify any roadblocks and find solutions accordingly.

# Anti-patterns in monitoring and observability

Observability is a backbone for efficient SRE practice. Without observability organization can never achieve software reliability. Observability means observing your system and reacting (or solving) to the anomalies or problems before the end-user notices. There are various best practices SRE teams should follow while designing their observability architecture, but here, you will understand some of the anti-patterns that organizations should avoid while implementing observability.

The following are some of those anti-patterns:

- **Excessive logs with no structure**: This is one of the anti-patterns that impact observability. Logs are an essential piece of observability and are the first point of initiating root cause analysis. However, when your application logs huge amounts of data, it becomes difficult to analyze the logs and pull any useful insights. Then, it becomes an anti-pattern, which creates a roadblock for SRE teams to investigate any error. Excessive logs analysis is time-consuming; with proper structure in logs, it becomes easier to identify any trigger events or errors in logs. To avoid such a situation, developers should always add event codes to analyze the mistakes or categorize them based on severity and timestamp. As mentioned, anti-patterns in software development can create roadblocks for SRE. It is essential to understand and remove these anti-patterns, for example, categorizing logs.

- **Noise in alerts**: It is similar to excessive logs, where excessive alerts are considered noise and impact monitoring systems. Too many alerts only sometimes mean better visibility; it can be overwhelming for SRE teams to monitor too many alerts. It is an anti-pattern as these false alerts misguide analysis and overload the system. If your application is alerting every second and most of these alerts are not required, then it is a signal that SRE teams should review their monitoring model. SRE teams should collaborate with development teams and identify such noise in the system. Some of the alerts can be improved by changing the code, and some can be improved by correcting the configuration in the alerting system. For example, repetitive sev4 alerts are firing, but the application does not see any underlying issue. It is an example of a false alert.

- **Multiple dashboards and monitoring tools**: Using the latest tools to monitor your system is helpful for the SRE team. However, using multiple tools and different dashboards to monitor applications can become an anti-pattern and a roadblock. Too many tools and dashboards will confuse SRE teams and consume a lot of time, as SRE teams will have to jump to multiple places to investigate any issue that can hinder the analysis and delay the solution. It is also an added cost to the organization. Sometimes, even after proper planning, organizations onboard new tools, and teams create multiple monitoring dashboards as the requirement grows. After some time, it becomes challenging to maintain numerous dashboards. Tracking, managing, and keeping these dashboards requires extra effort, time, and cost. So, the SRE team should regularly review the requirements of tools and eliminate tools that are not necessary. The team should always try to club multiple dashboards to give a unified view for better observability. For example, configuring multiple open-source monitoring tools is more expensive and time-consuming than purchasing an enterprise tool that can fulfill all requirements at a lower price.

- **Using wrong metrics to measure the system**: Metrics are a critical part of SRE. It helps you measure your system, so you must choose these metrics carefully and adequately. The more metrics you have for every service, the better you can measure and understand your system. However, sometimes right metrics are used with wrong data sampling, which can mislead the system's performance. Incorrect data sampling means collecting data during the wrong window or collecting very few samples that impact performance measurement. For example, a job runs in a system that saves some data in the database. The job always takes 1 hour to complete. The anomaly detection tool takes data sampling of 30 minutes and generates anomalies if jobs run beyond 30 minutes. Though the data model works fine for other jobs, this needs to be corrected for data sampling. Various tools available in the market help automated data sampling and anomaly detection.

- **No correlation in alerts**: As your system grows, it means more services, which means more logging and alerting. As a SRE team, you will try to implement tools that help you monitor and self-heal alerting. However, if your alerts are not co-related, they can lead to a roadblock in investigation and analysis. Co-related alerts are different but generated due to the same issue, or the system triggers multiple alerts due to an outage in one service. If your monitoring system is not advanced enough to identify these correlated alerts, you can miss some vital information or be misguided. This is an anti-pattern as it impacts SRE's ability to identify the right alert on time and delay the required action on that alert. Correlating alerts is not straightforward. As part of the root cause analysis, the SRE team should list down the alerts triggered by the system and feed this data to the monitoring system to correlate the alerting. This is a reactive approach to solving problems. SRE can also follow a proactive approach in collaboration with the development team. Where identifying the errors or alerts a service and dependent service will throw for any failure. That will help the SRE team to determine the correlated alerts.

- **Ignoring upstream and downstream monitoring**: To have a 360-degree view of your system, you need to monitor the system from all aspects. That means monitoring upstream and downstream systems talking to your software application. Sometimes, upstream and downstream systems do not fall under project or organization purview, so you should consider monitoring incoming and outgoing data and services. Organizations with mature SRE model pay a lot of attention to monitoring; however, sometimes, they ignore systems that interact with their system. Your software can encounter issues even due to impact on downstream and upstream systems, so monitoring the interface between your system and other upstream/downstream systems, data flowing, and network traffic is crucial. This is also one of the hidden roadblocks that SRE teams ignore unknowingly. Even after implementing monitoring, applications fail reliability.

To solve some of the aforementioned quoted anti-patterns there are various solutions, such as:

- **Excessive logs you can categories logs**: Logs can be divided into info, debug, error or warn at code level. Along with that there are various tools today that help categorization of logs on top of what you already did in code. Example Datadog it helps in log aggregation for effective handling.

- **Noise in alerts**: The actual fix for false alerts is in underlying code. However, there are some tools that can help grouping alerts to reduce the noise. Example ELK stack, Kibana can help creating expectations rules in alert config to eliminate false alert firing

- **Co-related alerts**: Where multiple alerts or events that are generated due to one problem and all these alerts are grouped in single, this method is co-relating alerts. This is very useful in monitoring and observability. Using AI to corelate alert is one of the upcoming solutions.

# Anti-patterns in release and deployment

Release management and SRE go hand in hand and are tied together. A defined release management process ensures the system's reliability, empowering SRE to maintain the system through best practices. Due to their dependencies, anti-patterns impact SRE in release and deployment.

Some of the common anti-patterns in release management are:

- **Environment inconsistency**: Having different versions of code in the test and production environment is an anti-pattern as it breaks the best practice model of release management. Inconsistent environments make it difficult for the team to investigate issues, and tracing back any issue is time-consuming. Ideally, the test environment version should get deployed to production; however, if you are testing a different version, then what is running on production is different than the actual testing, and you will not be able to catch issues on time. The release management process should be able to identify version discrepancies between testing and production environments and block anything in production that is not tested. There are various tools that can help maintain environment consistency across multiple environments. These tools are called as **infrastructure as a code (IaaC/IaC)** tool. IaaC tools are used to automate infrastructure provisioning and management. Example Terraform, Ansible, AWS CloudFoundation, Puppet, Chef and others, these tools can help automate configuration of infra and the same configuration can be applied to all environments without any manual intervention.

- **Lack of automation**: After DevOps, release and deployment have advanced from a traditional approach to a modern one, which is all automated. However, sometimes projects still follow a manual approach. Big projects with multiple services running on different infrastructures sometimes land up into release and deployment, which is a mix of automation and manual. There can be reasons for automation and manual mixed approach, but this can lead to an anti-pattern. Managing deployment manually for big projects can delay project delivery, is challenging to manage, and is error-prone and time-consuming. This can lead to issues in delivery in a production environment. To solve this problem there are various tools available also in-house automation works best.

- **No gating for changes**: This anti-pattern is linked to the previous *lack of automation*. Manually triggering the release and deployment pipeline will lack automated gating, which means someone has to validate the changes going into the system and approve them manually. Manual validation always needs the knowledge and skill of the approving person. This dependency on a SME is time- and effort-consuming and can also be a roadblock. With fully automated release and deployment, gating is built-in, and code is deployed into production after validation. The most common and effective tools that can help automate CI/CD are Jenkins and GitHub Actions.

- **Using multiple tools**: It can lead to an anti-pattern if not planned systematically. By nature of big projects, multiple tools are required for release and deployment; however, if tools are not planned, it can lead to a roadblock. Multiple tools require a lot of managing, as they follow different standards for CI/CD, and this involves collaboration among various teams developing the code. In an ideal scenario, an organization uses one tool for release and deployment, but big software solutions that run on different infrastructures require tools that support their deployment. For example, an application with microservice architecture consisting of various sub-systems/applications running on different infrastructures. Though the application product is considered one, underlying code and sub-systems are running on different infra and need different tools to run the release and deployment pipeline. Having multiple different tools for one project can create confusion and require strong collaboration, extra cost of maintaining tools, time, and effort. This can delay the delivery of the application and can compromise the quality.

# Anti-patterns in change management

It is often the unspoken aspects of organizational changes that lead to software failures. Changes are inevitable and required for your software's growth, so yes, if you do not make any changes in the system, it will never break. Release management and change management go hand in hand. Change management decides the changes to be applied in the system, and release management executes those changes. As both impact the production environment, any anti-pattern can create a roadblock for SRE. Change management controls software application changes and is a critical part of software delivery to end users. Any anti-pattern in change management can disrupt running software and impact end users.

The following are some of the anti-patterns in change management:

- **Absence of documentation**: Documentation is one of the critical parts of change management, as it defines and categorizes changes. Organizations always document changes as best practice; however, they sometimes need to document ad-hoc changes, which is an anti-pattern. If ad-hoc changes break the system, then it will be difficult to track down the changes and what went into the system. If similar changes come in the future, due to the absence of documentation, you cannot track or pull evidence that the change created an issue in the system. It is important to plan your change management tool that can document planned, unplanned, and ad-hoc changes.

- **Lack of prioritization**: One of the most fundamental yet impactful parts is missed by teams, leading to a pitfall if no clear prioritization is called out in the change process. This can continue to release and deployment also. When your application is extensive with multiple sub-systems, upstream and downstream, there will be various changes required to go into the system. Some changes are priority over above, but if change management does not have a clear process on how to prioritize, it can lead to hours of discussions, misleading, and a waste of time. There can be chances to miss high-priority change and let go of priority change. These all are examples of anti-patterns in the change management process. It is essential to clearly define the priority in the process; you can solve this problem by using tools available today to determine what priority is for your system. For example, there are ten changes listed, including security vulnerabilities, code changes, and version upgrades. Security vulnerability changes are a priority as if not taken on time; it can compromise your software security. Your tool should be able to identify the category of the change and approve it without spending time on discussions.

- **Too many changes in a day**: As discussed earlier, changes are inevitable, and if your software is on a growth path, there will be multiple changes. However, too many changes can sometimes lead to a bottleneck for the software development team and SRE. Approving various changes in a day, including operating system upgrades, security patching, bug fixes, and certificate renewals, can conflict with each other, and it sometimes becomes difficult to investigate the root cause if any failure occurs by any of the changes. It also demands time and effort from release and SRE teams as they must implement and validate the changes. This anti-pattern is connected to prioritization. Prioritization controls change and help DevOps and SRE teams plan changes. Several changes in a day should be defined as part of the change management planning phase, and you should always keep a window for ad hoc changes.

# Operational anti-patterns in incident and defect management

Incident and defect management are pillars of an SRE best practice. It would be best to have planning and the tools to incorporate incident management. Any anti-pattern can impact the SRE process and, in turn, impact software application reliability. Though organizations follow best practices for incident and defect management, however, there are some anti-patterns that are sometimes hidden.

The following are some of the anti-patterns:

- **No correct prioritization of incidents and defects**: Prioritization is critical in any aspect of SDLC. When you have big projects, multiple teams, and a huge customer base, prioritization of tasks becomes one of the key factors. And missing the right priority is an anti-pattern. The operations team receives multiple incidents and defects in a system daily, and if SRE teams do not define the correct priority, it will lead to a pitfall. Teams will not be able to identify what incident to pick first for resolution, nor will they be able to identify the defect that needs to be fixed by developers. Sometimes high-priority incidents will be lying in the operation's queue while the team is working on low ones. The same is true for defects; if the ops team identifies defects and does not assign the right priority, developers will not be able to fix the critical bug on time. Prioritization also defines the escalation process, and no correct priority will block that escalation. Priority has to be defined and implemented at the very beginning of the SRE process.

- **No workforce assignment process for the incident**: This is not an important factor, but this is one of the biggest anti-patterns in big projects. Tools must automate incident management and assignment, but sometimes organizations ignore this part, creating an anti-pattern. When there is no proper assignment of team members for incidents, it creates chaos. Multiple members might work on the same incidents, or incidents are not at all acknowledged by any of the team members; there can be confusion in handing over incidents in operational shifts. This all can lead to unattended issues in production that can impact end users.

- **Multiple channels for receiving incidents**: Receiving incidents from multiple channels can create chaos, making it difficult to focus on one channel, and the chances of missing incidents are higher. If there are multiple channels, such as email, incident management tools, SMS, etc., the ops team will not be able to focus on one of the channels, which can lead to repetitive effort or might miss these incidents. If there are multiple channels, then they should be linked to each other so that if the ops team acknowledges an incident on one channel, there should be an automated back to all the channels for that incident. The best practice is to avoid multiple channels.

- **No automation for defect management**: defect management is mostly automated in organizations; however, creating defects when it is manual leads to anti-pattern.

When you have a big software application with frequent code changes, it depends on the fast-moving requirements. Code changes also lead to defects in the system. If you do not automate the creation of defects, your ops teams can miss tracking those defects. Let us take a scenario in a day of ops teams; during monitoring they identified a significant bug in the system, and a few support members started resolving or circumventing it. In parallel, other ops members identified two more noncritical bugs. The team was busy monitoring and circumventing significant bugs, so they forgot to create the low-priority defect. After a few days, one new code change impacted this former low-priority defect and created an outage. As the team forgot to create and track defects, the issue was not caught on time and affected end users. This is an example of anti-pattern impacting software reliability.

There are some good tools available to solve the issues of automation in incidents and defects, such as PagerDuty, ITSM, Opsgenie.

# Anti-patterns in error handling

Error handling is mostly part of development best practices. However, development teams sometimes do not handle errors correctly. Not planning error handling can be an anti-pattern impacting SRE during an issue's investigation.

The following are some of the common anti-patterns in error handling:

- **The common anti-pattern is incorrect categorization**: Errors are not correctly categorized in code, such as the error logs being printed as info logs. SRE will not be able to monitor and catch these errors correctly.

- **Not handling errors**: It is also an anti-pattern for software engineering. It impacts the system in production, ultimately impacting reliability.

- **Not printing the correct message in logging**: This will mislead the operations team who is monitoring the system.

Errors and logs are the critical part for investigating any issue and not having the right logs or lack of structure can consume lot of time in finding the solution to any issue. Let us take an example where error logs are getting printed in warn logs. SRE team started investigating one issue using logging tool. In the tool SRE engineer filtered on error logs, as the actual error logs were printing in WARN so engineer was not able to identify the actual log and thus no solution to the issue.

# Anti-patterns in communication and collaboration

Collaboration is the key to today's SDLC model. DevOps and SRE are all new methodologies based on collaboration and clear communication. Any anti-pattern in collaboration can lead to real pitfalls and roadblocks in the SRE journey. Some of the common anti-patterns are:

- **No clear channel for collaboration**: All the teams in SDLC should use technology and tools to communicate and collaborate. Not using a transparent platform or channel can lead to an anti-pattern, as it creates confusion, lacks proper tracking, and is time-consuming. Let us take a scenario where the development team needs to collaborate with the SRE and ops team. There is no explicit channel, so some team members are using internal communication tools used in the organization, a few are using email, and some are just using phone call options. Each of these members is tracking conversation locally by their means. One of the conversations is about updating certificates in code that are about to expire. The SRE member tracking conversation went off, and the certs were not updated on time, creating an outage in the system. This is just one example of needing a clear channel for communication.

- **Not automating collaboration outcomes**: Collaboration tools help SDLC teams to break silos and work together. Though organizations today use modern tools however, not tracking the outcomes of collaboration can lead to anti-pattern. Teams are collaborating to solve the problem, the problem is solved, but they need to track the steps taken to solve the problem. The next time, the same issue happened, and the team had to sit and find the solution again and invest their time in a repetitive problem that was solved in the past. Teams collaborated to create a new system design for a requirement; they created the design; however, brainstorming points were not tracked down. When a similar design requirement comes in, teams will have to start from scratch, which is extra time and effort. Though this does not seem an anti-pattern, it takes time and effort from SRE teams, which can be utilized for other purposes.

# Anti-patterns in culture and teamwork

Culture is an important factor; however it is difficult to build in teams. Culture does not change overnight, and it requires planning and effort, which takes time for any organization to reflect on. Having anti-patterns in culture and teamwork can negatively impact the system. So, it is very important to identify some of the common roadblocks in culture and teamwork as follows:

- **Not using technology to instill culture**: To follow a specific culture in a team, leadership has to push teams to use best practices. However, if organizations use technology to mandate best practices, they can have a better chance to build a particular culture, as elaborated in the following example:
  - ○ Organizations want to build a blameless approach and teamwork culture. The leadership defined the process of blaming, but only on paper. When an outage occurred, SRE and three dev teams collaborated to solve the problem. However, due to the absence of a tool, no one tracked down the issue. During root cause analysis or post-mortem sessions, teams started pointing out issues, but as no evidence was captured, they were not able to identify the real root cause. The issue rotates between different development teams, with each team pointing out and blaming others for their code. It created chaos

and demotivation among teams, and there was no RCA. It is a waste of time and energy for teams. On the contrary, if the tool is being used to track all the points, teams can refer to that later and find RCA without pinpointing.

- **No teamwork model**: All organizations today function on teamwork. A lack of teamwork can create uncertainty in the delivery of the project. Not defining the teamwork model for a team is a big anti-pattern, especially for SRE. When the teamwork model has not been specified, that means there is no proper tracking of work, the load between team members is not shared, few members are working in silos in the team, others are in multiple groups, and there is no acknowledgment of teamwork outcome, etc. Just asking your team to work on some tasks together is insufficient in today's fast-paced world. Leadership needs to define when and on what tasks team members need to work together, whether teamwork is required within teams or with external teams, what the timelines for teamwork should be, and how the teams divide individual vs. team effort. Not having this model can lead to a roadblock for SRE as their model is based on solving problems, culture, and teamwork.

Organizations should build strategies around building the right culture for a blameless approach, better teamwork, and transparent communication. Some of these strategies are:

- Root cause analysis model- each issue should be closed only after RCA is completed. This will help cross-functional teams to collaborate and avoid blaming.
- Feedback loop model- teams providing feedback to each other as a regular process to ensure transparency.
- Same metric model, all teams in software engineering should have the same end goal, and their metrics should match. That will help the team foster and work toward one goal and help avoid conflicts.

# Anti-patterns in system reliability and scalability

Anti-patterns are roadblocks. Any roadblock in software development impacts delivery, affecting system reliability and scalability. Some examples are poor practices followed by a quick fix, bad design, and not following processes, which might resolve the issues quickly but compromise quality and impact long-term solutions. Such practices are anti-patterns and create topics. In the previous section, you discussed identifying different anti-patterns, and each of them establishes issues with scalability and reliability as follows:

- **Anti-patterns in service design**: It means not following best practices. Design is the critical phase that defines a system's baseline. Any antipattern in design creates issues in software or interrupts software development progress. Bad designs introduce bugs in code or make it difficult to identify bugs that break systems. Even if solid monitoring is implemented, if the underlying code is terrible, it will create defects and outages, which decrease the system's reliability. If bugs are not caught on time, it impacts software reliability as end users will be affected.

- **Anti-patterns in observability and monitoring:** The impact of the capability of SRE to observe and investigate issues in the system is as follows:

  o **Observability is the key tool for SRE**: Observability and monitoring are tools that help the SRE team monitor alerts and anomalies and catch issues on time. Sometimes, they resolve these issues or collaborate with other technology teams to fix them. Any anti-pattern in monitoring blocks the ability of SRE to monitor and observe the system.

  o **Multiple levels of gating in SDLC in the form of best practices**: Let us say you introduced an anti-pattern during service design, and if you have best practices for observability, you can still catch issues on time. However, if there are gaps in monitoring and observability, you cannot identify and resolve issues on time. That will create an outage in the system and impact the end user, blocking the system from scaling.

- **Anti-pattern in release and deployment**: Means not controlling bad changes in the system. Bad changes in the system are the natural killer of software reliability and scalability, and release management plays a critical role in managing code releases in a system. Daily changes exist for extensive systems with 1000 microservices, and an anti-pattern in release management can negatively impact the system. Not following best practices as part of release management can introduce bad code deployment, and bad code in production can break the system or create an outage. Let us tie this up with an anti-pattern in service design. Bad design can introduce bugs in code, such as performance issues. With strong release management, SRE teams can stop bad code deployment. Some anti-patterns in release and deployment are created during the release cycle only, for example, deploying the wrong version of code in production. This is no issue with the underlying design, but we did not follow best practices and released the wrong version, which had problems. An evil code version can create issues in the system or an outage that will, in turn, impact the system's reliability.

- **Anti-pattern in change management:** It means not managing changes correctly. Change and release management are tied together, impacting software due to not controlling bad changes. Change management tracks changes, and release management builds and deploys those changes into the system. Anti-pattern in the change process means no control over what is going on in the system and no prioritization. It might not directly create bugs in the system, but it can mislead SREs and impact their ability to invest their time in solving critical issues, indirectly impacting reliability.

- **Anti-patterns in incident and defect management:** They directly impacts reliability as they are best practices for SRE and ops. These anti-patterns might not create a bug in the system, but these are reactive and proactive measures to catch and resolve issues in the system. Any bad practices in the incident and defect management process will block the ability of the SRE team to identify and fix defects or bugs early. This impacts the two main metrics for reliability, MTTR and MTTD.

  o  For example, there was no proper prioritization of incidents. Due to this, one critical issue was not picked by the team for resolution, which created an outage in the application, and end users could not access the app. This decreased the reliability of the system.

- **Anti-patterns in error handling:** They are purely the way software developers handle errors in code. As mentioned in the previous section, if errors are not logged correctly, they will mislead the SRE or ops team in the investigation. Any issue that can be solved in less time will need more time in troubleshooting and finding a solution without proper logging.

  o  For example, a developer logged an error in an info log. During the issue investigation, SRE, ops, and dev teams did not look at info logs; they focused on warning or error logs. This misled them, and they could not identify the root cause or origin of the issue on time. This brought down a few services in the system and impacted reliability.

- **Anti-patterns in communication and culture:** It is an overlooked but high-impact roadblock in organizations today. The culture of following best-practice, blameless post-mortem, not working in silo, collaborating, transparency between teams, resolving issues proactively, and many more. The tone and culture have to be set in the beginning, and leaders in the team should initiate an ongoing process. Sometimes, technology cannot solve the problem of culture, which impacts the daily activities of team members and, in turn, has a broader impact on the system.

# Hidden roadblocks to the SRE path

In this chapter, we discussed various roadblocks in the software development lifecycle model that block the SRE path to maintain the system's reliability. As said earlier, *no one size fits all*; all anti-patterns and their solution will differ between organization projects. However, some of the best practice will help achieve and maintain the reliability of your software. This section will further help you with hidden roadblocks impacting the SRE journey. These hidden anti-patterns are sometimes very lucrative and provide a quick fix to the problem. However, in the long term, these become significant roadblocks, and removing these roadblocks is way more challenging than solving the issue in the beginning. We will discuss some of these roadblocks in detail as follows:

# Culture

The culture of an organization defines success. A good culture promotes collaboration, empowerment, growth leadership, teamwork, continuous learning, and work-life balance. Anti-patterns in culture are hidden roadblocks that sometimes organizations overlook.

Culture building is an ongoing exercise; it takes time to build a certain culture and have all members follow it. During the culture change process, sometimes, a few best practices are ignored, impacting technology and business.

Let us take a scenario of an organization onboarded a project to modernize its old e-commerce software and move to new technology. The project started with all the latest tools stack, best practices for software design, software development, and SRE. All teams involved in the project tried to minimize anti-patterns, and they were able to implement some of that successfully. However, the software started seeing multiple minor bugs. SRE ops teams started circumventing all issues to avoid customer impact but did not get time to do and follow RCA with the development team. Over a few months, no RCA turned into a blameful approach within teams. SRE teams used to move bugs to the development team's queue and blame them for not having quality code, and the development team got overwhelmed with defects. And somewhere in this process, fixing and resolving issues were lost. Customers started experiencing many problems with the application, and the organization lost many customers to competitor applications. This is an example of not having a blameless approach (this is a vital cultural pillar for DevOps and SRE teams).

The example is a hidden anti-pattern in culture. Organizations followed best practices but overlooked one critical RCA practice, which created a bad culture among teams.

Culture is a critical factor that can positively or negatively impact if not paid attention to. One small lousy practice can lead to other harmful practices and ruin the good culture in the organization. If we take the above example, where teams start blaming each other for system issues, they get frustrated and do not get enough time to fix the problem, leading to a roadblock in continuous learning. Not having continuous learning is another hidden anti-pattern within the organization.

All these bad practices block growth, impact quality delivery, impact software performance, and ultimately impact the end user.

The above scenario can be addressed by working together between the SRE and developers to identify the issue and fix it rather than putting all the load on just one team. Collaboration and transparency can help a lot. Involving SRE in the beginning of functionality design gives a production perspective. It also gives SRE visibility into the effort put in by development teams to build any feature. It will help create a healthy culture of collaboration between teams.

# Measurement and choosing the right metric

If you cannot measure it, you cannot improve it. Metrics are an essential part of any SDLC process, and for SRE, it is one of the pillars. As part of best practice SRE, teams create metrics to measure the system's performance, but if the right metrics are not chosen, it can be an anti-pattern. The hidden anti-pattern is incorrect metrics. The SRE team uses two standard metrics to measure the system's reliability, MTTD and MTTR. The key to using these metrics is how you see issues in your system, and if you do not choose the right underlying metric for these two, it can mislead the measurement.

Though you are measuring your system, sometimes the denominator, baselines you choose, do not give you the actual measurement of system performance. This impacts overall system reliability. For example, MTTD measures the meantime taken to identify defects or bugs in the system that impact the customer. You need to prioritize the correct defects to be able to measure the meantime taken for actual impactful issues.

# Unrealistic SLO, SLI, and SLA

SLA, SLO, and SLI measure the high-level performance of any application. These are service level agreement, service level objectives, and service level indicators that help organizations measure the system's performance from a high level.

**Note: MTTD and MTTR are more granular.**

Each organization wants 100% availability and reliability as part of its SLA, but systems will always have issues. Sometimes, that impacts the SLA badly, even unnoticeable to end users (for example, one user sees the app hang intermittently). However, keeping your SLA 100% availability will put a lot of pressure on SDLC teams to follow it. These are unrealistic measurements and sometimes turn into anti-patterns that you might be unable to identify.

For example, 100% availability SLA. Dev teams are pressured to use best practices and solve all the issues before the end user notices. The SRE team should be able to catch problems and circumvent them, even if some are minimal issues that the customer may overlook. However, this will put pressure on teams and overwhelm them with work. They will end up compromising the quality with a quick fix. All these compromises will create a roadblock to the system's performance.

# Reusing tools

Reusing is always beneficial either in day-to-day life or in software development organizations. Today, there is a lot of focus on reusing software to avoid extra costs and effort. However, sometimes, organizations overlook the reuse as the use cases do not match. Not reusing the tools/services/software can create silos between teams, and that is one of the significant anti-patterns in today's software organizations.

Each team builds tools, services, and capabilities for big organizations with multiple products. Being different products, the use cases between products differ. So, to save time analyzing and identifying commonalities, training teams choose patches *built from scratch*. It might save some time and give more ownership to teams who are building. Still, in the end, organization land up having multiple similar tools, no standardization, teams not collaborating, and working in silos. However, this helps individual teams to deliver the expected but is a roadblock to the overall organization from extra cost effort. And if an organization suffers from technical debt, it will impact software delivery.

# Real time scenarios of anti-pattern and solutions

This section will explain some scenarios from real software projects that block development and delivery. It will also provide solutions for overcoming those roadblocks in the SDLC journey focused on SRE as follows:

## Single data input

A software organization picked a real estate project. The application will manage viewing, renting, selling, and virtual tours of the property. The organization already had legacy software that it wanted to migrate to the cloud as part of this new real estate project.

The following steps explain the **software development lifecycle** (**SDLC**) model and the problem in the model:

1.  The technology teams were formed, and the planning phase started. Some old services were moved to the new cloud, and others were built from scratch. The decision on the tool stack was made.

2.  As a further step, architecture designs were created. Various other processes were outlined, such as agile, PI planning, release management, and change management. Best practices across all the phases and teams were followed to build and deliver the software application.

3.  The first version of the software was rolled out to customers, and the rollout went well. The development team had a sprint model, where they released new features in code every two weeks. After two weeks, the second version of the feature rollout created some issues in the software app, and customers could not search for the required data.

4.  After investigation, it was identified that the data store service moved from an old platform to the new one is creating the issue. The old system was monolithic, and all data was entered manually into this data store. The same data store was moved to the new system, too, but with a manual process of updating data. So, engineers manually change the data store whenever requested, and after the change, dependent services use the updated data.

5.  Eventually, the data store becomes a bottleneck and the reason for data issues in software. SRE started seeing problems in the system, and this data store became a pain point for SRE. This decreased the system's reliability. Teams cannot even catch issues before failure in production. As the data changes, validation is reflected only after the data is called and referred to. Before that, monitoring tools could not catch any issues. This is an example of an anti-pattern in which development teams overlooked the data input service, which became the single point of failure.

The following figure represents how data flows from data store to services:

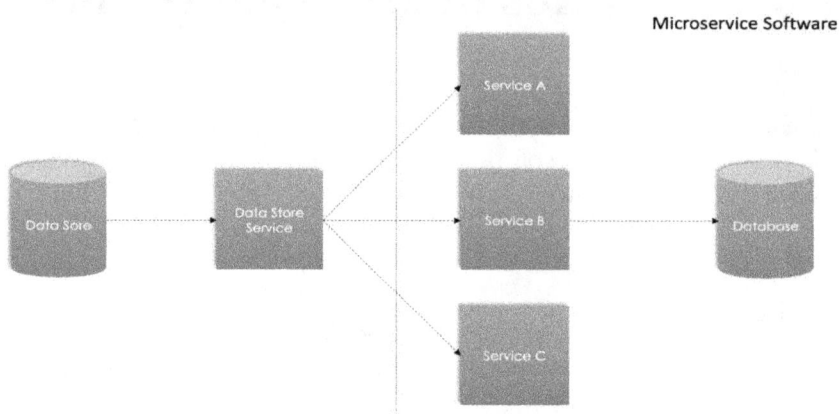

*Figure 5.3: Data store as an input source for services*

The solution to the problem looks straightforward. Remove dependency on the single data source. However, for systems that have legacy code and are migrated from old to new platforms, just lifting and shifting sometimes does not work.

The following are some of the solutions to the aforementioned problem:

1.  A short-term solution is to automate manual data entry in the data store. One option is to create an automation tool that will automatically update the data in the store as soon as the business gets a requirement. The business publishes the data requirement, and the tool triggers the data update. Data updating will be automated, removing human typos and errors and resolving some issues. Automation will remove the dependency on engineers updating data manually, and business requirements will be the source of truth. This will also resolve some of the system issues caused by data.

2.  The long-term solution is to break the data store service into two services. As part of the design, the data store has one service that fetches data. Breaking this one service into two will solve the problem of a single point of failure. One service will fetch critical mandatory data. Other services will fetch non-critical data. In such cases, if one of the services fails to obtain data, other services using the data from no-critical service would still be able to function.

    The following is the diagrammatic representation of a long-term solution of breaking down data store services into multiple services:

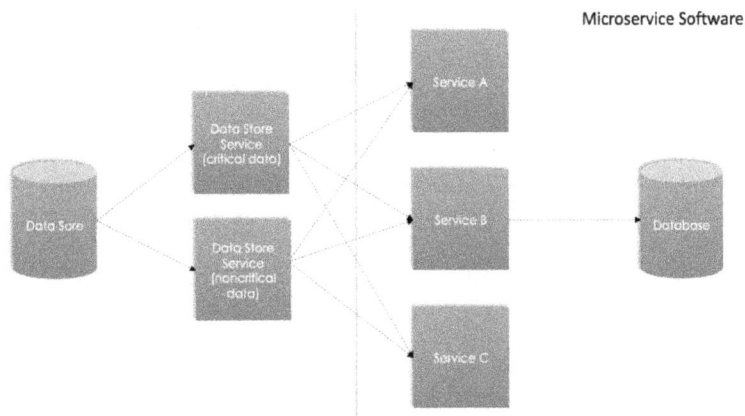

*Figure 5.4*: *Breakdown of data store service into two services*

# Lack of incident management process

This is a banking organization software project. The software is old, and the bank's customers have used it for over ten years. The organization plans to enhance its old software with technological advancements and increased customer demand.

The following are the steps explaining the **software development lifecycle** (**SDLC**) model, along with project onboarding and the problem in the system:

1. The organization started planning a migration from the old to a new platform. All technology teams, including architects, development, analysis, designers, testers, DevOps, and SRE, were formed. New tools were onboarded. The latest banking software was successfully launched in two years in three versions (or three installments).

2. The first two versions of the software went smoothly. Issues were identified in the software, but the team was able to fix them and roll out the final version. The final version included multiple new features in the software application and all the bug fixes of the previous version. This was a bigger-bang release for customers.

3. After customers started using software, organizations started getting tickets from customers. The tickets were daily general issues; there were no major functionality failures. The team was also getting tickets from the internal organization team and from upstream and downstream systems communicating with this software. For example, banking software sends reports to another system (another team maintains this).

4. Tickets such as how to use new software and tickets related to old data sometimes need to be visible. There were also a few major issues where customers intermittently needed help accessing some new software features. As the software was new, development teams were still building new features. The SRE team was

managing operations and the production environment. Getting tickets and having software issues is expected. No software is 100% robust or free of failures.

5.  However, after a few months, operations and SRE teams were overwhelmed with the number of customer tickets they received. This banking software team started seeing SLA miss in resolving tickets, which sometimes impacted customers. This decreased the reliability of software in the market. The problem was that there was no process for incident management. There were no clear guidelines on how to define the priority of tickets (as it was new software, new features teams were getting new queries, and they were not able to decide the priority of some of the tickets)

6.  As the priority was unclear, operations teams missed high-priority critical issues, creating outages. There needs to be a process for determining which engineer on the shift will work on which tickets or incidents. Operation engineers picked incidents based on their understanding and knowledge. Sometimes, two engineers worked on the exact tickets. This created a little chaos in operations teams, and as ops teams could not prioritize, SRE teams could not resolve issues on time.

7.  Incident management is a straightforward yet robust process. It defines how your team will address and track problems in the system. Sometimes, organizations need to pay more attention to the need for a robust incident management process. In the above scenario, technology was migrated, but the team used the same incident management process as earlier. The old process worked fine for previous software, but that does not mean the same process will work for newer ones. New software, technology, and customers are advanced. So, the organization should either revamp the old incident process to align with new software or use a whole new process.

8.  Organizations can incorporate some of the best practices from the old incident management process into the new one to save time. Change the priority and define a new prioritization process for tickets. For example, a customer who cannot send money should have different priorities than a customer who is opening a new deposit. The former is a high priority compared to the latter. However, a customer who cannot open a new deposit and a customer who is unable to update their address will have different priorities. Here, the former is a high priority compared to the latter.

9.  Automate the incident or ticket acknowledgment and resolution process. Instead of engineers manually pulling the tickets in their queue based on understanding, the process should be automated. Automation will save time, avoid confusion, and save rework.

The following diagram is the representation of incident management workflow:

# Incident management workflow

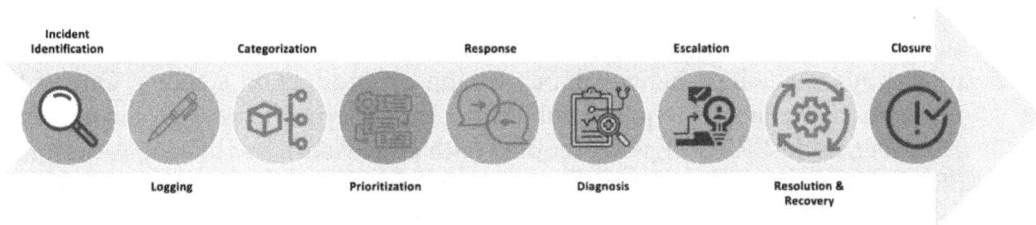

*Figure 5.5: Incident management workflow best practice*

# No control over changes

In continuation to the previous scenario (use case of banking software), assume that the incident management process is created and working fine. Various infrastructures are being used, and the new software is based on the latest cloud technology. The infrastructure stack includes a cloud platform, NoSQL databases, Cache (in-memory storage), event stream processing infra, CI/CD tool, monitoring tool, logging tool, alerting tool, and source code tool.

With so much infrastructure and new code, multiple changes are required for the platform, such as changes to security vulnerabilities, operating system (underlying OS for infra) patching, other patching on infrastructure and code changes, and hotfixes. As part of the change management process, all changes are first created and logged in the system (details about the change are logged).

The following are the steps explaining the problem:

1. Respective teams represent their changes in the **Change Advisory Board (CAB)** meeting, and depending on alignment, the change is approved by the CAB committee. Initial months went fine with the process, but the number of changes grew exponentially over the period.

2. As the new system has a large amount of infrastructure and services, multiple changes in a day were required to be implemented. After a few months, CAB meeting timing extended beyond one hour. As part of the process, all respective teams were supposed to join meetings and present their change. Some changes depended on other changes, which is why all teams were required to participate so that the CAB committee could review and take appropriate approvals.

3. Change meetings were getting overwhelming, and much effort and time could have been spent on these sessions. There was no window left for ad-hoc or critical

hotfixes changes. Sometimes, for ad-hoc changes, the team used to re-review all dependent changes that were reworking what was done at CAB meetings, which required a lot of extra effort. As ad-hoc changes were not tracked in CAB, sometimes, these changes created further issues in the system.

4. Over time, changes became uncontrollable and the reason for failure in the system. This overwhelmed SRE teams, as they had to validate all these changes in production and decide which could stay in the system for a day. SRE teams spent more time reviewing changes than working on production stability. One of the infrastructure changes required subject matter expertise to review and approve. However, as the SRE SME was occupied with other issues and available, the junior SRE approved the change. On the day of the change, this change conflicted with other changes, creating an issue in the system, which in turn caused an outage. This decreased the reliability of the system. Change management is one of the essential processes for DevOps and SRE. During the planning phase, the SRE or release team should clearly define the change management process.

5. The above problem is an example of an anti-pattern in change management that creates issues. The scenario quotes two problems. The first is too many changes. The solution to this is to automate the process of change management. The first team should identify the tool that will automate the process. Either use an existing tool and customize automation or use a new one (if no tool exists). As part of automation, respective teams should list details about the change at least two days before creating the request. The change request should proceed with an implementation step, validation step, and impact assessment. Once all details are mentioned, the requestor should assign the change for review to the SRE and CAB committee team.

6. The SRE and CAB team will select the list of changes in their queue and review and approve accordingly. As the changes are approved beforehand, this will save time in the CAB meeting. All regular changes can easily be approved beforehand. As SREs are the production owners, they always have visibility into the system and can help approve the change. CAB calls can be used only for critical changes.

7. The second problem is the impact of change. This problem can also be solved by automation. As part of automation, the requestor will have to mention the impact clearly and mention dependency only after details of the change can be submitted. After the request is submitted, the tool runs it through other changes in the same timeline and will further approve or decline it depending on what other changes are aligned for the day.

The tool's automation should also validate how two changes can conflict with each other so that only one should be approved. It should also be able to put changes on hold if further validation is required. The CAB committee should pull the report of all changes by tool and then discuss only changes on hold with other teams. Automation will be able to control and track changes in the system. As changes are validated thoroughly, they will help reduce issues due to changes.

The following figure explains the high-level process for the CAB. The process is sequential and should be performed in this manner to involve all stakeholders as follows:

## Change Advisory Board

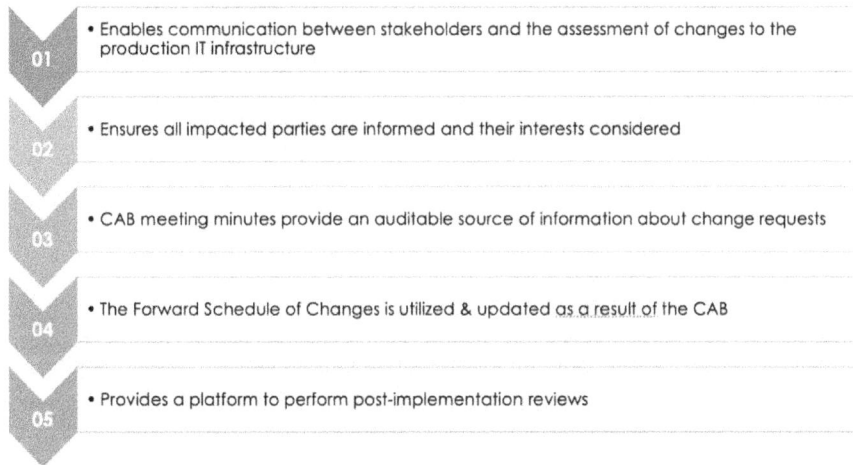

**01** • Enables communication between stakeholders and the assessment of changes to the production IT infrastructure

**02** • Ensures all impacted parties are informed and their interests considered

**03** • CAB meeting minutes provide an auditable source of information about change requests

**04** • The Forward Schedule of Changes is utilized & updated as a result of the CAB

**05** • Provides a platform to perform post-implementation reviews

*Figure 5.6: Change Advisory Board process*

# Key takeaways

Here is the takeaway and checklist to avoid anti-patterns and build reliable systems:

- Anti-patterns are small mistakes that look lucrative in beginning but eventually impact later.

- Use best practice in all phases of software development.

- Use tools to help automate and streamline various process.

- Tools are the best way to avoid various problems created due to manual and human error.

- Feedback loop and root cause analysis are two critical process to build culture.

- Measuring the system at each milestone and in each phase is the best way to track the performance of the software.

- There is no one solution fit all.

- It is beneficial sometimes to look at the smaller problems and solve them, to stabilize the system first. This help building quality product and then implement big features on top.

# Conclusion

In this chapter, we discussed different types of anti-patterns and how to identify those. This chapter covers the solutions to these anti-patterns and some industry examples, including anti-patterns. As discussed, you can avoid these roadblocks as part of your SDLC by using different anti-patterns and their identification. Additionally, this chapter helps you focus on best practices to maintain the system's reliability.

In the next chapter, we will discuss real industry scenarios of software organizations that will help us understand how SRE and its best practices helped the software industry to deliver and maintain quality products.

## Join our Discord space

Join our Discord workspace for latest updates, offers, tech happenings around the world, new releases, and sessions with the authors:

https://discord.bpbonline.com

# CHAPTER 6

# Real-world Examples of Successful SRE

## Introduction

The easy way to learn and understand any theory is through examples.

In this chapter, we will list some of the real-world scenarios for successful SRE implementation. These cases are real-world examples from various organizations of how IT organizations identified anti-patterns and solved problems by implementing SRE practice. The chapter will cover scenarios in all phases of the software development lifecycle that will help you understand the approach to various solutions.

## Structure

This chapter covers the following topics:

- Common terminology
- Avoiding alert fatigue
- Improving observability
- Reducing human toil by automation
- Implementing root cause analysis as the key process
- Building strong incident management
- Improving defect analysis and management

- Define SRE and ops roles to reduce burnout
- Implementing gatekeeping
- Metrics identification
- Early involvement of SRE in SDLC
- SRE as chaos and performance engineer

# Objectives

By the end of this chapter, we will discuss real-world scenarios of SDLC. All these examples are explained from the SRE perspective and how organizations plan their approach to various phases of SRE. By the end of this chapter, we will understand how organizations today solve some of the anti-patterns using the best approaches.

# Common terminologies

There are various acronyms and terms used in software development organizations as part of the development cycle and daily tasks. These terms are used industry wide. Before we start this chapter, let us discuss some common terms used across organizations.

We will use the following terms to explain all the examples in the chapter:

- **SMEs**: These are generally senior members of a team who have knowledge about that system, technology, and business flow. Some of the roles are architects, staff engineers, technical project managers, etc.

- **Engineering team**: It consists of the development team, testing team, and quality analyst. Some of the common roles are agile champions, project managers, scrum masters, etc.

- **Product team**: It consists of a business and analyst team that works with the engineering team on the process.

- **Infrastructure**: This means servers, databases, and other tools.

- **Resources**: This term is used for human resources and with respect to infrastructure also such as resource utilization for a server.

- **SRE**: Site reliability engineering.

- **DevOps**: In general, and in broader terms, this team is the bridge between development and operations by technology, such as creating CI/CD. Enabling both SRE and development.

- **CI/CD**: Continuous integration/continuous deployment.

The first example has a detailed explanation of various phases in SDLC along with the timeline, just to give you an idea. The same SDLC phases will be used in all the examples. However, they are not especially called out, but just for reference, these phases are briefly summarized.

# Avoiding alert fatigue

This case is from an alert management perspective. This example explains how SRE uses best practices in the initial phase to avoid alert fatigue later in the process (alert fatigue means unwanted alerts and wrong information in alerts that hinder the monitoring and detection of issues in the system on time).

Let us take the scenario of an e-commerce software application that is built from scratch.

The following are the planning and steps in the implementation of the project. These steps are in sequential order based on the timeline. There is no strict timeline called out in the example, as it solely depends on the organization. However, we will discuss the timeline to understand the process.

# Planning phase 1

This phase is planning at a high level with senior leadership on the feasibility of the product. And if we consider SDLC starting from the first month of the year, then the planning phase is supposed to start in quarter 1.

Business and technology leadership decided to build an e-commerce project on the latest technology. The business requirement is gathered, and the feasibility of creating a product is finalized. A high-level business requirement document is created.

Business and technology leadership outline revenue potential and cost of production. And allocate a budget for the project.

This phase can take 2-5 months depending on the type of multiple factors such as type of software, customer base, budget, and many others.

# Planning phase 2 (high level design)

After the business document, subject matter experts from engineering + infrastructure (DevOps) + product management, + SRE gathered to outline the initial architecture of the project. This includes a data flow diagram and an architecture diagram. This phase starts in quarter 2.

In this phase, SMEs make decisions on all tools and technology that will be used in building the project, including the software used by SDLC teams to develop the project, infrastructure, underlying coding language, and framework.

In parallel to planning, various team formations also happen, such as the dev team, QA team, DevOps team, and SRE team. Hiring resources as per requirement also happens during this phase.

The tool stack here is:

- **Infrastructure**:
    - **Cloud**: AWS web server and application servers from AWS. Load balancers on AWS, and IIM on AWS
    - **Database**: AWS NoSQL database, AWD relational database
    - **Storage**: AWS in memory storage
    - Event streaming software
    - Content delivery network
- **Dev tools**: GitHub, code development tool, Jira, Mural (data flow).
- Testing tools.
- **DevOps tools**: Jenkins (CI/CD), Terraform, Ansible.
- **SRE tools**: AWS monitoring tool, Grafana, Prometheus, ELK (logging), GitHub, ITSM tools.
- Product management tools.

# Planning phase 3 (low level design)

After all information is gathered during the planning phase, it is converted into requirements. This phase also gets executed in quarter 2.

Low-level design documents are created. This describes how each feature and component are tied with each other.

The product team creates features for development teams. This describes further low-level bifurcation of each data flow. Various tools are available that help the product team create and manage features. For example, Jira is commonly used for tracking.

In parallel, the DevOps team started creating low-level designs for infrastructure. This describes the design of creating and installing servers and databases. Also, configuring other projects' tools.

# Configuration phase

This is the intermediary phase after planning and coding, and this starts in quarter 3. In this phase, the DevOps/system admin/infrastructure team configures the development tools required by engineering teams.

The DevOps team set up a development and testing environment for the dev and QA teams for them to start writing code.

The DevOps team also creates CI/CD pipelines to build and deploy code.

All other tools and software are configured by the DevOps team, such as GitHub, Jira, and ELK.

# Implementation phase

This phase is the longest phase of SDLC, as the development of software happens during this phase, and starts in quarter 3 itself. The dev team starts building the code, and in parallel, the testing team tests the code.

Depending on the type of project, there can be multiple dev teams working on the same code base. Projects follow agile methodology, and so development and testing happen hand in hand. Dev build code, use CI/CD pipeline to deploy code to the dev environment, do the unit test, and build the code to merge into the main code branch.

In this phase, dev teams create their own branch and build and package code.

The DevOps team continues configuring the production environment.

# Testing phase

The testing phase is one of the critical phases of SDLC. It overlaps with quarter 4 and next year of quarter 1. In this phase, the **quality analyst (QA)** team creates test cases to test the code developed by the development team. Testing helps identify the quality of code.

The following are the sequential steps of the testing phase:

1. Once the code package is ready, the dev team also deploys the code to the test environment.

2. The tester/QA team then tests the code for regression and progression.

3. In parallel to step 2, performance testing also happens in this phase, where the application is loaded with data. This helps evaluate the performance and scalability of the application.

4. As defects are identified, the code is sent back to the dev to fix the bug and merge again into the test environment. Then, the testing team does another round of testing. This is generally done in a sprint of 2 weeks (the testing team takes 2 weeks to test regression).

5. The SRE team then does chaos testing on the regression-tested code. This happens after the testing team completes its regression. The SRE team uses various testing tools to mimic production scenarios to test chaos.

6. The development team walks through SRE on the various features. The SRE team will support the production environment. Walkthrough of features is important for SRE to understand how data flow and user journey happen from end to end. This is another best practice; the SRE team takes the walkthrough from the development teams and reviews the runbooks for each feature. Runbooks are manuals that explain how the service works, what type of errors the service will throw in case of any issues, and how to resolve errors if the service fails.

7. After the walkthrough of runbooks, the SRE team configures alerting and monitoring dashboard templates based on error codes defined in runbooks.

8. In this phase, SRE teams also create other tools and processes required to support production applications, such as the production support readiness manual, tooling, and capabilities required.

# Deployment phase (quarter 1)

As year 2 start, deployment phase also started. In the deployment phase, developers ensure that the software is ready and available to use. That means the software is packed and deployed to the production environment. Once the code is certified by testing and the SRE team for regression and chaos, the dev team deploys code to the production environment using CI/CD pipelines created by the DevOps team. After the successful deployment of code in a production environment, the application is first tested for sanity by SRE teams. Once the SRE team validates basic sanity and gives a go-ahead for opening gates (taking the application live). After the application is live, the SRE team also continues their alert and monitoring dashboard configuration.

# Sanity testing phase

As its name suggests, the sanity phase tests the sanity of the application. With year 2, this phase moved to quarter 2. That means validating the basic functionality of the overall application to certify that the software is running ok. The deployment phase overlaps with the SRE sanity phase. As of the $2^{nd}$ month of quarter 2, SRE continues its alerting and monitoring tasks. Alerting and monitoring are critical phases from an operational perspective. If wrong and unwanted alerts are configured in the system, it will mislead the SRE/ops team and hinder their ability to investigate any issue. So, the SRE team follows best practices here, such as collecting alerting data from the testing team as part of their testing phase. Then, the SRE team analyzes those alerts along with alerts mentioned in runbooks (created by dev teams for all features). Once the SRE team has all the data, they start incorporating it into their alert and dashboard configuration. The data analysis is done by tools available, or sometimes SRE teams build their own tooling and ML algorithm to analyze data.

After alert and monitoring dashboard creation, the SRE team starts their sanity testing on the production environment. This is another test that the SRE team performs to make sure the application is working with basic functionality. As part of sanity testing, the SRE team again validates alerts, such as whether the right alerts are firing; they check if any unwanted alerts are also firing, the channels of alert notification are configured correctly, and self-healing is configured correctly. If SRE teams identify issues during their sanity testing, depending on the type of issue, they collaborate with various teams, such as the code issue dev team, to fix the code and redeploy it in production. And the cycle of hotfix repeats (dev-test-prod). For infra issues, the SRE team resolves on their own and retests the application.

Once the sanity test passes all validation criteria, the SRE team signs off the application to go live. Generally, the go-live date is pre-planned by leadership. In parallel, dev leadership again starts collecting requirements for new features. The cycle starts with planning.

# Maintenance phase

The maintenance phase in the agile and SRE world is more akin to a monitoring application phase, also referred to as the operational phase. Though this is an ongoing phase, it is considered the end phase, and as per SDLC, this has moved to year 2, quarter 3. In this phase, the SRE and ops team monitor the application, and if any bugs are identified, they either fix or report them to developers. For the initial launch of the application, this phase is treated as first-time maintenance. However, this is part of the ongoing software development cycle. Where new requirements flow from the business, and the software development team develops and deploys the new code to the production environment. Then, the ops team monitors the system with these new features.

Once the application is live, the SRE and ops team support the application and infrastructure. The ops team takes care of daily tickets, queries from end-users, and other issues. The ops team also collaborates with SRE teams to resolve technical issues. In this phase, SRE and ops both have overlapping responsibilities to monitor the performance of the system.

The following are two of the important roles of SRE and ops in this phase:

- The ops team monitors the dashboards and alerts created by SRE. The ops team then informs SRE about the technical issues they are seeing in the system, and the SRE teams work on the resolution.
- The ops team also solves some non-technical issues as per the runbooks given to them. Technical issues are generally solved by SRE teams.

Let us take an example of technical issue, customer data not visible on the customer's account as the underlying service is throwing out of memory error intermittently. As per the runbook, ops teams restarted the service, but that also did not solve the problem, so the ops team reached out to SRE. The SRE team checked the code and fixed the issue by increasing memory. Let us assume that it also did not solve the problem, then SRE teams reached out to the development team to change the logic in the code. Then the code was changed and was deployed to production (this is again a cycle of development, testing, deployment).

The SRE team continues to monitor the reliability and availability of the system. They create various tools to reduce the toil for the operations team so that ops do not spend time on manual tasks. Whenever any error occurs in the system, the SRE team collects the data and root cause of the issue and tries to build solutions for early recovery of the issue, early detection of the issue, or if the issue can be fixed permanently. This is an ongoing exercise for the SRE team.

As part of an ongoing exercise, the SRE team regularly collects data from alerts and works on improving alerts.

The following figure gives you the high-level flow of the process:

- The planning phase is the system design phase.
- The development phase refers to the implementation phase.
- Build and Package refers to the configuration phase.
- The release phase is the deployment and maintenance phase.

The product owner is just a representation of architects and SMEs who design the data flow and architecture of the system.

Then, as per the agile approach, product owners of the team divide this architecture into various features for the development team to build the code.

SRE is involved in chaos and performance testing as follows:

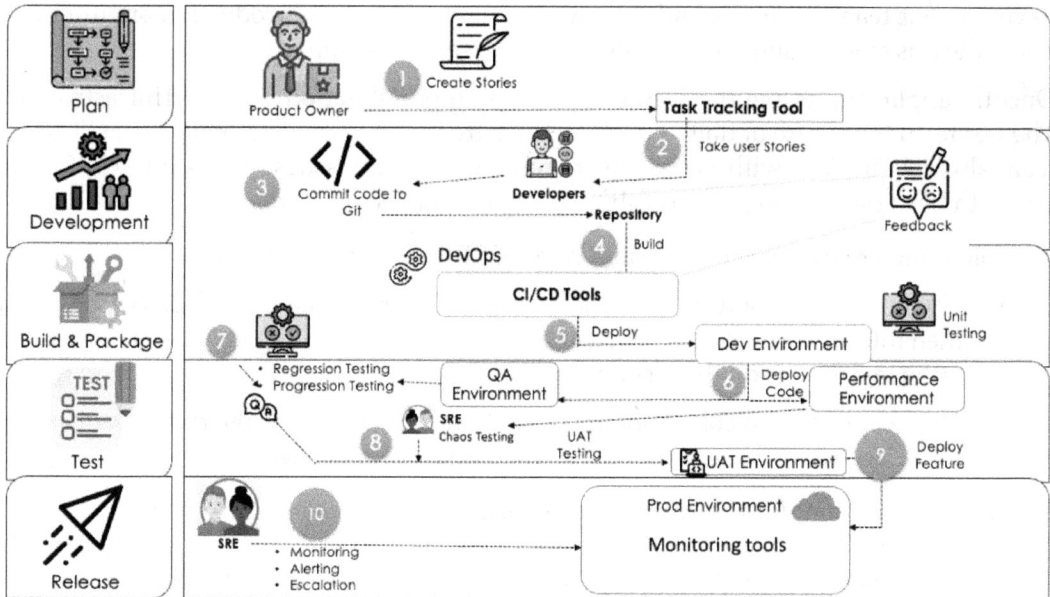

*Figure 6.1: SDLC process with all teams involved*

# Improving observability

This is an ongoing example of a previous case. Inspired by real-world scenarios. In the previous example, you learned how using best practices early in the SDLC phase can help improve the reliability of the system. Where the SRE team used best practices for alerting and monitoring and was able to solve alert fatigue anti-pattern, in continuation of the aforementioned example, let us see how the application is working after its go-live. This example will help you understand how improving observability will help improve the performance and reliability of the system.

The e-commerce software application is live now and customers are using the application. Businesses are getting new requirements, and to compete in the market, organizations have to keep on updating their applications with the latest technology and features, along with maintaining the high performance of the software.

The following are the various phases of SDLC from an observability perspective.

# Planning phase

Businesses have new requirements for the application. The business and technology team gathered requirements and passed on the requirements to the technology team.

As tech teams were preparing for new requirements, the SRE team reported multiple issues in the system.

# Maintenance phase

SRE monitored the system for 3-4 months and collected data from alerting and logging. We also made a list of all tickets received by the ops team from customers and other downstream/upstream systems. The SRE team used data analysis tools and analyzed the reported issues.

The result of the data analysis shows:

- Few services do not have correct error and logging.
- Few services do not have the right metrics added to the code to measure the average response time.
- One of the critical payments microservices does not have metrics to measure performance.

The aforementioned issues impacted system performance and became a blocker in observability. Due to the unavailability of the right logs, alerts, and metrics, the SRE team was not able to resolve issues. They did not catch the issues on time. For example, the payment service was failing intermittently, and users were not able to pay during checkout of the product. SRE teams had no data to capture the performance of payment service as the metric was not built in code.

Now, in parallel, the SDLC process has started for new requirements.

Before SMEs start creating the design of new features, the SRE team reached out to tech SMEs with the above analysis.

The SRE team shared the recommendation of creating metrics in code to measure the performance, adding the right entry-exit points to capture correct errors, and correcting logging.

Dev teams fixed the existing services as per SRE recommendation.

In parallel, technology SMEs incorporated the recommendation of SRE in the design document for new features. This approach is called **observability-driven development**.

# Implementation phase

The development team got the architecture document. The document listed data flow, business flow, services communication, and metrics to be added. Dev teams started the development of these new features with an agile approach.

As per process and standards, the dev builds the code, deploys the code to the dev environment, and performs unit tests.

After unit testing of all features, the code is deployed to testing env. The testing team starts their testing.

# Testing phase

Along with testing, the SRE team also performs chaos testing and performance testing on the new features. Tested code deployed to the production environment. The SRE team started monitoring the new features along with the application.

During monitoring, the SRE team captured a high response time for one of the critical services. As the metric was integrated into the code, this helped the SRE and dev team to observe the system proactively and catch issues on time.

The ODD approach helped teams observe the system's performance and reduce MTTR. Capturing real-time data from metrics helps SRE teams observe the system from an end-to-end perspective. So, adding the right metrics in code rather than building on top of the code helps better in observability. This is an example of how SRE teams improved system reliability by improving observability.

# Reducing human toil by automation

The example will explain how automation achieved organization reliability and performance for their software system. Let us take a use case from the healthcare industry. One of the big healthcare entities wanted to revamp their old software application that is currently used in hospitals for electronic health records, used by pharmacies, and used by doctors to view and track patient health records. The software is running on old infrastructure and is also not scalable and not performant with the current number of customers/end-users, so leadership decided to migrate the software to new technology and implement new features to help doctors and hospital staff better manage the health records of patients.

The process of software development is the same as shown in *Figure 6.1*. To give a brief recap of SDLC refer to *Figure 6.1*.

The following are various phases of SDLC from an automation perspective.

# Planning phase

The business and technology team got the requirement to revamp old software. They captured the requirement, finalized the budget, checked the feasibility of the product, decided on high-level technology to be used, and gathered % of the customer base to understand the scalability of the software.

In part of this phase, SMEs get together to design the architecture of software, create data flow diagrams, and business flow diagrams, listed all tools and technology to be used.

Leadership started recruiting engineers on the basis of the new skills required.

# Implementation phase

Project and product management teams created standards and processes following the agile approach.

The DevOps team started configuring the environment and CI/CD pipelines for engineering teams to use. They started configuring other tools required.

Once DevOps completes the environment configuration. Then, development teams were formed. All requirements were logged in the task tracking tool in the form of features and user stories (these are agile terminology used for development).

The development team got the requirements, and they started building the software. Coding and unit testing and merging code using CI/CD pipelines created by DevOps.

SRE teams started configuring monitoring dashboards and alerting templates.

# Testing phase

In this phase, the testing team tested the code for different types of testing. After one round of testing by the testing team, SRE teams started chaos and performance testing. There were a few issues identified in testing. The code was sent back to developers for fixing and retesting.

# Deployment/release phase

After the code was fully tested and certified by the testing and SRE teams, it was packaged and deployed to the production environment. The SRE team did sanity testing. Business users also tested the software before it was launched to end-users. Once certified by business users, as per the live date, the software was launched for end-users.

# Maintenance phase

Ops teams and SRE teams started monitoring the system. After 4 months of launch, ops teams started receiving multiple issues in the system, for which they had to follow a manual workaround to circumvent the issues.

Two of the examples of issues:

A lot of the patient's historical data was not visible in the app. The ops teams loaded the data manually in the new database and circumvented the issue. However, this was not a one-time occurrence. In 2 months, the ops team had to circumvent the issue around 10 times manually.

This is not an error or bug in the system, but the current configuration does not have automated failover. So, the software runs on multiple regions to support the load and increase performance. If there is a problem in one region, traffic must be moved to another region without impacting end-users. The current configuration of the system is such that automated failover is not possible for the full system, as some validation has to be performed before traffic moves. So, this started creating problems for the ops team. Any time there is a planned outage, planned release, or unplanned issue, the ops team has to spend time moving traffic manually. This is error-prone and time-consuming, too.

Both of the aforementioned errors consume the time for the SRE and ops team. More time to circumvent, meaning more time to recover from any issue. That could lead to an impact on customers and decrease the reliability of the software.

Let us see how the SRE team resolved this problem by automating using the following examples:

- **The root cause of the issue**: As part of data migration from the old to the new DB, some of the data was not copied, and that is why the new database has data missing.

  To solve the problem permanently, the database team had to copy data again, but it was tricky as they had to first identify the missing delta data and then copy it to avoid duplicate data. And that needed some time to plan and approach.

  Meanwhile, the SRE team builds automation, where as soon as they get an error of data missing, they check the old DB and copy the data from the old to the new DB. And restart the service after the copy. Though this was a temporary solution, it helped save downtime for customers.

  After a few months, when the database team copied all delta data, SRE's automation still helped; after full migration, one of the errors came where, by mistake, the team loaded data in the old database (there was a requirement from the business to keep old database also for 2 years as backup) and same error happened again. So, SRE automation helped the team to solve the issue.

- **The root cause of the issue**: Some of the services in software use flags in properties that drive what region the service should run. This is not part of the current load balancer, as this is an app configuration. So, the load balancer cannot fully move traffic to one region, and the ops team has to manually take care of failover.

  To solve the problem, the SRE team built a tool that validates current traffic, checks when the load balancer is moving traffic to another region and triggers this tool automatically. This tool takes care of moving the traffic for these few services automatically.

SRE teams used Python and integrated their code into a pipeline that ran automatically. This saved a lot of time and no human error in changing flags.

Resolving manual toil by automating the SRE team reduced MTTR, increased the reliability of software, and helped create a seamless experience for end-users.

# Implementing root cause analysis as key process

Root cause analysis is the heart of software reliability. Unless you identify the root cause of the problem, you will not be able to solve it permanently, and unless you solve it permanently, the problem will reoccur. Reoccurring problems create fatigue, decrease performance, and waste time. Even if you try to solve reoccurring by automation, the underlying problem persists. So, root cause analysis for any problem is very important

Let us extend the previous example to this scenario as well.

After healthcare software was live for end-users, it ran in maintenance mode. Along with that, new requirements are also getting built into software. Now we see two issues in the previous example where one of the issues was due to data sync between the old and new databases. Let us examine that scenario and explore how root cause analysis serves as a key process.

The following are the various phases of the SDLC from an RCA perspective.

# Monitoring and maintenance phase

SRE builds automation to sync data whenever an error is received. However, this is a temporary and reactive solution. It will remediate the problem but not solve it.

To solve the problem, root cause analysis is required. The SRE team collaborated with the database team. Created RCA document. After the root cause, the SRE team worked with the database and application team and synced all the data.

The application team built an auto-sync service between two databases. That proactively checks the delta data and syncs. The dev team also implemented a wait time in the service that calls the database. This means that if a service does not find data in the database, it will wait for the data to sync up and return the result.

Implementing the aforementioned fix at the database and service level fixed the problem at the root level. The aforementioned scenario explained that any problem in the production environment, if fixed at the root level, will help solve it permanently and improve system resiliency.

Let us take another example.

There was an issue identified in the payment service, where it failed intermittently, and end users were not able to pay for medicine purchases. The SRE team identified the issue through an alert, and as per self-healing, the service got restarted. After 2 days, another alert was identified in the payment service again. Where the purchase receipt was not updated in the database. To circumvent the issue, the SRE team restarted the service, and the issue was resolved.

Then, SRE started the RCA process. Where the defect was raised to the dev team with high priority. The dev team investigated the issue and identified the root cause of failures in the payment service. Meanwhile, the SRE team rolled back the service to the previous stable version till the issue was resolved. Once RCA was done, the dev team fixed the issue in the code. The testing team tested the issue, and the fix was deployed in production environment. Now, the issue was fixed at the root level, and the payment service did not see any failures after that.

This example explains that including root cause analysis in SDLC and SRE methodology helps improve the resiliency of the system. Once the process is set and integrated into the system, it will help the SRE team not to invest time in operational work and circumvent issues as follows:

## RCA Process

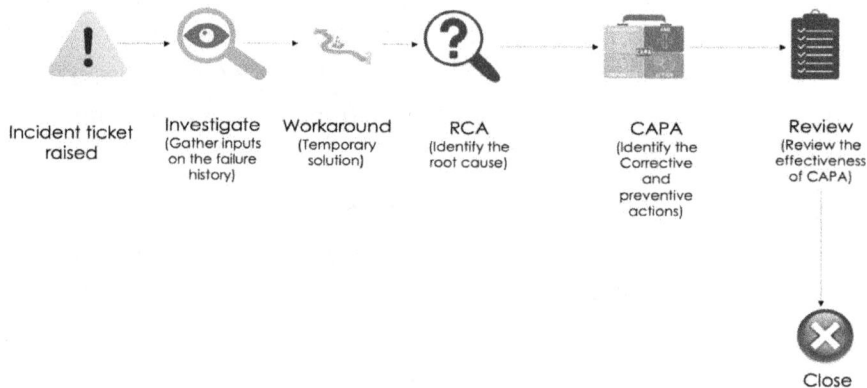

*Figure 6.2: RCA process in SRE approach*

The aforementioned figure represents the RCA process and how it is integrated into the SRE approach. The figure raises the incident to the SRE team, which investigated the incident and performed the workaround to circumvent the issue. Then, the incident is moved to the development queue to find the root cause of the issue. The root cause was reviewed by the dev and SRE leadership on its effectiveness. Then, the issue was fixed in the code and deployed in a production environment. This fixed the problem permanently.

RCA process is ownership of SRE and development team both. In the traditional SDLC approach, the RCA process was missing, but with the modern framework and new technology, organization and thinking also changed. They are focused on solving the issues at the root level and implementing this feedback loop between SRE and dev teams.

# Building strong incident management

Incident management is part of SRE and operations' day-to-day life. In previous chapters, we read about the importance of the incident management process in the SRE lifecycle. Let us see the example of how a strong incident management process helped improve the reliability of the system.

This organization has security software used by a lot of people who live in high-gated apartments, where apartment management and residents use software for visitor control, paying bills, grievances, and communication. It is a good, reliable software; engineering teams build it with all the best practices incorporated. One day, the business decided to acquire an online grocery delivery organization and integrate the grocery app into the security app. To give their customer a single platform for their daily tasks. SDLC process was started on this project.

The following are the various phases of SDLC from incident management perspective.

## Planning phase

Business and technology collected requirements as the software was already available, only integration on two software to be planned. Some of the teams from this other organization were hired, too.

Engineering teams started creating designs for integration. We decided on the tools to be used and what features to modify in the existing application to integrate with the grocery application.

## Implementation phase

Databases were synced to use a shared customer pool.

The DevOps team implemented new CI/CD pipelines to build and deploy the integration service and reused the pipeline from the grocery organization for their application.

SRE teams also reused some of their alerting and monitoring dashboards and integrated them with existing ones to give a centralized view of dashboards.

Dev teams integrated two software, tested, and then deployed to production.

## Testing phase

After the development, the code was merged with the existing code. The testing team performed regression and progression testing. SRE executed performance testing.

# Monitoring phase

This is the phase where the SRE and ops team started monitoring the system.

The following is an example, with the problem and solution:

- **Problem**: After a few months, the application started seeing multiple bugs. SRE teams got 1000+ incidents in their queue, and they were not able to address all incidents. That impacted the reliability of the software, and customers started opting out of the application.

- **Solution:** As the organization has SRE best practices and processes. They started collecting the root cause of the problem.

After root cause analysis of some of the incidents, the SRE team identified that these incidents reported are not impactful issues. Most of them are queries and questions from end-users. The SRE team released the incident management process that they had implemented earlier as the bottleneck and overwhelming the SRE and ops team. Due to this, they are not able to focus on the real high-priority issues.

After analysis, the SRE team identified that the current incident management process is a real problem for SRE to not able to focus on another high priority issue.

The current incident management process was introduced for security software functionality. The security software customer base is only people staying in rising apartments in metropolitan cities; the categorization of tickets/incidents was different than online grocery software. Online grocery software has a customer base of metro and non-metro cities customers. After integration, security software is just an added functionality for customers who do not live in apartments.

Also, the infrastructure for both applications was different. The incident management process was built considering the customer base, infrastructure, and design of security software.

As per the current process, the priority 1 incident was categorized as system unavailability, customer queries, and critical service unavailability. SLA for priority 1 was set to 10 hours. There was no automated assignment of incidents as the security software was stable, and they used to receive fewer incidents. The model was working fine with the security application.

With the integration of an online grocery application, the current design failed. A high customer base means more tickets from customers, and having a priority 1 category for simple queries is the wrong design. So, the SRE team changed the category of incidents. Now, customers' simple queries were marked between P2 and P3.

Due to the volume of incidents, the SRE team builds an automated tool to acknowledge, assign, and resolve incidents automatically.

After making changes and following best practices, the SRE team was able to manage tickets/issues/incidents. All high-priority issues were addressed first and were integrated into the root cause analysis process. The new process helped resolve issues and improved reliability in a 4-month time period.

The aforementioned example explains the importance of the correct incident management process. And how just improving the process can help improve the reliability and performance of the software. Though this will not solve the defects/bugs in the system, it will empower SRE and other engineering teams to focus on improving the reliability of the system.

# Improving defect analysis and management

The defect management process is another pillar and a part of best practice in the SRE approach. Like incident management, defect management empowers not only SRE but also the development and testing teams to work toward a failure-free system. Incident management is more operational tasks, and defect management is development. However, both of these processes go hand in hand for SRE.

Let us see how defect analysis and management helped SRE to achieve reliability. Take the previous example and extend it to this example.

Let us discuss the maintenance or monitoring phase.

The following are the sequential steps for this phase:

1. After improving the incident management process, SRE teams are able to focus on working towards improving reliability.

2. The software was running in the maintenance phase of SDLC, where SRE teams monitored the system, worked on improving observability, and reduced toil. Helped development teams provide them with the required capabilities to replicate scenarios in a production environment.

3. The SDLC phase started again, where, in parallel, the business captured new requirements to be implemented in the application.

4. SMEs created the architecture of new features and data flow and integration with existing services. During this time, the DevOps team focuses on improving their tasks, such as improving the CI/CD pipeline, creating automation for quick infrastructure scaling, and helping the development and testing team in their day-to-day needs related to infrastructure (hardware and software).

5. The development team then developed new requirements and moved the code to the test environment.

6. The testing team tested the new feature's functionality with the existing system. And identified bugs in the system. Some development team members also focus on fixing defects reported in a production environment by the SRE team.

Even after best practices, the software started getting multiple defects/bugs. Some of the bugs were identified by SRE monitoring, and end users reported a few. SRE teams started noticing the same defects occurring multiple times, and eventually, it created problems.

- **Problem**: reoccurring defects/bugs in the system impacting system availability and overwhelming SRE teams, as their 100% of capacity was getting involved in firefighting bugs to protect end-user impact.

- **Solution**: Let us see the step-by-step approach to solving the aforementioned problem as follows:

1. The SRE teams started analyzing the pattern of defects/bugs in the system. Some incidents reported are also getting converted into defects in the underlying code. Some alerts identified by proactive monitoring are also converted into defects.

2. As part of the process, the SRE team used to create defects for any issue seen in a production environment. And then, SRE and development teams used to pick the defects as per categorization. All functional defects fall under the development team bucket and non-functional under SRE. Functional defects: end-user is not able to make a payment as the online payment is not working. Non-functional defects, ex, warn logs, are getting printed as info logs.

3. After analysis for a few weeks, the SRE team identified that though they are creating defects and assigning them to the development team, defects are still not picked up on time, and issues are still reoccurring in the system. Sometimes, the SRE/ops team used to do a workaround by restarting services. However, the problem was not solved at the root level.

4. The SRE and development SMEs collaborated and identified the current defect categorization is not correct in the process. That means SRE teams are creating defects but not assigning the correct category, and so development teams are not picking up the defects to fix. One example is the payment service down defect, which was created by SRE with the category as a normal priority, as there was a workaround to restart the service. The current defect process is if the workaround is available, then the defect will be marked as normal priority. Development teams will first pick high-priority defects and then normal priority. Also, the team analyzed that there is no ownership and regular connection within development teams on defect discussion. So, few defects in critical services were fixed without SME consultation, which introduced other defects in the system.

5. After the analysis, SRE and development team leadership planned to improve the current defect management process.

6. Defect categorization was redefined. All production defects impacting end users are marked as resolved immediately.

7. After seeing a high number of production defects, development team leadership allocated added capacity for dev teams where 20% of the team will focus on solving production functional defects. Development team names were redefined to give a

clear indication of defects while assigned by SRE teams. For example, the SRE team creates defects with the correct priority and correct dev team name so that they can be picked on time for fixing. Weekly SRE and Dev SME connect was set up to discuss defects and tracking.

8.  Once the process was implemented, SRE teams started seeing traction on the defect fixes. Development teams were picking correct defects to fix and test by testing the team and deploying the fix in a production environment. Within 3 months of the new process implementation, defects frequency was reduced. No issue occurred again in the application. This, in turn, increased the performance and availability of the system. Also, that gave back time to the SRE team to work on other daily tasks rather than operations.

The aforementioned example explains the importance of the right defect management process in SDLC. This is an ongoing process, and teams should regularly review the old processes. As with time, when software grows, the customer base grows, and the requirements of software also change. So, it is very important to have flexibility in software and processes around SDLC. Leadership should empower engineering teams to take a leap of faith and change as per requirement.

# Define SRE and ops roles to reduce burnout

SRE and operations in technology are used interchangeably sometimes. Some organizations have different SRE and ops teams; on the other hand, in some organizations, SRE teams also do ops tasks. However, it is very important to define clear roles and responsibilities for SRE and ops to avoid overlap, conflict, and burnout. Supporting live applications is referred to as operations in technology terms. This can be overwhelming sometimes, depending on the type of software, as the team must be available all the time. For example, an application that is used by end-users 24*7 across the globe needs to be monitored 24*7, and any outage can lead to losing customers, in turn, losing business. Customer service, L1, L2, and L3 support come under operations, and sometimes SRE performs L2 and L3 tasks, too.

Let us see one scenario. There is a travel company that wants to revamp its old software. With time, they have grown and acquired a good customer base across the globe. The SDLC process started for the project.

The following are various phases of SDLC from SRE perspective.

# Planning phase

Business and technology leadership gathered requirements. Finalized budget, the feasibility of the project, and high-level timeline.

Engineering SME designed high-level architecture and data flow model for the new software.

Tools and technology were finalized. The team decided to use a public cloud platform.

The underlying coding language and framework were decided.

Some services were planned to be reused in the new model.

Teams were decided, and new resources were hired per the required skillset.

As part of SDLC, dev, testing, analysis, SRE, and DevOps teams were onboarded. Among these, dev, testing, and ops teams were reused.

# Implementation phase

Ops team members of the DevOps team started creating CI/CD pipelines for dev teams to start building and deploying the code. The dev team got the features from the planning phase, and they started developing the code. The dev team starts once the DevOps team builds the initial infra for the dev team. The SRE team also started configuring dashboards and alerts. Started creating metrics to be used to measure applications. SRE builds incident management and defect management processes.

# Testing phase

Once the code is ready by the dev teams, it is deployed in a testing environment. The testing team started the progression and regression testing. The SRE team started chaos testing and performance testing. The testing team identified a few bugs in the system and sent back the code to the dev team to fix them. Then, mini SDLC happened again here, where the dev team fixed the code and deployed it in the testing environment so that testing teams could retest.

# Deployment/release phase

Once code is fully tested for functionality and performance, it is packaged and deployed in a production environment.

# Maintenance/monitoring phase

In this phase, the SRE monitor system is used. Identifying any issue and reporting to the development team if a fix in code is required.

The software went live, and customers started using it. As this is a revamp of old software, it is a kind of new software. That means issues are expected. No software is 100% error-free. Though best practices were followed after 3 months, SRE and ops teams started getting multiple issues in the system, and both of the teams were seen only firefighting the situation all the time. This created burnout for the SRE team.

- **Problem**: Not able to control issues in the system and missing SLA for some of the issues.
- **Solution**: The following is the step-wise approach for solutions.
    1. SRE leadership started analyzing the errors in the system. The incident and defect management process were re-reviewed, too.

2. After analysis, it was identified that even though there was good capacity for SRE teams, they were overwhelmed as the team was still following the old process of doing operations.

3. The SRE team was just renamed from the ops team, but there was no clear role the SRE team defined. This means the SRE team was doing L1, L2, and L3 support and had many automation tasks in the backlog. To solve the problem, a few SRE skilled engineers were hired for the team, and the team was internally divided between operations and SRE. Where old ops team skills were utilized, the role of ops was defined as a team that will do L1 and L2 support. They will monitor the system, resolve low-level issues as per the runbook, enhance alerts and monitoring dashboards, and create day-to-day automation to reduce toil; for any technical help, they will collaborate with SRE engineers.

4. SRE role was defined as L3 support, available as backup for ops teams whenever required, creating tools and capability, fixing non-functional defects in systems, participating in system design review with dev teams, solve problems at the root level.

5. Once the roles of SRE and ops were clearly identified. The team was able to handle the load in a shared manner. Now, ops are used to solve low-level issues. They were also trained to implement alerting and dashboards. As SRE was not involved in support for each and every issue, they were able to focus on reducing toil. Help developer to give them perspective from production to add in their while fixing defects. For example, while fixing any code, SRE suggested considering the self-heling scenario. That is, any failure in service should be able to recover automatically without ops manually restarting.

This problem does not look or sound that big, but if not solved on time, it can create a problem for the SRE and ops team. As mentioned earlier, the ops team is the front face of the organization, and that is direct contact with customers and end-to-end visibility of software. Their job can be overwhelming if the underlying processes are not defined clearly. Today, many organizations also focus on moving towards automated operations, such as implementing self-healing and auto resolutions of errors to reduce human involvement and effort. However, this again needs skilled engineers to build and depend on the complexity of the software.

The following figure shows the SRE and ops roles:

*Figure 6.3: SRE and ops roles*

The aforementioned figure shows the high-level roles of operations and SRE teams and how the information flows from SRE to the development team. In an organization where SRE and ops are two different streams, the ops team takes care of L1 support customer care and also creates alerts and a monitoring dashboard. The SRE team takes care of L2 and L3 support. The ops team reaches out to SRE if they need further investigation on issues. The SRE team also takes care of the development and automation of manual work. Development teams collaborate with SRE to track the production defects and fix them defects.

# Implementing gatekeeping

Gatekeeping means making sure no erroneous code goes into production. Gatekeeping is not always SRE's best practice, and it can sometimes slow down the speed of development. However, in some situations, having SRE as gatekeeping helps achieve goals. Gatekeeping is reviewing what is going on in production, and that does not mean having an engineer review each change going on in the system. It means building tools as gatekeepers that can review the change going on in production as an added step without slowing the speed of development.

Let us first see the gatekeeping process. This is the flow of code review in the SRE approach, where the SRE reviews all the changes and acts as a gatekeeper before production.

*Dev building code | tester testing code | CI/CD pipelines validated code | SRE as gatekeeper review code | approve to deployment in production, as shown in the following figure:*

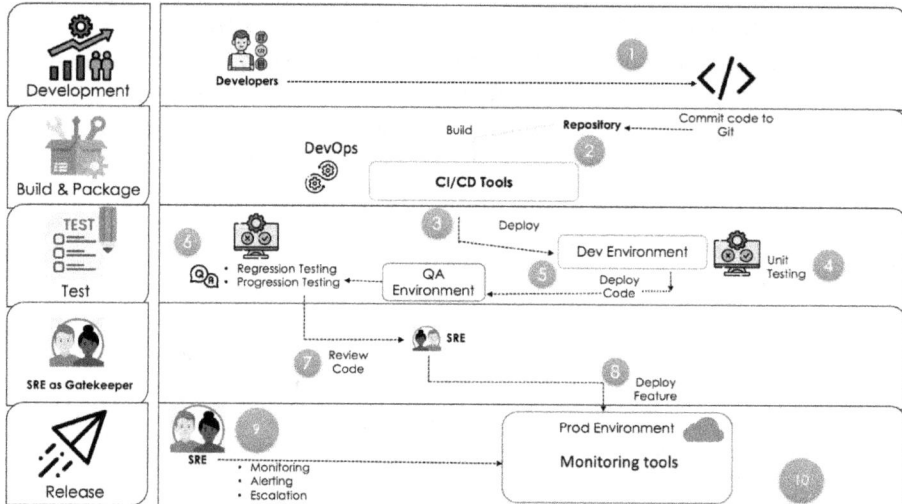

*Figure 6.4: SRE as gatekeeper*

In the aforementioned flow, as SRE is reviewing each change, it will delay the code deployment in production. SRE and the dev engineer will have back and forth as part of the review, which will further delay the code to production. So, instead of the SRE engineer, there should be added validation steps in the pipeline itself to certify the change/code/infra to be ready for production.

This is the SRE review process for changes going into production.

*Dev building code | tester testing code | CI/CD pipelines validated code | added validation and review in pipeline | automated approval| approve to deploy in production,* as shown in the following figure:

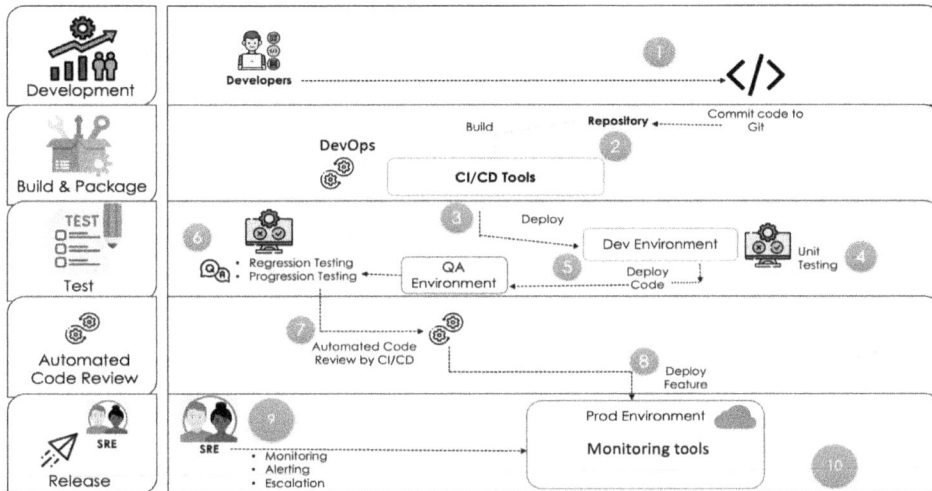

*Figure 6.5: Automated code review acting as gatekeeper*

Let us take previous examples and see how gatekeeping helped SRE to improve the performance of the system. The following is a list of some of the pros of gatekeeping:

- Software running in the maintenance phase. Ops and SRE team monitoring system and reporting code issues to dev teams.

- The SRE team is also working on enhancing their automation tools, improving alerting and monitoring in collaboration with ops teams.

- In parallel, new features are also being built by dev teams.

- As the system grows, more changes are required to be implemented in the system. Changes include infrastructure and application, such as security vulnerability patching, underlying operating system upgrades for servers, database server patching, and app code bug fixes. These all are called changes.

- More changes in the system mean more chances of errors and outages.

**Problem**: After a few months, the system started seeing many outages. Each outage resulted due to the changes that were implemented in the system.

**Solution**: The following is the stepwise approach to solutions:

1. The SRE team reviewed all outages. Toot cause analysis of outages and errors was identified.

2.  After review, SRE noticed that 90% of the time, outages are related to the change that went into production. For example, one of the code fixes in the service was introduced out of memory, and services started failing.

3.  They reviewed the change management process and identified the gap in there.

4.  As there was no involvement of SRE in the review of change before going into production. The SRE team worked with the DevOps team to implement extra validation in the CI/CD pipeline. Such as the pipeline will validate regression test case results, global configuration correctness, underlying infrastructure configuration, etc. Only once the change passes the validation will it be moved to production.

5.  After implementing the gatekeeping in the pipeline, SRE noticed a reduction in issues in the system. It also helped development and infra teams to fix issues on time. Issues were identified before the customer reported. This increased the overall reliability and performance of the system.

Gatekeeping is not for every project, and it depends on how big the project is. The bigger the software is, the more changes will be there. So, the team should weigh in to see if it is worth implementing gating or using testing team validation. Implementing gating in the pipeline requires skill, and organizations might need to train or hire people accordingly.

# Metrics identification

*If you cannot measure it, you cannot improve it.* This metric is one of the pillars of the SRE methodology. It not only helps SRE but also all SDLC teams to measure the performance of the system. The performance of the system is the direct reflection of the effort and performance of all teams involved in implementing any product. However, identifying the right metric for your system is a very important and demanding task. Even if you measure the system, if the metrics you choose are not right, that will not give the right picture of the performance of your system.

Taking previous examples of travel software applications. After implementing gatekeeping, SRE was able to control the outages caused by the changes. New features were still coming in as new requirements. After one year of the software's life with the end user, leadership reviewed the system's performance. This data was provided by the SRE team, as the SRE team pulled the measurement from the production environment, such as % of availability of software, % of SLA breaches, MTTR, MTBF, and MTTD. However, the results pulled by the SRE team did not match the data from customer complaints.

- **Problem:** SRE measurement showed 100% availability, but customer data showed 95% availability. After seeing 100% availability, the business reduced the tech budget as the system was stable enough and only needed little maintenance.

- **Solution:** The following are the steps for the solution:

    1.  As per SRE metrics, the system was 100% available, but we have learned in previous examples that there were multiple issues reported. There

were various bugs also identified by SRE teams in the system. However, the metrics were not showing the right result. The problem here is that the metrics selected to measure the system did not give the right picture. 100% availability means that even if there were errors, they were auto-resolved, and the system never went down.

2. Another metric, MTBF, showed that there was a 70% improvement in failures. That is, the mean time was very high between the two failures. However, during operational monitoring, SRE teams have seen multiple failures within 3 months of time.

3. After analysis, the SRE team identified that they were not using the right metrics to measure the system and that is giving the wrong picture. The MTBF was set to only consider if the same failure occurred again; they never measure different failures. The system was mostly seeing different failures. The SRE tool to capture availability was not set for the right data. The tool also took customer tickets into consideration for availability. But that is the wrong data to capture. Even if the customer did not reach out to the service center, the service was still down, and that impacted the availability of software.

4. The SRE removed the customer's ticket logic from their availability measurement tool.

5. The SRE also collaborated with the dev team to implement metrics in their process of identifying defects as MTTD. Earlier, SRE just calculated MTTD on the basis of alerts configured and how soon alerts were identified by ops. However, the SRE team never considers that alerts are coming from underlying error code logic setup in the application. Due to this, the SRE metric was showing good results, though SRE was missing detection of some failures unless the customers reached out.

6. The SRE collaborated with the dev to improve the error code logic for some of the services, and the dev team added MTTD to their process. This helped the dev also to identify some of the defects in their code before it reached the testing environment.

7. Once SRE redefined the metrics, leadership got a clear picture of the performance of the system. It was reported that the system is still in a nascent phase. Though overall performance is good, there are still multiple areas to improve.

Choosing a metric is critical, but it can be difficult to define. It is not just the job of the SRE team; it is a collaborative effort between all the SDLC teams. Some of the commonly used metrics are MTTR, MTBF, MTTD, availability %, and SLA %. MTTR, MTBF, and MTTD should be defined very clearly, as every application will have a different flow, and sometimes, even within an application, multiple services might differ in their measurement.

For example, 2 services, 1 of which functions to trigger multiple other jobs in the system. And that service goes down automatically as soon as the function ends. Service 2 has to be always up and running. Now, if MTTD is set up on service health, then it will give wrong data for service 1, as service 1 does its job and goes down. There is no error in service 1, but the metric will show the wrong result, and SRE will have to spend the unwanted effort to investigate the failure.

Other than the four golden metrics of SRE (latency, saturation, traffic, error), some of the common metrics used are as follows:

- **MTTR**: MTTR from any failure. Less time to recover from failure reflects how efficient the systems are, as they can recover within a few minutes from any failure. These metrics are for developers to measure the self-healing of their code and for SRE to measure their tools and observability that help recover the system faster.

- **MTTD**: MTTD any failure. The time it takes to identify defects in the system, the better the observability is. These metrics are for the SRE and ops team to help measure observability and tool efficiency. The efficient alerts and monitoring are fast, and SRE will be able to catch the defect in the system.

- **MTBF**: The more time between two failures reflects the efficiency of the system. This metric is for both dev and SRE, as fewer failures means efficient code as well as good self-healing.

- % **availability**: what % of the system was available for end-users? This is a direct reflection of reliability. High availability means high reliability. The error rate metric is linked to MTBF as the higher % of error rate means less MTBF.

- **Lead time to successfully implement the system change**: This metric is solely for the SRE team and reflects how good their tooling and processes are. The less time it takes for a chance to go to production shows the speed of the project. Some of the projects have new requirements every month, and they follow a 1-week sprint cycle to develop and release code.

# Early involvement of SRE in SDLC

The SRE team is responsible for ensuring the reliability of the system. So, they have a birds-eye view of a system that is live in the market. They monitor the system from the user requests perspective, infrastructure health perspective, and underlying application code perspective. SRE teams have end-to-end visibility of how the system is performing, and using their knowledge in the early stage of development can help development teams build their system, keeping production aspects in mind, such as scaling, auto-recovery, handling high loads, error handling, etc.

In continuation of the previous examples of online travel software, we will understand how involving SRE in the early stage of SDLC helped this organization achieve reliability in its application.

- **Scenario**: Let us take one scenario involving SRE in the early phase. After various improvements in a project, such as right metric calculation, gatekeeping, and defining roles, the team improved the performance of the system. They were able to manage defects efficiently, and system recovery also improved. With new requirements, the system started seeing more defects.

- Some of the defects are as follows:

    o Search and compare hotels' prices, service timing out as not getting a response for dependent service of a downstream system (a system that takes care of hotel details on the competitive platform).

    o Payment service fails whenever the database is down.

    o Reward service failing intermittently multiple times.

The development and testing team tested all the cases before moving the code to production, but in the first defect, the service was timing out due to another system in the same organization. The development team and testing team simulated the defect with a dummy response from an external system. A dummy response is not the exact replication of the scenario. But SRE has visibility of the system end to end, and they can suggest that the dev and testing teams design the functionality as per issues seen in production.

The following is the step-by-step process of how SRE involvement in the early phase of SDLC helped solve the aforementioned problem:

- **Planning phase 1**: Architects and analysts got requirements from businesses on the new requirements. They divided these requirements into different features for dev teams to build.

    High level data flow diagram was created by SMEs for new features.

- **Planning phase 2**: Dev SMEs started an architecture forum to discuss the design of new features. And the SRE SME also participated in the discussion.

    The high-level design of **search and compare service** (consider it as service1) is service calling to external service2, service2 responding back, and service1 will wait for 5 secs, and if no response is received, service1 time out.

The following is the diagrammatic representation of the search and compare service:

**Search and compare Service Data Flow**

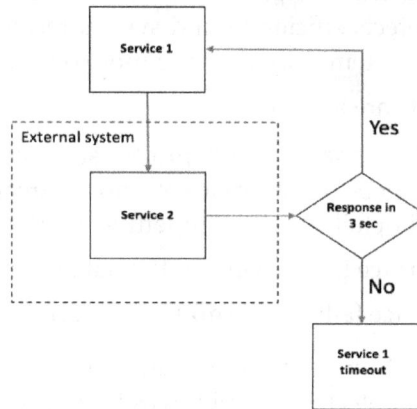

*Figure 6.6: Search and compare service data flow*

The SRE team has the to-end visibility of the system and its dependent system. So SRE suggested that the dev team implement a retry in service1, where if after 5 seconds the service fails due to no response, there should be a second retry. There can be network latency sometimes or some issue with service 2 responding late. As service 2 is outside of the current project, we cannot control their system, but we must improve our system. The dev team incorporated this design change in the search and compare service to address the first defect in the system: search and compare hotel price service timing out as not getting a response for dependent service of the downstream system (a system that takes care of hotel details on the competitive platform).

The following is the high-level data flow for the payment service:

**Payment Service Data Flow**

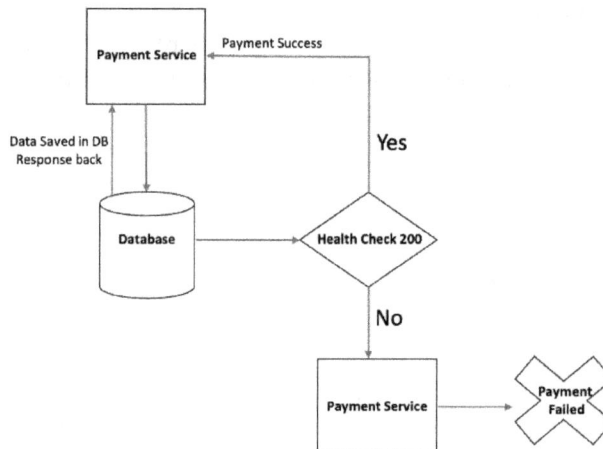

*Figure 6.7: Payment service data flow*

Before we jump into design, there are a few things to remember, it is a high-availability system. All servers have multiple nodes to handle the load. The application is running on multiple regions (also called data centers). Load balancers are installed on top of applications that take care of managing load by moving traffic between different servers and different regions. In this design, the payment service is doing a health check on DB, so if one of the nodes of the DB server is down, then the service will automatically move to another available node.

However, the dev team did not consider the chaos case, where the full database cluster is down. In that case, the payment service will fail, and the customer will not be able to book any hotel or flight. The SRE team is also responsible for performing chaos scenarios. The SRE team suggested a design change where, in such cases, the payment service should get *400 responses* from the database and automatically move the service to another region so that customers do not see any impact. After incorporating auto failover in the application, the problem of payment service failing whenever the database is down will be solved.

The following is the high-level data flow of the reward service:

**Reward Service**

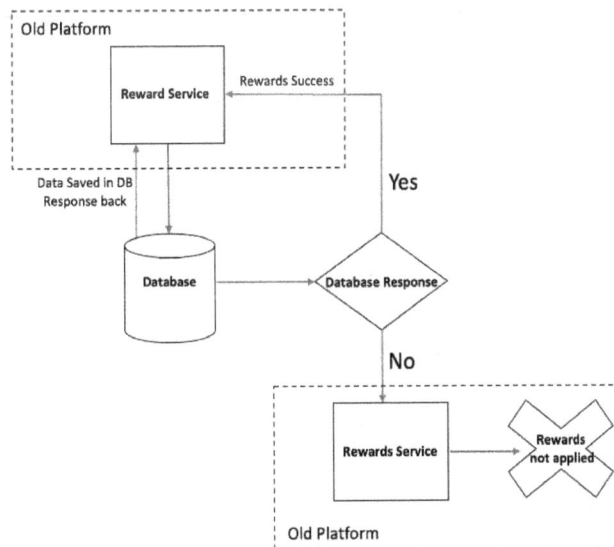

*Figure 6.8: Reward service data flow*

This is a slightly different case, where the reward service was still running on an old platform, and all other features of the travel app were migrated to a new platform. Initially, while planning, the technology team decided to take this service next year in a plan to migrate. However, SRE started seeing multiple issues with this service. As per design, the rewards service is running on the old platform but calling the database from the new platform. Due to the old framework, the service was not able to scale up enough and was timing out while searching data in the database. SRE suggested dev teams either plan to migrate reward also to a new platform or temporarily create an overnight data sync service that will store data in the cache to be available to reward service. This will not solve the problem permanently, but it will increase the reliability of the application. In this scenario, as SRE has visibility of all issues in the system, they were able to suggest design changes to the dev team.

- **Implementation phase**: All the implementation and development happen in this phase. After planning was completed, dev teams built the code. SRE teams added new alerting and monitoring for new features before time. As they were involved in planning discussions, it helped them to understand the flow better and create observability as per the design.

- **Testing phase**: After development, the software goes into the testing phase. The testing team performed a round of testing for new features. The SRE team performed chaos testing and added new chaos scenarios for new features in their test suite. Being involved in planning helped them get better information about the system design.

- **Deployment phase**: This is the phase where tested code is packaged and deployed/ installed on the production environment (when software is live to users). Once the code is certified, it is deployed in a production environment.

- **Maintenance/monitoring phase**: This is one of the important phases where engineering teams monitor the performance of live software. SRE teams started monitoring new features along with the existing app. The SDLC cycle started again for new features. The following figure represents the involvement of SRE in the planning phase.

The following figure shows the position of SRE in the planning phase and how the software development lifecycle flows when SRE is involved in the planning phase:

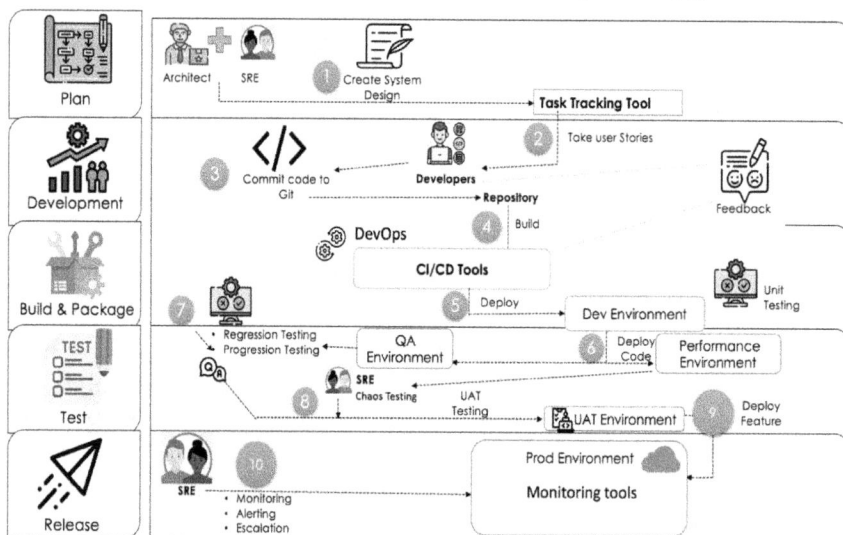

*Figure 6.9: SRE involvement in the planning phase of SDLC*

# SRE as chaos and performance engineer

In all the previous examples, you have learned SREs' involvement in chaos and performance testing. In the traditional model of SDLC, performance testing was performed by a dedicated performance team. They were either part of a testing team or a new team hired only to perform performance and load testing. Chaos was not part of any testing in the old SDLC model; maybe a few test cases were covered as part of load testing. With modern technology and modern frameworks, DevOps and SRE adoption increased. Over the period of time, the roles and responsibilities of SRE also evolved, and many organizations started involving SRE in chaos and performance testing. SRE has end-to-end visibility of software; they have knowledge of how systems perform in a production environment where various other factors are also to be considered, such as system communication to other systems over a network, network latency, % of real traffic, error rate in the system, etc. This bird's-eye view helps SRE to simulate the cases in the lower environment to better catch bugs on time and fix them.

Take the previous example and online travel software. You have learned that SRE was involved in chaos testing in a previous scenario, which is a defect; *Payment service failing whenever the database is down*, how SRE helped the development team in changing the design of the existing service to fix this problem.

Consider another use case where a few members of the testing team were hired to perform chaos testing. The testing team listed out chaos scenarios and executed all scenarios. However, one of the chaos issues happened in a production environment.

- **Problem**: The hotel search service failed as it did not receive any response from the database.
- **Solution**: The solution to the aforementioned problem is explained with two scenarios below, along with the diagrammatic representation.

The following is the data flow of the search service:

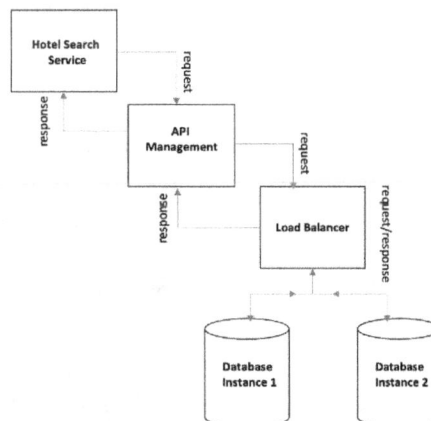

*Figure 6.10*: Search service data flow

The following are sequential steps for a chaos scenario:

1. Customers searched for hotels for particular date ranges and places.

2. The customer got page cannot be loaded in the first search. The customer tried again and got the same error. Multiple customers reported the same error to customer service.

3. The SRE team noticed http 400 error for service in the backend.

4. After an investigation by the SRE team, they identified that the underlying database is not giving a response to the load balancer. After further drilling down the issue, it was identified that one of the database clusters was not available. When the load balancer tried to move the load to another database instance, that request also failed. Though it does not seem like a chaotic scenario, it is as in this case, the database is not available, and the load balancer is not able to respond back to service with the right error.

The following are the chaos scenario steps tested by the testing team:

1. Hotel search service requested to the database. As part of the test case, one of the database instances was brought down.

2. The load balancer moved the load to another database instance. Service got the response back, and the test case passed.

3. The testing team did not incorporate a database cluster-down scenario, and that is why the load balancer was able to balance the traffic to one instance.

In the aforementioned two scenarios, the testing team did not test the scenario where the full database would be unavailable. So, the dev team did not add this error handling in service. Now, SRE has real-time, throughout the book visibility of production issues. So, if SRE had tested the chaos, they should have included this scenario. The dev team cloud has added error handling for the service, where the service could save data in the memory cache and display results from the cache. An error can be displayed on the screen that the app is under maintenance, so proactively inform customers.

# Conclusion

By the end of this chapter, we discussed various examples of how SRE's best practices helped organizations to achieve reliability and performance of the system. The chapter walks through examples from different domains of software applications and their different problems. The solution explained for each example will help you understand real world SRE. By now, you will learn different SRE practices and how incorporating these practices helps build better software.

In the next chapter, we will discuss some of SRE's best practices and the core values that SRE and DevOps share. These practices are the foundation of software development that will help build resilient and performant systems.

# CHAPTER 7
# Best Practice for SRE

## Introduction

This chapter will explain some of the best practices for SRE from a Business perspective. In previous chapters, we discussed various best practices for SRE. However, this chapter specifically focuses on the core values. These practices are derived from real-world scenarios from organizations following the SRE path.

## Structure

This chapter covers the following topics:

- Software design and software code
- Core values of DevOps and SRE
- Business and SRE

## Objectives

By the end of this chapter, we will cover the best practices for successful SRE teams and discuss some core values you should focus on for reliability. This will help us understand that if the root of any methodology/approach is strong, it can help you achieve good results.

# Software design and software code

Quality of software is directly related to the reliability and performance of the software. Best practices followed during software designing and coding help deliver quality. These two pieces are the core of SDLC.

Software design has multiple phases. This is one of the initial phases of SLDC after planning.

At a high level, software design is divided into three phases, interface design, architectural design, and detailed design. Interface design is a high-level design where internal systems are ignored, and only the input system and end-user are focused. Architectural design is a layered system architecture where all major components of the system are designed. The communication of different components is also designed. As part of a detailed design, every component is designed. Every specification of each component is defined. Data flow and interface between every component are also designed.

These three are internal phases of designing. As discussed in the previous chapters, designing is the crucial phase of SDLC. Organizations also create smaller strategies for software design, following best practices. This phase is the link between the problem and the solution.

One of the best practices followed for software design to help fulfil the next phase is software coding. So, best practices and standards followed during design help build better software from a coding perspective, and quality coding, in turn, increases software reliability and performance.

Some of the best practices for software design are:

- **Think about each component**: Breaking down the system into smaller components and listing every component. Then, you create communication between these components. Breaking down your system into components will help you understand the system better and how data flows between each component. You also get to understand the approach to be followed while coding the software. It helps you list down the tools and technologies to be used as part of building the software. Each component in software design here means services, interface between services, data communication platforms (such as API to API communication), storages, firewalls, load balancers, communication to outside systems, and all such components.

  There can be multiple designs in the process. As you progress in SDLC, architecture also changes, so breaking down components helps change your software design according to growing or changing requirements. This proves to be a good practice for software design.

- **Platform agnostic**: this means your software can run on multiple platforms and technology. For example, your software was built to run on the AWS cloud platform, but with a few changes, it can easily be configured to run on the GCP cloud platform.

Making your software agnostic is not easy, and there will never be a lift and shift of your software. However, during design, one of the best practices is to design your system in a way that does not overlap with the underlying architecture. It helps create a flexible system and can be migrated to another platform if required

- **Creating a prototype**: Building a prototype is a good way to see how your system is performing. The prototype allows you to see the system; if it fails, then repair it early on time. As part of failure, you would know if any component in the system needed to be changed and as you are early in your SDLC, it will help you to minimize the effort in changing the design. The first few iterations of the prototype might not be perfect, but that allows the creation of a perfect system (as no system is perfect).

  Though prototype creation is also part of development sometimes, it can also be added as part of designing. In designing, you break down your system into sub-systems and develop prototypes to validate the concepts designed. Prototyping has disadvantages for big systems as it can consume time and effort and add complexities.

- **Non-functional requirements**: These are high-level requirements for the overall project, which means outside the function of the software. For example, the system's performance, scalability, profitability, and extensibility. These are some of the non-functional requirements. During the designing of software, you should also consider non-functional requirements. The functionality of software directly impacts non-functional requirements and defines the performance of software.

While designing all components and data flow, you should always consider how each service will perform with load, how reliability works by defining load balancing, how auto failover of software will work, etc. These non-functional requirements drive the architecture of the system.

The following figure is a brief description of the best practices of software design:

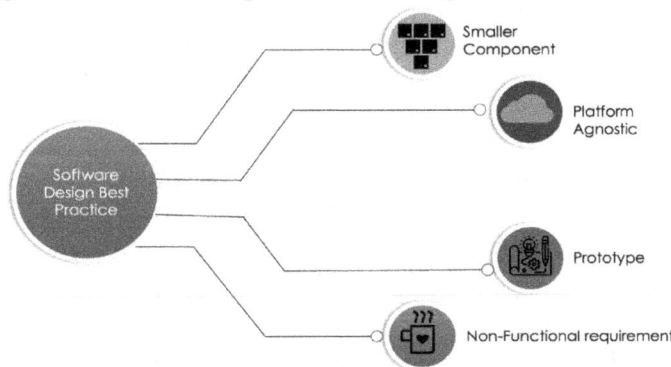

*Figure 7.1: Software design best practice*

Some of the best practices for software coding:

- **Design system architecture**: Software design and coding are tightly coupled. Right software design is one of the best practices for designing, but it also impacts software development. The better and more detailed the architecture, the more convenient for developers to understand and write the code. Good design starts from the right understanding of the requirement, functional and non-functional, and then maps these two. Divide and rule policy wins here, that is, diving architecture into slices will help plan and design software that meets the delivery outcome.

- **Code reviews**: After the designing phase, development teams divide the system into multiple features, and each feature is further broken into smaller stories that are further broken into smaller microservices. These stories are picked by developers, and they code into software. As best practice, each code after development should be reviewed by peers. You should clearly define the standards to be followed by development while writing code, such as the naming convention of their service, no hard-coded values, virializing dynamic values, etc. As part of code review, all standards are reviewed, and if the code does not follow standards, then it is rejected, and developers have to rewrite the code.

- **Develop test cases**: As part of development, the team should create unit test cases to increase code coverage. The more you test the code, the more you will get visibility of the code's functionality. Though unit tests do not give enough visibility for end-to-end functionality, they give you a view of the performance of smaller pieces of code. And it is easy to fix the smaller code for any issues.

- **Performance testing**: Include performance testing as part of your testing. This best practice generally comes under SRE or QA teams, but it is part of SDLC. This is one of the best practices to understand the system performance end to end. Issues identified as part of this testing can be fixed before deploying the code to production.

- **Documentation**: This is one of the key best practices for developers. Documenting defines detailed information on how the software works. As part of designing, you should document each feature that will help developers to understand and write the code. Along with this technical documentation, developers should also document their services, such as what the service does, input, output, data flow diagram, how to troubleshoot the service, user manuals, etc. For example, adding brief comments about the code during programming such as mentioning the new function that was added as part of this feature. These comments will help developers to track back in case of any troubleshooting.

- **Version control**: Software versioning is important as it helps developers and software keep track of different versions. When multiple developers work on the same piece of software code, it becomes essential not to conflict with and overwrite each other's code changes. Keeping versions of code will help avoid this conflict. If developers wanted to roll back their changes, they could easily choose an older version. Various version control software is available that can be used across organizations.

The performance and reliability of software depend on multiple factors. However, the quality of the code is the core reason for the software's performance. Code quality improves the effectiveness, usability, and reliability of the software. Software organizations follow various best practices at each stage of SDLC to build performant and reliable systems. As underlying code is one of the key variables for any software, best practices followed for software design and code will help increase the reliability of the system.

Best practices for software design and code will improve code quality; code quality reduces bugs in the system, and bugs mean fewer outages and high reliability.

The following are some of the best practices to improve code quality along with the aforementioned explained best practices:

- Practice designing each component with detail helps developers understand data flow that, in turn, helps them to build quality code.

- Practice adding code review to help catch issues on time before even it is published to the repository.

- Practice adding test cases will help code coverage and catch issues on time. That gives developers time to fix these issues before the code is published in the production environment.

- Practice planning and designing non-functional requirements to help understand the overall aspect of the system. This gives teams perspective to look at software from outside and how other factors impact code, such as load, failure in an external system, disaster recovery situation, reaction to outages, impact of technology changes in the market, etc.

- Practice building a feedback loop between all SDLC teams helps understand the system better, reduce turnaround time for bug fixes, reduce recovery time, and, in turn, reduce impact on end users.

If you fix the core of the problem, the end results will eventually be positive. So, the following described best practices during the initial phase of SDLC will help build a quality software system:

| 1 | Define requirements and scope clearly |
|---|---|
| 2 | Create Use Cases |
| 3 | Use Agile Methodology |
| 4 | Implement version control |
| 5 | Implement access control |
| 6 | Create detailed and full coverage unit test cases |
| 7 | Define requirements and scope clearly |
| 8 | Document your service as part of runbooks |
| 9 | Document issues and progress |
| 10 | Right software for development |
| 11 | Collaboration with DevOps, SRE, QA, Business |
| 12 | Document all changes in collaboration with SRE |

*Figure 7.2: Software development best practice summary*

Let us take a real-world example of how software design best practices help SRE achieve its goals.

A banking software organization is working on launching one of the big features of its existing software available in the market.

- The architect teams got the requirements from the business and started designing the new feature.

- The feature was broken down into multiple smaller components. The architecture diagram was designed with data flow between all smaller components.

- The architecture was passed to the software development team. Detailed component design helped development teams understand the design.

- Design each component:

    o Breaking down into smaller components helped teams identify non-functional requirements.

    o Engineering teams were able to design failovers within services and add test cases for performance testing.

    o Detailed designing of all components helped development teams divide features into multiple small services for clear development.

The development teams started building the code. As they build code, they use the CI/CD pipelines built by the DevOps team to package it, deploy it, and test it.

- **Code review**:

    o As part of best practice, the senior developer reviewed each code change, and only after their approval was the code merged into the repository. As part of the code review, it was identified that one of the codes is missing the critical configuration required to run in the production environment. After the review, the configuration was fixed and merged into the code.

    o During the code review, the SME identified that the wrong version of the code (branch) was requested to be merged into the main code. So, the SME rejected the code and asked the dev to correct the version.

    o Code review helps developers identify and eliminate bugs in the code at an early stage.

    As part of the SDLC process and best practices followed by DevOps, the dev team used automated test cases integrated into CI/CD and identified bugs early in the phase. Devs fixed the bug, redeployed, and retested.

- **Testing**:

    o QA did their broader testing of the feature. Also, integration testing is a whole application.

    o  Bugs identified as part of QA testing were sent back to dev teams to fix and retest.

After testing, the feature was deployed to production.

- **Monitoring**:
  - o  As best practice was followed during software design, not many issues were observed in the code for new features.
  - o  The service was also built as an auto-failover. There were retries also implemented in the code.
  - o  Though SRE teams observed some issues, best practices followed during software design and development helped the team deliver quality code. That, in turn, helped maintain the application's reliability even with new features. This also saved operational overhead for SRE.

The following is the diagrammatic representation of the example explained, where incorporating best practices helped build and deliver quality software:

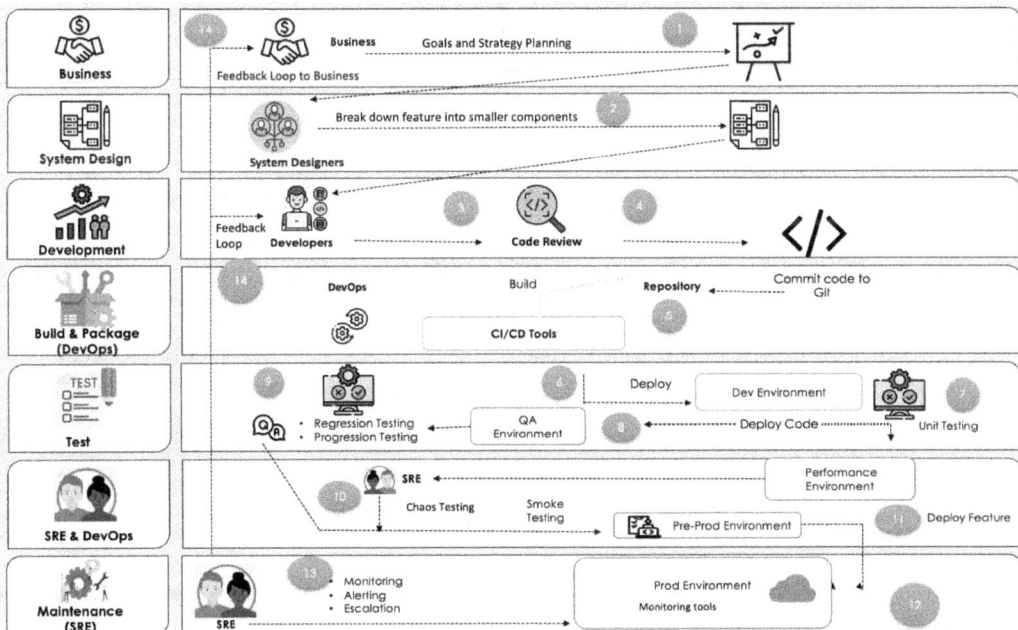

*Figure 7.3: SDLC process, including business and system designers*

# Core values of DevOps and SRE

DevOps and SRE are the most used approaches in today's software development and operations. Each organization has its own definition of DevOps and SRE. Sometimes, they overlap with each other, sometimes also used interchangeably; oftentimes, they are both used as two separate divisions. However, an underlying principle for the two remains the same.

DevOps focuses on agility. The methodology is to unite the entire software development journey, design, building, testing, and deploying; by breaking it down into smaller pieces to increase the delivery of the product.

SRE focuses on resilience and reliability. The methodology is to collaborate with the development team to design a system that runs smoothly even during stress.

DevOps is a fusion of development and operations from a deployment perspective. It focuses on deploying the code smoothly. Here, a team that develops the code is also responsible for maintaining the code in production using an automated cycle.

The core principles of DevOps are as follows:

- **Collaboration**: Break down silos by connecting the development and operations teams, using automation cycles for building and deploying.

- **Catch failures**: Building automated CI/CD pipelines to build, test, and deploy the code. Automation test cases catch failures on time and are fixed before releasing them to production.

- **Control changes without slowing speed**: The DevOps team builds automated pipelines that help deploy changes in an incremental way regularly. This helps break down big changes (such as big builds) into smaller packages and deploy them. This helps faster deployment and quick review of changes.

- **Automation**: The DevOps team builds CI/CD pipelines using automation tools. They add various controls and test cases as part of CI/CD to catch issues on time.

- **Measurement**: DevOps team always measures their outcome using various metrics. Error rate, build failures, change failure rates, etc.

- **Feedback loop**: give and seek feedback for continuous improvement. Give feedback to development teams on errors encountered during the build, test, and deployment of code. Seek feedback from dev teams on how to improve CI/CD pipelines.

SRE is the team that makes sure to develop a system that is highly available and reliable. It also brings development and operations together from an operational perspective. It focuses on measuring and building the performance and reliability of the system using various automation. The SRE team develops various approaches to increase operational visibility for the development team so that they can build quality code.

The core principles of SRE are:

- **Collaboration**: Break down the silo between development and operations teams focusing on operations. That helps developers give more context to production performance.

- **Catch failures**: The SRE team builds various monitoring dashboards, alerting to catch failures. And feedback loop to share the information back to developers. This helps developers fix the problem in code and use DevOps's pipelines to deploy fixes quickly, which in turn increases reliability.

- **Automation**: The SRE team builds various automation to reduce operational overhead by reducing toil. Automation to identify issues in the production system, failover system during any issue, and create an RCA loop for developers.

- **Measurement**: This is key for the SRE team. They create various metrics to measure the performance and the availability of the system. Three major metrics are SLA, SLO, and SLI.

- **Feedback loop**: Give and seek feedback for continuous improvement. Give feedback to development teams on types of errors encountered in the production environment that impact reliability. The feedback helps dev teams to analyse and fix it permanently. Seek feedback from dev teams on tooling and how to help dev teams speed up their development without compromising quality.

The following is the diagrammatic representation of the core values of DevOps and SRE and how they overlap:

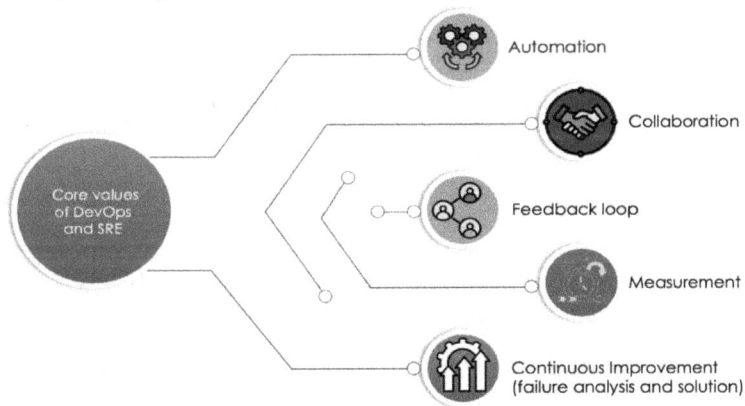

*Figure 7.4*: *Core values of SRE and DevOps*

The core values of both DevOps and SRE are the same, but both focus on different aspects of SDLC. The goal of both teams is to create a stable and reliable system.

Some of the differences between DevOps and SRE are:

- **Roles and responsibilities of both teams**: The DevOps team works on providing a platform for building, testing, and deploying the code. The SRE team works on providing feedback to the development and testing team. SRE manages operations.

- **Focus**: SRE focuses on maintaining the availability of the system. They focus on customers and end users. DevOps team focuses on faster building and deploying code. They help the development team.

- **Metrics for measurements are different**: SRE uses SLO, SLI and SLA, MTTD, and MTTR. DevOps uses lead time for change, deployment frequency, time to restore, and change failure rate.

- **Managing tickets**: SRE focuses on customer-focused incidents. DevOps focuses on internal tickets for development teams.

The best practices for DevOps are:

- **Agile methodology**: Building pipelines that follow continuous integration and continuous deployment. CI/CD pipelines that integrate building, testing, and deploying code automatically.

- **Continuous monitoring**: Implementing monitoring at various phases of development and deployment. To catch failures and other issues on time.

- **Feedback loop**: Implement a feedback loop between development, testing, and SRE teams. And also seek feedback from these teams to continuously improve the services.

- **Collaboration**: This is the key practice for the DevOps team. To break silos and build transparent collaboration between teams. To give full perspective to all teams about the software progress.

- **Automates testing**: Testing is the key to measuring the quality of code. The DevOps team integrates test cases in the CI/CD pipeline to help automate testing. Automated pipeline to build infrastructure along with code. This comes under automation as a best practice.

The best practices for SRE are:

- **Automation**: Automate all manual work to reduce operational overhead. Automate incident management process. Automate the RCA loop. Automate change management process.

- **Define metrics**: Define and create metrics to measure the performance of the system. Metrics are one of the key practices for SRE. You cannot improve your system without measuring its current performance.

- **Monitoring**: Building dashboards and alerting to monitor the system in real-time and passively. Dashboards are proactive, and they give an overview of the system's health. Alerting is reactive; engineers take action after receiving alerts.

- **Collaboration**: Collaboration is the best practice for any teamwork. For SRE, collaborating with the development and product teams to give a full perspective of system performance. Collaboration involves understanding each team's perspective, empowering them, and building a system that considers all aspects of SDLC teams.

- **Engineering**: Building tools and capabilities for non-functional requirements to help the reliability of the system.

The following is the summary of DevOps vs. SRE that you learned above. There are high-level differences and similarities between the two:

| Factors | DevOps | SRE |
|---|---|---|
| Collaboration | *Dev and Operation/SRE* | *Dev, QA, Business* |
| Automation | • *CI/CD pipelines for building, testing and deploying*<br>• *Automated Infrastructure configuration*<br>• *Tooling around deployments* | • *Incident management*<br>• *Auto failover*<br>• *Alerting, Monitoring*<br>• *Tools and Capabilities*<br>• *Operational Toil removal* |
| Measurement | *Error rate, build failure rate, change failure rate, MTTR, MTBF, MTTD* | *SLO, SLA, SLI, Error Budget, MTTR, MTBF, MTTD* |
| Feedback Loop | *Dev and QA* | *Dev, QA, Business* |
| Continuous Improvement | • *Catch failures as part of CI/CD*<br>• *Feedback loop to dev for fixing the bugs* | • *Catch failures as part of alerting and monitoring*<br>• *Feedback loop to dev and business* |
| Role and Responsibilities | *CI/CD, infrastructure as a code* | *Operations and reliability* |
| Focus | *Faster build and deploy* | *High availability and reliability* |

*Figure 7.5: DevOps and SRE*

# Business and SRE

The goal for business and SRE is to build and deliver reliable and available systems. Adopting the SRE approach has changed the business mindset toward IT operations. By applying SRE principles, businesses can achieve high availability, reduce incidents, and faster resolution. This helps increase customer satisfaction and, in turn, increases productivity.

The best practices followed at SRE help businesses achieve their goals. Though SRE is part of the technology domain, its methodology has increased the visibility of the system for business. Business and SRE go hand in hand. The organizational goals are defined by the business and followed by technology teams, including dev and SRE. Then, the SRE team builds a feedback loop about system stability from production to the engineering team. The feedback goes back from engineering to product to business, which gives visibility to the business about the real picture of system performance. This loop helps business review their goals, keeping operations in mind.

Let us see how SRE enables businesses to scale their system:
- **Measurement**: At the start of any project business, define high-level goals for engineering teams with respect to software development and delivery. And all SDLC teams follow those goals. Once the software is delivered and used by end users, SRE creates various metrics to measure system performance. This measurement helps businesses understand the system better so that they can align how and when to add new requirements and features.

SRE creates key metrics at the service level. These key metrics are SLA, SLO, SLI, and error budget. Service level agreement defines the availability of the system. The service level objective defines the desired level of reliability of the system. Service level indicators are measurements of the performance of the system. An error budget is a measurement of the reliability or downtime of the system within acceptable limits. By using these metrics, an organization can align its engineering efforts with business objectives.

- **Incident management**: It is part of the operational process, but it also enables SRE to define the error budget. The error budget allows the team to define the permissible error rate for the system. The feedback loop within the SRE process allows engineering teams to visualize the error rate. This helps the engineering team to prioritize production reliability issues and also helps them balance between existing production issues and new feature development. As the engineering team gets the requirements from the business, they can give the error rate back to the business, and then the business can balance out between reliability and new requirements.

  The error rate in the existing system also helps define the business IT operational budget. This gives the business a 360 view of engineering plus operations progress.

- **Operations as a value creation**: SRE's key focus is to maintain the system's reliability. In the process, they create multiple automations to reduce operational overhead, faster system recovery, automated failovers, quick capture of issues and solutions, and continuous improvement. SRE contributes to the overall business strategy and helps drive innovation. As SRE has 360 views of the production/ live system, they act as growth enablers, providing support to infrastructure and application, providing visibility and support to the development team to deliver high-quality software code, and building operational tools and capabilities to help the development team focus on building code at speed.

  SRE empowers engineering/development teams to deliver quality, and that helps the business meet its goals.

At a very high level, any software organization's business goal is to deliver a quality experience to its customers in order to grow. Keeping this goal in mind, the business breaks down into various measurable, smaller goals for engineering teams. The overall strategy of an organization always flows from top to bottom. Here, business is at the first level of this chain, and SRE is at the last; this flow of goals into strategy changes multiple times in between, but the end goal is the same: to make sure customers are satisfied. That is why SRE plays a very critical role in achieving organizational strategy. SRE measures the reliability and performance of the system; the measurement gives visibility to businesses on where to improve in case customers are not satisfied.

Let us look at the following real-world scenario on how SRE helps businesses achieve organizational strategy:

- **Project**: A software organization planned to build an e-commerce platform.
- **Goal**: To deliver seamless service to customers 24*7.
- **Timeline of project**: 2 years.
- **Process**:
  o Technology stack listing.
  o Budget allocation.
  o Teams onboarding.
  o Processes and standards creation.
  o For software building, consider the SDLC process with Agile methodology. Multiple teams are involved in building, testing, and delivering the product. (Refer to previous chapters for SDLC in Agile.)

Engineering teams built the product keeping the organization's strategy in mind. The first version was launched after 2 years. Six months after the launch, the SRE team shared their analysis of the system's performance. The proactive and detailed analysis helped businesses avoid unforeseen situations. Take a detailed look at this problem.

The following steps will walk you through finding the root of the problem:

1. As best practice, SRE created various metrics to measure the performance of the system.

2. Availability of the system was measured as 99.999%. That means there is no problem with the application's availability to customers.

3. As part of the incident management system, operations teams were able to resolve operational queries of customers on time. So, incident management was also not the cause of customer dissatisfaction.

4. Data captured by SRE, as part of reliability and performance metrics, showed some degradation of service. The two metrics were configured to capture the request/response time of each service and the error rate for each service. As part of these two metrics, the SRE team identified that there is an intermittent failure in payment and search service. Also, a pattern where at a particular period in a week, they see higher response time from search service.

5. After initial analysis, SRE collaborated with infrastructure SMEs to capture logs on the network side. As part of best practice, the network team has also configured metrics for the latency. However, there was no lag noticed in the network logs.

6. The analysis was further shared with engineering/development teams (as part of the feedback look).

7. The engineering and SRE team collaborated and identified high memory in logs during higher loads.

8. The SRE team re-reviewed their load test cases and found out that they did not estimate the number as real live applications are seeing. So, the application was never tested beyond a certain traffic.

9. The SRE team updated their test case and was able to replicate the scenario.

10. Engineering teams identified the root cause of the issue and fixed the underlying code by changing the multithreading and caching logic for payment and search services.

11. This scenario also acted as a trigger point for the development team to proactively review other services using similar logic in code.

12. The feedback loop was shared with the business, and they updated their measurement to increase their customer's traffic estimation.

13. This also helped businesses estimate the infrastructure's size for the future and allocate respective budgets to onboard added capacity for the infrastructure.

The aforementioned is one of the scenarios on how SRE best practices helped organizations to quickly catch issues and resolve them on time. This helped maintain the reliability of the system and, in turn, customer satisfaction. Without SRE measurement, businesses might still be able to identify the issue. However, that identification will be more reactive, that is after the problem has impacted customers.

In some organizations, business works directly with SRE teams and involves them in the initial planning and strategy of a product. This is also one of the best practices for an organization to follow to get a 360 view of the product.

The aforementioned problem is the best example of *if you cannot measure it, you cannot improve it*. Creating the right metrics at every level of software building is one of the important steps that is also critical in choosing the right metrics to measure your system.

Best practice for a business to follow:

- Clearly defined objectives and goals for the organization.

- Create a detailed roadmap with smaller achievable milestones and timelines.

- Conduct market research before starting to onboard any project. This helps business to identify their target audience, too.

- Keep a buffer for operational overhead. That means businesses should always keep added capacity for operational tasks. Businesses should be able to allocate resources effectively.

- Risk management is one of the key factors when deciding an organization's strategy. No product is 100% reliable and available. There will always be outages in the application. However, the business should align its strategy, keeping these operational outages in mind.

- Regular review of goals and strategy with engineering teams. Businesses should split broader goals into smaller milestones. And review those smaller milestones to track the performance of the delivery.

- The business and engineering team's metrics should always match. For example, if MTTR and MTBF are the metrics to measure the overall system's performance, then the same should be followed by all SDLC teams for their individual services and systems.

- Prioritization of functional and non-function requirements based on system performance and reliability. It also prioritizes non-functional requirements to meet the system's reliability.

- Prioritization of features based on user needs and business goals.

- Incorporate a feedback loop for continuous improvement.

The following is the diagrammatic representation of the aforementioned best practices for businesses to follow in software development. It explains how business and SRE collaborate through feedback loop that helps build and deliver quality software:

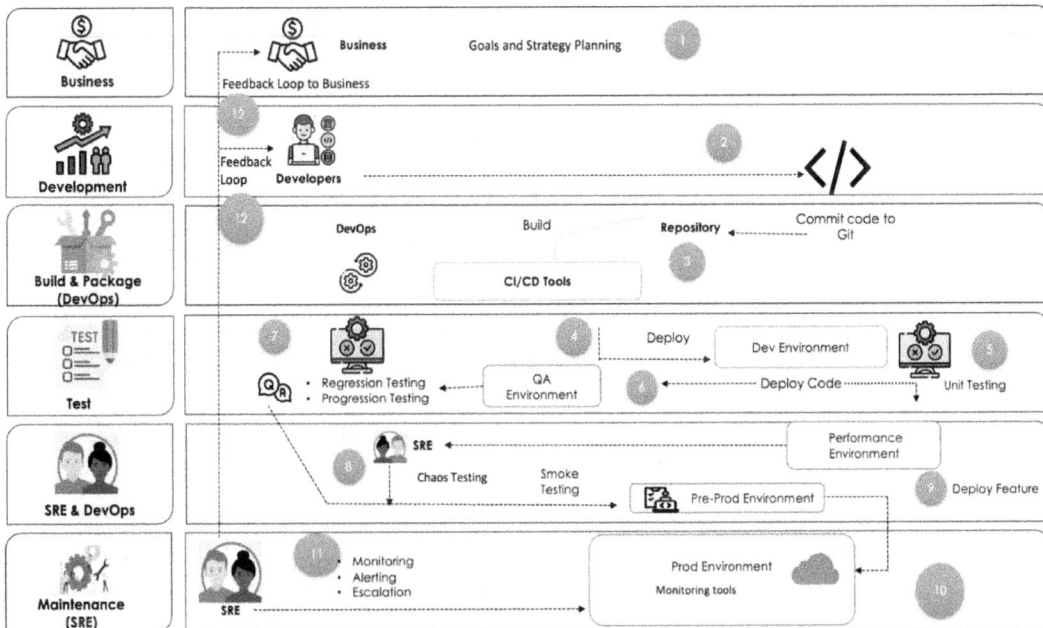

*Figure 7.6: Business to SRE and feedback loop*

The aforementioned figure is the summary of the software development lifecycle model. The data flows from top to down, business to engineering teams. It shows various stages of information passing from the business to the software development team, then to QA, and further to the SRE. The system design stage is hidden to emphasize business and SRE communication.

Stage 12 shows the feedback loop from SRE to developers and also businesses.

This loop is a measurement of system performance, issues encountered, and reliability of systems. These details help developers and businesses to gain insight into production system performance.

Let us look at a real-world scenario of how a feedback loop helped an organization build a reliable system and deliver a good product. Also, highlight the importance of SRE teams and involvement in each phase of SDLC.

For example, the health care product that is live in the market and is used by various hospitals and direct customers to manage medical records, online medicine delivery, patient data, doctor's information, online booking for consultation, and in-hospital emergency booking.

The following points show technology teams identified various problems in software on time and solved those to give seamless experience to users.

The software's initiative was only for hospital usage, where hospital representatives used the software to track and manage patient medical records.

Over 1 year, the organization built and delivered two more capabilities in the system, i.e., online booking and delivery of medicine and database search for hospitals and doctors to direct users.

In 2nd year, the organization builds further capabilities for users, such as online booking for consultation and in-hospital emergency booking.

Six months after the release of multiple features, the software started seeing some performance lag. As part of performance metric capture, the SRE team identified a 5% degradation in performance. However, this 5% did not impact the availability of software. However, the operations or support team received some 0.5% of queries from customers on the slowness of the application.

The above point of performance degradation is an alarm for the organization to re-examine the design of the software and take appropriate action to solve the problem before it impacts the reliability of the platform. That, in turn, impacts customer satisfaction.

Take the aforementioned figure, where SRE had a direct feedback loop to the development, product, and business teams. The advantage of a direct feedback loop is no loss of information and on-time information delivery to the teams that plan delivery, i.e., business.

The performance data captured by SRE teams through their tools were shared with development teams and businesses within 2 days (SRE took 1 day to analyse the data and shared initial analysis).

The organization had a regular cadence of meetings between all technology team's leadership. However, the data shared here was alarming to the product, businesses got notified, and a meeting was called between the development and SRE teams to discuss further solving the problem.

Teams analyzed that there was an increase in user requests concerning online booking and that degraded the performance of the application. The current booking module was not able to handle the load. A quick and easy fix to increase the memory of the system was implemented with proper testing.

Again, 2 two-month analysis of the system shared by SRE to the business team looked good and in control.

However, 3$^{rd}$ month, the SRE team captured 5% more degradation than last time. That means even after increasing memory, the application was not able to handle the load. As the customer request increased by 30% this time and application load time increased by 10%, that is a red flag on the reliability of the system.

The SRE team captured two instances of application crashes during high load. However, due to the self-healing capability in the application, the service was auto restarted, causing minimal impact on users.

The SRE team also captures the increase in customer compliance from the support team on application slowness.

As part of the feedback loop, development teams were given data on open bugs in the system. The business team identified the urgent need to fix the current bug in the system and de-prioritize any feature in progress. The development team paused the development of 2 new features, and the engineer's bandwidth was allocated to fix open production defects.

This gave visibility to the business, they stopped the new feature requirement and shifted strategy to focus on improving the existing feature.

The timeline was defined as 2 weeks to fix all issues on system performance.

After 2 weeks, the technology team delivered the fix to the production system. SRE closely monitored the system's performance and identified an increase in the application's performance even during high load.

During defect fixing, engineering teams were also able to solve customer queries.

This scenario is the best example of solving the reliability of the system through a feedback loop and capturing the right data through metrics. This also shows the importance of collaboration and transparency between the product and technology teams that can solve big problems.

# Conclusion

By the end of this chapter, we covered three major aspects of SRE best practices. This chapter helped you understand how SRE helps businesses to achieve their goals by aligning with organisational strategy. The mentioned real industry scenario helps you visualize SRE's role in various phases of SDLC.

This chapter also helps you understand the importance of the feedback loop and how it can be used as one of the best practices throughout the Agile process to improve the reliability and delivery of software products. We also understood how DevOps and SRE are helping businesses achieve their goals.

In the next chapter, we will discuss about the tools available in the market that help SRE to build and deliver reliable and quality software. The chapter will also explain the cheat sheet for SRE, serving as a useful guide for those starting their career in SRE as well those already working in the fields.

# Join our Discord space

Join our Discord workspace for latest updates, offers, tech happenings around the world, new releases, and sessions with the authors:

https://discord.bpbonline.com

# CHAPTER 8
# Tool Kit for SRE

## Introduction

In this chapter, we will discuss some of the best tools available on the market that can be used as an SRE tool kit. This chapter will be a cheat sheet for a successful SRE. The chapter will help you learn the high-level daily tasks that SRE does to ensure successful reliability. Readers will understand how an SRE team is formed by diverse skill sets.

## Structure

This chapter covers the following topics:

- SRE tool kit
- Cheat sheet for SRE

## Objectives

By the end of this chapter, you will have a high-level understanding of SRE. Also, you will learn the tools available in the market today that the SRE team uses. These tools might change in the future as technology changes. Still, in current scenarios, they are some of the most used tools and technologies by software organizations that have an SRE methodology.

# SRE tool kit

There are multiple enterprises and open-source tools available in the market today that are used by SRE teams. Some organizations also build their in-house tools, and some of them use open-source tools and customize them as per the requirements. Automation is at the heart of SRE teams, which means they automate all the manual, repetitive work to reduce toil, and in the process of automation, they also build their daily tools.

The following tools mentioned are some of the most used by organizations today. These tools have been categorized according to their usage and functionality.

Before shortlisting a tool, consider the following things that can help choose the right tool:

- **The problems you are trying to solve**: Start by identifying the gap or problem. Once you have the problem, then try to see if the tool has the required feature that can solve your problem.

- **Who will need to use the software**: Evaluate cost and requirements and consider who will be using the software.

- **Other tools required to be used along with the current tool**: Can the tool alone solve your requirement, or will you need another tool integration? Or is there any other tool available that has all the features?

- **Important outcomes**: Once you have the problem or the gap, try to see what tool will deliver along with solving your problems.

- **The learning curve**: Will the tool require learning from scratch? Do you have people on the team who already know the tool? Is ramping up on the tool easy, or does it require any certification or learning course?

- **Implementing the tool**: Will the tool require just installation and basic configuration, or will you have to configure every feature of the tool? What expertise do you need in configuring the tool, and what will be the cost of installing/configuring?

- **Popularity of the tool**: This can be misleading sometimes; however, if other organizations similar to your business model are using the tool, then it is worth considering the option.

The following are the service management tools.

# Incident management

The following are the details:

- **ServiceNow IT service management**: This tool aligns with **IT service management (ITIL)** practice and is used for end-to-end management of service delivery.

  o It is a cloud-based enterprise. It also has a dedicated cloud.

  o It has multiple and scalable workflows.

- o Easy user interface
- o Provide various dashboards for reporting
- o **Paging**: Notify the right people by identifying real-time issues
- o SRE teams mostly use the tool for incident management
- o Support on-call rotation for the team
- o Needs skill and time to configure

- **PagerDuty**: This tool also manages operations.
  - o It is a cloud-based tool.
  - o It manages operations by collecting real-time data signals, applying machine learning, and notifying the right people for faster resolution.
  - o Easy user interface.
  - o SRE teams use the tool for incident management.
  - o Support on-call rotation for the team.
  - o Easy to configure.

- **OpsGenie**: This tool also provides incident management systems.
  - o It is based, but costs less than others.
  - o Provide 24*7 on-call rotation.
  - o Incident notification by collecting real-time data.
  - o This tool has more flexibility, such as alert management and deployment/ rollbacks.
  - o Very easy log tracing.
  - o It is part of Atlassian products like Jira.
  - o Easy to configure.

- **Jira service management**:
  - o It is cloud-based enterprise software.
  - o Jira is mostly used for agile project management. Jira service management is used for operational tasks.
  - o It is a new software compared to ServiceNow. It is a rebranding of its Jira software.
  - o Lightweight and easy to configure.
  - o Provide real-time incident management.
  - o Provide detailed reporting.
  - o Jira tasks (used in agile) can be linked to incidents in Jira service management. This provides better tracing.

- **SolarWinds**:
  - ○ Its cloud-based.
  - ○ The tool is mostly used as a network monitoring tool. But SolarWinds ITSM is another functionality.
  - ○ It provides incident management with ITIL best practices.
  - ○ Configuration of alerts is easy.
  - ○ On-call service.
  - ○ Service monitor.

- **Zendesk**:
  - ○ One of the oldest cloud-based software.
  - ○ Used as **software as a service (SaaS)**.
  - ○ Provide incident management.
  - ○ Customer support and Live chat.
  - ○ It is more of a ticketing system and a help center-focused tool.

- **TopDesk**:
  - ○ Well-renowned ITIL-compliant IT service management software.
  - ○ Suitable for medium and large enterprises, it manages their workflow, customer communications, and assets.
  - ○ Good reporting and analytics. Gives insight into IT performance and areas of improvement. Unique feature of the knowledge management repository.
  - ○ Cloud-based enterprise solution, and it is not open-source.

- **SymphonyAI IT service management**:
  - ○ Cloud-based enterprise solution.
  - ○ One of the new software with advanced features such as AI-enabled, analytics, a good dashboard, multi-language support, and a persona-based user dashboard.
  - ○ It is good for reporting and analytics. Organizations that need extensive reports on the performance of their software can use this tool.

There are various open-source software also available, such as Atlassian, FreshService, SysAid, InvGate, Spiceworks, and Cherwell. The usage of these tools solely depends on your project, budget, usage of the tool, data security, compliance, and organizational decision.

# Change management

- **ServiceNow**:
    - o This tool is also used for change management.
    - o It is cloud-based enterprise.
    - o Strong workflow integration with incidents.
    - o Good report dashboards.

- **Jira management tool**:
    - o Jira is also used as a change management tool.
    - o It is also the enterprise version.
    - o It can also be integrated with Jira Agile and Jira service management. This gives better tracing.

- **ChangeGear**:
    - o It is more of a service desk ITSM tool.
    - o It has both on-premise and SaaS versions.
    - o Easy and customizable dashboards with a single pane.

- **ChangeGrab**:
    - o Cost-effective tool. Its free version is also available.
    - o Easy customization.
    - o Better reporting and good integration with tools such as Slack and Twitter.

- **SpeKit**:
    - o Real-time analytics to uncover insights.
    - o It has the knowledge base to consolidate all data and remove unwanted or poor-quality data.
    - o Various customizable templates for change management features.
    - o Real-time alerting.
    - o Uses AI to translate calls and meetings transcripts and summarize them.

# Alerting and monitoring tools

ServiceNow, Jira, and PagerDuty can also be used as alerting tools. These tools will alert users if they encounter any alerts as per the configuration. However, organizations use tools that cater to all these functions for tracking, logging, alerting, and monitoring. Choosing the right alerting and monitoring tool is very important for SRE. The earlier you are notified about any outage, the easier it is to trace, and the more it will help you resolve the issue.

- **Elastic Search Logstash Kibana: Elastic Search Logstash Kibana (ELK)** is an observability tool stack
  - This is a stack of three tools that capture the data, log it, and alert on issues.
    - Elastic search provides analytics on it
    - Logstash collects and aggregates the data
    - Kibana gives a user interface to monitor the logging
  - It is a cloud-based open-source software
  - Kibana is used to configure alerts and notifications on various channels, such as Slack.
  - Elastic Search is based on indexing data to display on Kibana
  - Kibana has good monitoring dashboards that give a single view of the health of the application.
  - Can be used for application and infrastructure monitoring.

- **Splunk:**
  - This is a proprietary security and observability tool.
  - Splunk can be used to ingest various formats of machine data, format it, and display it on the user interface.
  - It offers better and flexible monitoring dashboards.
  - It is a cloud-based paid software.
  - Can be used for application and infrastructure monitoring.

- **Dynatrace:**
  - It is a cloud-based open-source tool
  - It is **application performance monitoring (APM)**. Used mainly for application logging and monitoring.
  - Dashboard creation.
  - Provide application log traces.

- **AppDynamics**:
  - It is a cloud-based paid software.
  - It is also an application performance monitoring tool similar to Dynatrace.
  - Easy dashboard creations.
  - Supports many platforms and is easy to set up.

Some of the other tools are NewRelic, Datadog, Prometheus, Grafana, and Nagios.

# Release and deployment tools

- **Ansible**:
    - o It is an application deployment, configuration management, and continuous delivery tool.
    - o It is mainly used as **infrastructure as a code (IaaC)**.
    - o It helps in the provision of target infrastructure and the deployment of the application.
    - o Mostly used by DevOps and SRE for their in-house tools.
    - o An open-source tool.

- **Jenkins**:
    - o It is an IT automation and **continuous integration/continuous deployment (CI/CD)** tool.
    - o An open-source tool.
    - o Used mainly by DevOps and SRE to build and deploy the application.
    - o It is also used extensively by SRE to automate manual tasks.
    - o It has various plugins available to integrate multiple platforms.

- **AWS code deploy**:
    - o AWS in-house tool
    - o Used for automated application deployment
    - o Comes with an AWS purchase (no extra pricing for deploying apps on AWS)
    - o Easy pipeline creation and configuration
    - o Provide monitoring of application health and easy rollbacks.

- **Azure DevOps**:
    - o Microsoft product for automated deployment, project management, and release management
    - o Easy integration with Microsoft-based software system
    - o It is an end-to-end solution for the DevOps team. However, SRE is also used for tracking and reviewing changes in production.

- **GitLab**:
    - o It is one of the powerful open-source tool.
    - o It is based on git and a DevOps platform that helps developers monitor, test, and deploy the code.
    - o It has an in-built CI/CD pipeline.

- Along with building and deploying code, it is also used to automate using CI/CD.

- **Terraform:**
  - It is an infrastructure-as-code software tool. It facilitates provisioning and managing infrastructure on-prem and in the cloud.
  - It helps define infrastructure using declarative language.
  - It can be easily extended to a plugin-based architecture.

It is not open-source and is paid. However, for smaller project the free version of the tool can be used.

- **GitHub Actions:**
  - It is one of the upcoming CI/CD tools with integrated CI/CD solutions coupled with GitHub repositories.
  - This tool works on workflows, where developers can easily create workflows to run multiple jobs.
  - GitHub Actions and Jenkins can be used together, though they are independent. But complement each other.
  - It is used to deploy applications to multiple clouds.
  - GitHub Actions is free for standard GitHub-hosted runners in public repositories. But for private repositories, GitHub Actions is paid.

# Chaos testing tools

- **Litmus:**
  - It is an open-source tool
  - Provide a library for testing containers, hosts, platforms for Azure, AWS, GCP, and other cloud platform.
  - Web UI to review the test cases.
  - Good Integration with observability tools.

- **AWS Fault Ingestion Simulator**:
  - The underlying platform is AWS
  - Works best with AWS applications and infrastructure
  - Easy to configure test cases

- **Azure Chaos Studio**:
  - Similar to AWS FIS, this tool has an underlying platform, Azure
  - Works best with applications and infrastructure on the Azure cloud.
  - It has a learning curve to configure and use the tool

- **Chaos Monkey**:
  - ○ This is one of the oldest tools used for Chaos testing.
  - ○ It has limited test cases compared to other tools.

The following are some development tools:

- **GitHub**: Source code repository.
- **IntelliJ**: For writing code.
- **Visual Studio Code**: For writing code.
- **Sublime text**: Writing code.
- **Eclipse**: Used for code written in the Java language

Along with the aforementioned tools, there are various other tools and technologies used by SRE for their day-to-day tasks. SRE teams are developers who use various coding languages such as Python, Java, Golang, and others to develop tools and capabilities for non-functional requirements.

As part of the SRE tool kit, the skills required by engineers for day-to-day tasks are:

- Knowledge of containerization, such as Kubernetes and Docker.
- Knowledge of cloud computing.
- Software development for microservice architecture.
- Networking.

As we know, *no one size fits all*. Each organization has different requirements, and they should choose these tools based on their requirement. However, some common things to consider before you choose any tool are:

- What % of your requirement will the tool cover.
- The effort required to configure the tool, and the support required.
- What type of customization is required in the tool.
- Skill set required to configure the tool. Such is if you need to hire people to just configure the tool, then what is the cost of hire vs cost you will save in long term by using the tool?
- Cost to configure. Open-Source vs. Enterprise version.
- Can the same tool be used across organizations by other projects as well.
- Integration of the tool with other software used in an organization.

# Cheat sheet for SRE

The cheat sheet is a concise note for site reliability engineers. It gives you a high-level overview of the SRE role. In previous chapters, you learned in depth about how organizations use various best practices to maintain the reliability of software.

This topic is also a summary of the best practices the SRE team uses in each of the various categories to excel in reliability and performance.

The following are the various categories for the SRE role:

- **Automation**: It is the key to SRE and DevOps. Though identifying manual tasks and their automation consumes time, it saves time for SRE and DevOps teams to focus on other priority tasks in the long term.

  One of the top tasks for SRE is to automate tasks that take up a lot of time, are repetitive, and are prone to human error.

  The following are the key features of automation:

  o Automating manual tasks that are performed to keep the production environment up and running.

  o Creating self-service tools for other cross-functional teams to help them pull data from the production environment.

  o Automating alert resolution and incident resolution.

  o Automation can be any language. The most commonly used software languages to automate are shell script, Python, and Java. Automation is sometimes known as a description, depending on the requirement. Sometimes, scripting can also automate and remove the toil. Sometimes, you need to build a new tool to automate, and you can choose any programming language to build the tool.

- **Service management**: The management of any form is one of the key features for any organization, irrespective of software, automobile, bank, etc. Even if you have the best team and tools available to build software, without good management, the processes fail and impact the overall delivery of the product.

  The following are the best practices to follow in service management:

  o Another task is to have strict standards and processes around ticket tracking, such as:

    ▪ Incident management includes handling incidents, resolving incidents, and tracking them.

    ▪ Defect management for production defects to raise defects for production bugs, tracking defects with dev teams for fixes, and validating fixes.

o **Root cause analysis (RCA)**/ post mortem is another key to SRE to fix the issue at the root. Embedding RCA into the incident management process helps achieve good software reliability.

o The goal is to prevent incidents from occurring and, if they occur, prevent them from further occurring. Problem and incident management are correlated and go hand in hand.

- **Alerting and monitoring**: Monitoring a system is critical to ensure its performance. If any lag in the performance of the system is identified, then alerting on that lag is another critical step in the operational process.

  The following are some of the best practices to follow for alerting and monitoring:

  o Creating metrics to measure the health and performance of the application.

  o Collaborating with developers to identify the severity of alerts.

  o Configuring alerts.

  o Deciding on monitoring and alerting tools.

  o Creating monitoring dashboards for application health.

  o Continuous enhancements of alerting and monitoring with new feature releases in the application

  o Integrating alerts with incident tools for notification to the right people.

- **Observability:** This is related to alert and monitoring; however, it is a little more advanced, as shown:

  o Building machine learning to co-relate various signals and alerts for production applications.

  o Building self-healing alerts. This helps the software to auto-heal

- **Security and compliance**: This category is sometimes hidden or ignored. However, when you are working in the production environment, you should add this to your daily tasks suit.

  The following are some of the factors to consider while building software:

  o As SRE mostly takes care of production applications, security is one of the key things the SRE team must take care of.

  o Access policies across applications and infrastructure

  o IAM policies for the application.

  o Credentials, password management, and automated renewal of these credentials.

  o Audit control on application and infrastructure

  o Audit and compliance reports

- **Change management**: Generally, organizations have separate teams for change management, and SRE does not participate in it. However, SREs who support production should know what change is going into their system and how that change can impact them.

  o   Review changes and implement changes sometimes.

  o   Tracking changes in the production environment.

- **Release and deployment**: This is also another important category for SRE to keep in daily tasks. It is tied together in the SRE function along with release management. Sometimes, release and deployment are part of the SRE function; sometimes, they fall under the DevOps bucket. A strong release and deployment strategy helps control poor quality changes via reviews, automation, etc.

  The following are some of the points on how a strong release management process can help achieve reliability in the system:

  o   Review code changes and bug fixes for the production environment

  o   Build and release tools and capabilities used for non-functional requirements.

  o   Rollback changes in the production environment

  o   Collaboration with the development and testing team on the release cycle and hotfix cycle

- **Chaos engineering**: In some organizations, this category is owned by a dedicated team. However, for better chaos results, SRE should own this, as they work on production in and out and understand various chaos scenarios better.

  o   Listing chaos test cases

  o   Performing chaos testing to simulate production chaos scenarios

  o   Collaborating with the development team and infrastructure team on fixing the bugs identified as part of testing.

- **Capacity planning**: Planning of capacity for human and infrastructure resources is always a good practice in software development. Along with planning your team size and skill sets, it is very important to plan the capacity required to build and run your software. Also, capacity is required to extend the software as per future demand.

  The following are some of the best practices to follow in capacity planning:

  o   Collaborate with the development team on the capacity of the infrastructure required for the application to run.

  o   Requirement analysis for production applications such as CPU, mem, number of instances, number of cross regions, etc.

  o   Continuous monitoring and analysis of the usage of infrastructure such as CPU, Mem.

- **Availability**: This is the first tool to be picked from the SRE tool kit when someone asks how SRE is performing. If the application is highly available, that means the SRE team is doing their job well.

  The following are the points to consider while measuring the availability of software:

  o Identifying SLI, SLO, and SLA.

  o Identifying and configuring metrics to measure the performance of the system

  o Measuring the availability of the system through various metrics

- **Non-functional development**: This is the practice that means helping your development team focus on coding the app, and the rest will be taken care of by SRE. It gives back time to the dev team so they are not stuck in operational tasks and increases trust between the two teams. The following are some of the non-functional requirements:

  o Building tools and capabilities

  o Fixing non-functional bugs in a system, such as correcting wrong alerts, removing false alerts, cleaning up extra logs in the system, etc.

  o Performing sanity checks on production applications for new features

- **New product onboarding and planning**: This is one of the important pieces, so have SRE as part of the initial planning process. As SREs are generally involved during the end phases of SDLC, a mature SRE organization keeps SREs in every phase of SDLC and involves them from the first phase. This is one of the best practices for achieving reliability in the system. The feedback loop from SRE is direct problems in production and can provide great insights for designers, planners, and business teams when they plan the architecture of any new product.

  The following are the points on how to involve SRE in the beginning:

  o Participate in architecture discussions with the development team for new features

  o Collaborate with dev to build the system design for new features

  o Review the new service manual and sign off before releasing it to the production environment.

- **Application production support**: This is one of the key roles for SRE teams. Though it is operational, SRE should spend 50% of their time in development and another 50% in supporting the production system.

  The following are some of the tasks SRE performs as a production support engineer:

  o Troubleshooting issues/bugs in the system using tools

  o Performing circumventions for issues that impact live applications.

  o Incident management is part of operations and support

- o Perform root cause analysis of the problem, collaborating with cross-functional teams.
- o Building an alerting and monitoring dashboard for daily monitoring.
- o Creating standards and processes around incidents and defect management.
- o Continuous feedback loop of production to other SRE engineers and dev, test teams.
- o Collaborating with release, change management, and dev teams, run-time, while circumventing issues.

- **Infrastructure production support**: Application and infrastructure production support go along. Both are part of one role for SRE. Some big organizations divide SRE into various sub-functions; however, in some organizations, it is one single SRE team that performs various roles.

  - o Monitoring infrastructure health
  - o Troubleshooting and resolving infrastructure issues in a production application
  - o Upgrading infrastructure versions

- **Planning**: There are multiple best practices called out for various types of planning. It is very critical also.

  - o Build best practices for each category
  - o Create standards and processes to bring best practices into the team's culture
  - o Build a transparent and blameless culture
  - o Best practices around tools and technology

- **Collaboration**: This is the baseline of SRE methodology. When SRE and DevOps were formed as new process to build software, one of the key problems was silos. Lack of collaboration between teams. In past when each SDLC team used to work in silo, there was no clear communication or collaboration between teams, big projects used to fail a lot. Collaboration is the new culture for any organization that wants to build high-performance and reliable software. The following are some of the key points mentioned on how collaboration can be included in daily tasks of SDLC teams:

  - o Day-to-day collaboration with development teams for new features, bug fixes, investigating, and postmortem.
  - o Collaboration with testing team to review defects in lower env that can occur in production
  - o Collaboration with DevOps to configure CI/CD pipeline. Also, to configure infrastructure
  - o Collaboration with product management team for building best practices for full SDLC
  - o Collaborate with the business team to understand new requirements

Each of the categories defined earlier has best practices to follow. SRE teams generally run on standards, processes, and best practices. To start creating your own SRE team, you should first list the categories (such as what role SRE will perform) and then build best practices around each category. There can also be other categories depending on the project type, size, budget, etc. It also depends on how granular you would like to go in the SRE process while defining categories.

The following figure shows some of the top categories to start with while creating an SRE team. It also helps redesign the existing SRE teams if required:

**BUILDING BLOCKS OF SRE**

| | | | |
|---|---|---|---|
| AUTOMATION | ALERTING & MONITORING | INCIDENT MANAGEMENT | DEFECT MANAGEMENT |
| CHANGE MANAGEMENT | OBSERVABILITY | SECURITY & COMPLIANCE | RELEASE & DEPLOYMENT |
| CHAOS ENGINEERING | CAPACITY PLANNING | AVAILABILITY MEASUREMENT | NON-FUNCTIONAL DEVELOPMENT |
| NEW PRODUCT ONBOARDING / PLANNING | APPLICATION PRODUCTION SUPPORT | INFRASTRUCTURE PRODUCTION SUPPORT | COLLABORATION |

*Figure 8.1: SRE building blocks*

# Conclusion

By the end of this chapter, we get a high-level overview of the SRE role.

We discussed the various tools SRE uses across organizations and the categorization of these tools. Moreover, we discussed the daily tasks that SRE can follow.

In the next chapter, we will cover the daily roles and responsibilities of an SRE engineer. Also, the chapter will describe the skill sets required to be an SRE engineer.

# Join our Discord space

Join our Discord workspace for latest updates, offers, tech happenings around the world, new releases, and sessions with the authors:

https://discord.bpbonline.com

# CHAPTER 9
# Day in the Life of SRE

## Introduction

This chapter will explain the roles and responsibilities of SRE and give a glimpse of the daily tasks of SRE teams. This chapter will help you understand what skills to learn to become an SRE.

## Structure

The chapter covers the following topics:

- Skillsets and technology background of SRE
- Roles and responsibilities of SRE

## Objectives

By the end of this chapter, you will learn about various real-world scenarios of SRE daily activities to give you a glimpse of the skill sets of SRE engineers. This chapter aims to help you understand the starting point to become an SRE and how an SRE team functions in today's Agile approach.

# Skillsets and technology background of SRE

As the name suggests, SRE is site reliability engineering, a team that builds and maintains system reliability. The end goal for any organization is to build and deliver a reliable product to satisfy customers. Though the SRE team builds and maintains the reliability of the system, it is the responsibility of each SDLC team to build a reliable system. Goals for every function in the SDLC are designed to incorporate the reliability aspect. For example, development teams follow best practices while developing code, ensuring a reliable software code. The testing team incorporates end-to-end data flow test cases to ensure full code coverage during testing. The design team incorporates scalability in system design, ensuring the reliability of the end product.

The question that arises is, why do we need a separate SRE team to build reliability when reliability is incorporated in every phase of SDLC?

Sire reliability engineering falls at the end of the SDLC cycle, which means more visibility of the end product and end user. The SRE team gets a 360-degree view of the product/ system just before its delivery and also after its delivery to customers. Each SDLC team follows reliability as part of its function, but the SRE team gets the view of reliability for the whole product when all pieces are merged.

Consider the following example:

The design team builds the design of the system, incorporating scalability and reliability. As part of development, multiple development teams are involved in building different modules and software. These different services are merged and tested as one product by the testing team. All three teams follow best practices to ensure reliability in designing, coding, and testing. However, various other factors need to be considered when the final product is delivered, such as external system integrations, third-party integrations, real customer load, the behavior of the system with customer load, the system's behavior during unwanted disasters, etc. The SRE team monitors the system end to end, including upstream and downstream systems impacting the product. This end-to-end monitoring gives 360-degree visibility to the SRE team, which helps ensure reliability. They build recovery tools for a seamless customer experience.

Let us extend the above example and take one scenario where a new feature was developed by the development team. The code was tested by the dev and testing teams. The new code was validated for scalability by SRE tools, and it failed in one of the validation cases. So, the code was sent back for redesigning and testing. This scenario explains how SRE controls the code quality and ensures the reliability of the system by avoiding wrong code changes going into the system. SRE teams take care of reliability on top of the product by building tools.

The SRE team is a set of various skills. The site reliability engineering team consists of members with different technology backgrounds and skills.

Let us look at some important site reliability engineering skills that we will need to fulfill the role:

- **Software coding**: As an SRE, you need to be proficient in coding. It could be any coding language. SRE is required to code to build tools, sometimes SRE teams are required to develop non-functional requirements in the system, and sometimes SRE collaborates with development teams to fix non-functional bugs in the system. The most popular languages today are Python, Go, and Java.

- **Automation/scripting**: As SRE, you will need to automate all the manual tasks and reduce toil. Scripting is handy in automating daily manual tasks such as writing scripts for health check servers, writing scripts to alert for any anomalies, etc. The most popular scripting languages today are Python, Linux/Unix Shell, and PowerShell (mainly for Windows operating systems). Scripting is a little different than coding. Coding involves building tools and non-functional requirements. However, scripting involves automating smaller manual daily tasks.

- **ITIL**: Information Technology Infrastructure Library (ITIL) is a framework designed to standardize the planning, design, delivery, and maintenance of overall IT service within a business. Knowledge of ITIL comes in very handy for SRE.

  The two major aspects of ITIL are:

  - **Release and change management**: Understanding the release and change management process is very important for SRE. As SRE, you will have to collaborate with development teams to review and release the changes; for that, you will need deep knowledge of the release and change process. Change management implies managing multiple changes in the system without interrupting business, and release management is grouping all major features in one release for faster rollout of production without interrupting business. As SRE, you will have to participate in the process to review, validate, and implement the changes in the system.

  - **Incident management**: As SRE, you will work on tickets and incidents from customers. Sometimes, SRE will work with separate operations teams, and sometimes, SRE themselves will take care of incident management. As SRE, you are required to have an understanding of how to manage incidents reported, how and when to act on incidents, how to prioritize, how to define the severity of incidents, and what actions to take to resolve these incidents. Some of the common tools used are ServiceNow and Jira.

- **CI/CD pipeline designing**: Continuous integration and continuous deployment. Most DevOps teams are responsible for creating CI/CD pipelines using tools such as Jenkins. However, as an SRE, you should also know what the CI/CD process is and how to create a CI/CD pipeline. In some organizations, SRE team is responsible for building these pipelines. Sometimes, to automate daily manual tasks, SRE teams build pipelines using CI/CD tools. Such as building pipelines for display server configurations, so that you do not have to login into multiple servers all the time to check configurations. CI/CD pipeline creation involves a lot of scripting also. As SRE, you will have to create pipelines to configure end-to-end infrastructure also, including installing servers, databases, containers, and other software. Some of the tools used for CI/CD for application and infrastructure are Jenkins, Ansible, and Terraform.

- **Cloud computing**: Today, most of the applications are designed to run on cloud platforms such as AWS, Azure, and GCP (all are public cloud providers). There are other private cloud providers also, such as *Oracle* and *Red Hat*. As an SRE, you need to have knowledge of any one of the cloud computing platforms, how cloud-native applications are designed, and how to deploy these applications on the cloud. As SRE, you will work on deploying and maintaining this application on the cloud; you will monitor the infrastructure for this application that is running on the cloud. For example, applications running on servers configured on the AWS cloud platform. As SRE, you will monitor this application on AWS, build pipelines on AWS, and build dashboards on AWS.

- **Database management systems**: Databases go hand in hand with applications. As SRE, you will need to work on relational and non-relational databases. Where you will monitor database performance, run queries on the database to troubleshoot problems, update and insert data in the database as part of any change, and many more such tasks. For all these tasks, you need to have knowledge of databases. Most of the used databases are non-relational, Couchbase, MongoDB, Apache Cassandra, and Oracle NoSQL; and relational, Oracle, Postgres, DB2, MySQL.

- **Distributed infrastructure engineering**: Most organizations today maintain distributed systems to achieve high availability and scalability. Distributed systems mean applications using resources across multiple infrastructures. Even if one infrastructure or node is down, the application will use other resources and continue to perform its function without impacting business. As an SRE, you need to have a deep understanding of distributed architecture. This overlaps with an understanding of cloud computing and operating systems. As an SRE, you will monitor the system end to end, and to solve any problem in the system, you need to know how the distributed system architecture works.

- **System administration**: As SRE, you will have to perform various system administration tasks such as installing and configuring software and networks, ensuring the security of the system, monitoring system performance, identifying system requirements, and upgrading systems with the latest versions. So, knowledge and hands-on experience in system administration is one of the important skills for SRE.

- **Tools**: As SRE, you will have to work on various tools. Day to day, SRE will monitor the system, troubleshoot issues, solve app and infrastructure issues, and do coding and scripting. To perform these tasks, SRE will use various tools.

For example:

- o **Monitoring tools**: Grafana, Prometheus, AppDynamics, DataDog, Dynatrace, Splunk, Nagios, NewRelic, etc.
- o **Logging tools**: Splunk, FluentD, Logstash, SumoLogic, SolarWinds. Version Control tools – GitHub, GitLab, Bitbucket, Azure DevOps, SourceForge, etc.

- **Communication skills**: Communication is one of the key soft skills required by SRE teams. SRE was formed on the lines of collaboration and removing silos. To eliminate silos, you need to collaborate and communicate with various cross-functional teams. As an SRE, you will have to participate in designing discussions, reviewing processes, defining metrics processes, and setting processes. For all these discussions, you need to have great communication skills where you can understand technical and business knowledge and convey your message.

- **Problem solving**: As SRE, every day, you will be involved in solving problems. Problems related to system code, system designing, system reliability, performance, collaboration problems, customer issues, etc. So, the skill of being able to solve problems quickly and effectively is essential for any site reliability engineer.

These are a handful of skills required if you are looking to be an SRE. However, you do not necessarily need to have all the skills; if you have 50% of these skills in your portfolio, you can be SRE. SRE teams consist of multiple team members having different backgrounds and skill sets. Team members will also have different levels of experience, starting from entry-level to senior to leadership.

The background of SRE engineers includes software developers, software testers, DevOps people, system administrators, Infrastructure engineers, production support engineers, and architects. If you have experience in any of these skills, you can choose the SRE career path. For entry-level, if you have a basic level of understanding of development, cloud computing, and operating systems, you can choose the SRE path.

# Roles and responsibilities of SRE

The SRE team consists of team members with diverse backgrounds, as mentioned in the previous topic. It is a mix of skills within the SRE team, and all team members perform different functions within the team.

To understand the roles and responsibilities of SREs, let us discuss their daily lives. The following are the various roles SREs play daily. Before we start, let us assume that this SRE team takes care of both engineering and operations.

# Case 1

The details are as follows:

- Site reliability engineers start his/her day by logging into the ITSM tool. Tools will automatically assign tickets to the engineer.

- The engineer then logged into the monitoring dashboards and started monitoring the health of the system.

- In parallel, he/she keeps an eye on alert notifications received on the collaborative platform.

- Two new tickets were automatically assigned to the engineer. After monitoring the dashboards, the engineer reviewed the tickets. After initial review, the engineer identified that the ticket is low priority and has an SLA of 4 hours to resolve.

- The engineer noticed some HTTP 500 alerts in one of the services. As the ticket was low priority, the engineer started investigating the **http 500** alerts.

- Then, he/she logged into the logging tool and started pulling the logs for the service, throwing http 500 alerts.

- As a part of the investigation, he/she logged into change management software and reviewed any changes that went into the system for this service in the last 24 hours.

- He/she also logged into the knowledge base tool to check if any such alert was reported in the past for this service.

- The engineer identified one of the changes that went into the system but for another downstream service but is still a potential candidate to cause alerting.

- The engineer logged into the source code and reviewed the change in the code in production.

- He/she clones the piece of code to his/her local system and debugs it.

- As part of troubleshooting, it was identified that the latest code change to the downstream system was causing http 500 alert for the upstream system.

- SRE collaborated with the development team to collect more information about the change and used a CI/CD pipeline to roll back the change.

- Meanwhile, SRE used their in-built tool to move traffic to another working region to avoid any interruption in business. Rolling back the change circumvented the issue.

- The SRE engineer then created a defect for the development team to fix the new code.

- Soon after resolving the http 500 alerts, he/she picked the tickets from the queue and started working on them.

- After half day, the engineer logged out from ITSM, and another engineer was onboarded to take over operational tasks.

- The former engineer then logged into the collaboration tool to start working on the engineering tasks assigned in the queue.

- He/she picked up automation of manual tasks. As part of automation, he/she then logged into the development tool and started writing code for the tool.

- At the end of day, all the SRE team meet and discussed briefly the daily tasks performed by each team member and added note to their knowledge base for future.

- Tools and skills used are development in Python using VisualCode, ITSM, change management, monitoring and logging using Splunk and Kibana, GitHub, Java debugging, Jenkins CI/CD

# Case 2

The details are as follows:

- Another SRE engineer started his/her day by logging into the ITSM tool. And then started looking into the tickets assigned to the queue.

- Similar to the previous case, this engineer also logged into the monitoring dashboard to proactively monitor the health of the system.

- Later, after some time, the engineer noticed that one high-priority ticket was assigned.

- He/she communicated to the team to keep an eye on the dashboard as he/she will be working on the high-priority ticket.

- The ticket was a customer complaint about not being able to access a functionality in the app.

- The engineer then started troubleshooting the issue by logging into the monitoring and logging tool.

- As part of troubleshooting, he/she enabled temporary debug logs for the service (for which the customer raised a complaint) and collected logs for the past 3 days.

- He/she was able to identify the problem in the debug logs. But also noticed that no alert was received for this error that the customer saw.

- So, the engineer created a ticket for the SRE team to review and configure alerting for this use case.

- After identifying the problem in code, he/she informed the development team to fix the issue on high priority and also informed customer on the status.

- He/she then picked the earlier ticket of alert configuration and started working on creating a custom alert for this particular use case. Updated the runbook for the service and added this newly created alert.

- Engineer, then logged out from operational tasks and reviewed other engineering tasks assigned to him/her.

- From the engineering queue, he/she picked up the chaos engineering tasks.

- As chaos engineering, SRE started creating use cases and chaos, and then using testing tools to configure these test cases in the tool.

- SRE collaborated with the QA team to list down other chaos scenarios noticed by the QA team in the testing environment. In order to incorporate those scenarios too, in chaos engineering.

- After creating new chaos test cases, he/she executed some chaos test cases and identified that in one of the use case application is not able to recover when one of the database node is down.

- SRE shared the finding with the team, and the SRE team collaborated with the development team to understand the connection configuration for the service.

- As part of the solution, the SRE engineer configured a health check on the database from that service to fix the chaos case.

- This case covers monitoring and alerting creation, chaos engineering, troubleshooting, and coding.

# Case 3

The details are as follows:

- SRE engineer started his/her day with non-operational tasks. As part of the daily activities of SRE, the engineer logged into the monitoring dashboard to review system health.

- He/she then checked the calendar for upcoming meetings. The first meeting of the day was a collaboration with architects on designing new features. SRE engineers and architects discussed this, and for SRE recommendations, it was decided to incorporate auto failover of service for this new feature.

- Then, the SRE engineer joined another meeting for knowledge transfer of new service getting onboarded in the upcoming month. The SRE engineer participated in the meeting and reviewed this new service for retries, alerting and logging. It is also recommended to add alerting and metrics in code.

- Then, the SRE engineer was notified by one of his/her team members about an outage reported in a production environment.

- Then, he/she, along with one other SRE engineer, joined the war room to circumvent the outage.

- He/she started troubleshooting the issue by looking at the logs. As part of best practice, he/she looked for recent changes that went into the system.

- After investigating the issue, the SRE engineer identified the cause of the outage and collaborated with the development team to fix the issue.
- This use case covers system designing, new service review, troubleshooting, collaboration, and coding knowledge

# Case 4

The details are as follows:

- Another SRE engineer started the day by looking at pending tasks in the queue.
- One of the tasks is to review all open issues in a production system that are impacting the reliability of the system.
- The engineer listed out all defects and started working on fixing non-functional defects on the list. For example, adding an alert on the last retry, changing the log level for services, or adding a health check on a database from a service.
- Then, the SRE team got a request to review one of the upcoming ad-hoc changes. This SRE engineer participated in the review call and validated the change. As a part of validation, SRE reviewed the change, its impact, and what region change is planned. The change did not mention the impact, so the SRE engineer rejected it and asked the requestor to raise it again with rollback in case of impact.
- After the review, the engineer went back to fixing defects.
- For the day, he/she worked on completing defect fix tasks.
- This use case covers change management, coding, and monitoring.

The aforementioned cases explain the daily activities of the SRE engineers. They include various roles and responsibilities of the SRE team. The SRE team is a mix of diverse skillsets, and each team member has a defined role according to expertise. Some team members are more involved in operational tasks such as monitoring, alerting, and automation. Others are responsible for coding and infrastructure management. Some participate in change, release management, and design review.

However, the core for each SRE is collaboration, problem solving, and development. The level of coding may differ depend on the years and type of experience.

# Summary of key tasks and skills of an SRE

The roles and responsibilities of the SRE team are:

- Monitoring and configuring dashboards.
- Identifying bugs and resolving those bugs in the system, this is a very broad role and includes fixing system design, architectural changes, code changes, infra configurational changes, etc.
- Infrastructure configuration and management.

- CI/CD pipeline creation.
- Chaos engineering.
- Change review.
- Incident management.
- Collaboration.
- Communication.
- Planning.

The career path to becoming an SRE is the skills in your tech stack. It could be a mix of the following 2-3 skills:

- Software development
- Software designing
- Scripting
- Infrastructure configuration
- Cloud knowledge
- System administration and database administration
- Production support

# Conclusion

This chapter will help you choose a path forward to SRE as a career.

By the end of this chapter, we discussed the various roles that SRE engineers perform and their background experiences. This will help you decide what technology to learn to become an SRE engineer.

In the next chapter, we will cover the future of SRE and help readers understand how to begin a career in SRE. It will also help readers understand how and what skills to ramp up as an SRE engineer.

## Join our Discord space

Join our Discord workspace for latest updates, offers, tech happenings around the world, new releases, and sessions with the authors:

https://discord.bpbonline.com

# CHAPTER 10
# Future of SRE

## Introduction

This chapter concludes with key SRE features that readers learned through this book. It also gives comprehensive SRE goals and some food for thought to readers on how and where to begin the SRE journey.

## Structure

We will cover the following topics in this chapter:

- Recap of SRE
- Goals of SRE
- SRE career path
- Future of SRE

## Objectives

This chapter aims to focus on the SRE career path and how you can become an SRE. The chapter will start with a brief recap of SRE's key features and move toward the tools and technology required to learn for a successful SRE career.

In the previous chapter, we briefly discussed the roles required to choose to be an SRE, and this chapter is a continuation of that in detail. In this chapter, you will also learn about the future of SRE.

# Recap of SRE

In the previous chapters, you learned various facets of SRE and SDLC. You learned the importance of SRE and its evolution with technology. The following are some highlights of SRE:

- SRE is not a replacement for DevOps. They both follow different approaches but share the same core values.

- SRE and operations can be the same team but have different roles.

- SRE engineers are strong developers who can develop code and also manage production system performance.

- SRE engineers build reliability in the system by adding scalability and availability on top of functional code.

- SDLC has grown a lot over the last 10 years. With new technology and an agile approach, SRE has become the core function of SDLC.

- SRE is not only taking care of production/live applications. The SRE process starts from the very beginning in SDLC.

- SRE is not only maintaining scalability on the already built app, it is building that scalability in the code along with business functionality.

- Development and SRE both focus on building reliable systems. However, SRE focused more on long-term reliability, unlike feature releases by development.

- Planning is one of the important pieces in the SRE approach.

- Collaboration and communication are core values of SRE. Without these two pillars, we will go back to old school methodology of silos.

- You should follow best practices to avoid any anti-pattern.

- As best practice, you should always measure. This means SRE should define metrics to measure the performance of the system at every level. Also, SRE should collaborate with the development team to integrate some of these metrics into the code.

- SLA, SLO, SLI, and error budget are key metrics for SRE to measure system performance.

- Knowledge of ITIL comes in very handy within the SRE function.

- Problem-solving is another key skill required for an SRE engineer.

- Automation is key for SRE.

# Goals for SRE

The main objective of SRE is to deliver a highly reliable and scalable system. To achieve this goal, SRE needs to act as a bridge between development and operations. SRE goals should always align with high-level organization goals. In theory, all SDLC teams should follow and align with high-level organisational goals.

Some internal SRE goals are:

- **Efficiency**: Increase the efficiency of the system. To achieve this high-level goal, the internal goal of SRE is to increase the efficiency of daily tasks, such as building standards and processes, incident management, defect management, and change management.

- **Automation**: The key goal of SRE is to automate manual and repetitive tasks. Automation increases the efficiency of SRE's daily work.

- **Give time back to the development team**: By taking non-functional development work, SRE gives time back to the development team to focus on building new features.

- **Reliability**: Another key goal for SRE is increasing the reliability of the system. To increase reliability, SRE builds reliability in the system, along with that, SRE standardises various processes to follow, such as performing chaos engineering, performing root cause analysis, and creating a feedback loop from production to QA to development.

- **Monitoring and alerting**: These are key tools of SRE to reactive and proactive identify issues and resolve them on time.

# SRE career path

The previous chapter briefly explained various skill sets and toolkits required to be an SRE. In this section, you will find some tools and technologies that the SRE should know about.

For entry-level:

- **Data structure**: SRE is an engineering role that requires coding and system design. To perform these activities, it is important to understand basic data structure concepts. As an entry-level, you might not perform system designing but knowledge of data structure will help you understand the system design flow and help you build the code. One of the good books for learning data structure and algorithms is, *Introduction to Algorithms by Thomas H. Cormen, Charles E. Leiserson, Ronald L. Rivest, and Clifford Stein.*

- **Coding**: This is one of the important aspects of SRE. As part of daily activity, SRE develops code and builds tools and capabilities. If you are starting fresh, start with learning data structure (as mentioned previously), oops concept and hands-on any language. As an entry-level, either backend or frontend programming language is sufficient to start with. Some of the most used backend programming languages are Java, Python, Go, Ruby, and .Net. Popular platforms for learning coding and participating in challenges include HackerRank, LeetCode, Codeforces, TopCoder, and CodeChef. You can create your account on these websites and start using the platform to learn coding. This platform enables you to code in multiple programming languages.

- **Scripting**: Coding is the primary skill for SRE, however learning scripting on top of coding will help you get the SRE role better. Automation is the key for SRE engineers, where they automate manual and repetitive tasks via scripting. Some of the most used scripting languages are Bash, Perl and Python.

- **Operating system**: Knowledge of operating systems is important if you want to start your career as an SRE. Learning OS will help you understand the interaction between users, software and hardware. This knowledge will help you understand the system and infrastructure architecture. Linux, Unix, and Windows are commonly used operating systems for building servers and databases. As an entry-level, you should know these features for any OS: memory management, file management, security, user interface, and multiprogramming. One of the good book available to read is, *Operating System Concepts by Abraham Silberschatz, Peter Baer Galvin, and Greg Gagne*: This textbook provides a comprehensive introduction to operating systems and is widely used.

- **Database management**: No software runs without a database. Knowledge of databases is one of the key skills for any engineering role. If you want to get into the role of SRE, a database management system comes in handy. As an entry-level, you should know the fundamentals of databases and hands-on writing of database queries.

There are two types of databases used RDBMS (relational database) and NoSQL database, and you need to learn the basics of both types. You can pick any one of the following databases to begin with.

Some of the commonly used databases are:

- o **RDBMS**: Oracle, Postgres, MySQL, DB2, Amazon Aurora
- o **NoSQL**: Couchbase, Cassandra, MongoDB, Amazon DynamoDB, Cosmos DB

- **Cloud technology**: Today, many organisations rely on cloud computing for their business need and running applications due to its cost-efficiency, scalability, and collaborative technology. Cloud in itself is huge with multiple tools and technologies. As a beginner, if you know programming languages, databases, and operating systems, then it will help you start learning cloud computing better. Once you learn the aforementioned skills, you need to start learning about the fundamentals of the cloud, such as:

    o  What is cloud technology?

    o  Different service models in the cloud.

    o  Deployment model in the cloud.

    o  Cloud architecture.

    o  Basic cloud computing platform.

There are three major public cloud platforms available Amazon AWS, Microsoft Azure, and GCP. To begin learning about cloud computing, you can start with any of these platforms. You can also start with any one of the following certifications:

    o  AWS-certified cloud practitioner

    o  Associate cloud engineer certificate GCP

    o  Microsoft Azure Fundamental Certification

- **Communication skills**: SRE approaches are based on clear communication and collaboration. Irrespective of entry-level or experienced professionals, you need to have good communication skills. Good communication skills are active listening, the ability to convey your message, confidence, giving and receiving feedback, clarity and volume, and responsiveness.

For experienced professionals:

- **Coding**: the ability to code and develop software is the core at SRE. If you are an experienced software developer, then SRE is also one of your career paths forward. Knowledge of development and its best practices comes in handy for SRE functions. As an experienced developer, it is good to have backend and frontend development experience as a full-stack developer.

    o  Backend languages are Java, Python, .Net, Golang

    o  Frontend languages are JavaScript, React, Angular, Django

- **Scripting**: the ability to script is also one of the core requirements for the SRE role. SRE engineers automate daily manual and repetitive tasks. As these tasks are small runtime programs scripting is mostly used to automate. For example, automating regular health checks for servers and alerts during any anomaly. There are various languages used for scripting. Experience in any one of these can help you land an SRE role.

    o  Shell

    o  Perl

    o  Python

- **System administration**: It focuses on servers and computers. System administrators have various roles and responsibilities but if you know some of these tasks as part of system admin you can move to SRE as your path forward. Some of the system admin roles experience good to have for SRE:

- o Backup and disaster recovery
- o Database administration
- o Installing and patching firmware or applications
- o Security administration
- o Network administration
- o System health monitoring
- o System maintenance
- o Cloud computing

- **Infrastructure engineering**: it focuses on designing, building, coordinating, and maintaining IT environments for organisations that need to run their software and other applications. In today's time infrastructure engineering on the cloud is in great demand and someone who has experience in designing and building infrastructure on the cloud can choose SRE as a career path forward. System admin and infrastructure engineering roles overlap in some functions. Infrastructure engineering can be a path forward for system administration too.

   Some of the layers for infra engineering are:

   - o **Cloud infrastructure engineering**: Design and build infra on the cloud.
   - o Network infrastructure engineering
   - o **Infrastructure architect**: This role is designed for big projects, where the architect is involved in planning and designing.

- **DevOps**: DevOps and SRE are two different profiles, however, if you are DevOps with development experience then SRE can be your best next path forward. Some of the DevOps roles that are used in SRE are:

   - o **CI/CD**: Creating CI/CD pipelines using tools like Jenkins, GitLab, Azure DevOps, GitHub Actions, and TeamCity.
   - o **Infrastructure management automation**: IAAS (Infrastructure as a code. This is also one of the roles of infra engineering). Automate infrastructure provisioning using tools such as Terraform and Ansible.
   - o Releasing code to production environment.
   - o Collaboration with development and operations.

- **Change management**: It is one of the key functions of SRE. Knowledge of the change process is important. If you are in a DevOps role, then you will have experience in change management, and that can help you choose the SRE role. However, if you are a software developer, then you might need to learn the change management process to become an SRE.

   Here are some of the change management certifications you can obtain:

   - o ITIL: IT Service Management

o   Change management foundation certification

o   AIM Change Management certification

- **Cloud computing**: all the above roles can be performed on the cloud as well. So if you are a developer, developing applications cloud will give you experience with cloud applications. If you are an infra engineer provisioning infra on cloud that will help you learn how servers and databases work on cloud. Similarly, system administration on the cloud gets you knowledge of servers on the cloud.

- **Production support**: If you are a production support engineer with L2 and L3 support model, SRE can be your career path forward. As an L2/L3 production support person, you will have skill to troubleshoot, incident management, change management, scripting and all these comes in handy with SRE.

- **Collaboration and communication**: If you are an entry-level or an experienced person, collaboration and communication are key for the SRE role. For experienced engineers, you are expected to have collaboration experience and experience working in non-silos teams and agile methodology. For example, if you are an experienced developer, then collaboration with operations will come in very handy to crack the SRE role. Collaboration gives you understanding of different functions in SDLC.

The aforementioned are some of the key roles that fall into the SRE domain. SRE teams have diverse backgrounds and experiences. It starts from entry-level to 8+ years of experience. In the above roles defined the experienced professionals are in range from 4-8 years of experience.

# Future of SRE

In today's cloud-native era, which is continuing to grow, SRE plays a very important role in maintaining the reliability of the system. SRE as a role has evolved over the last 10 years and will continue to evolve. The roles and responsibilities might change in future however, the focus of SRE will be on process, strategy and culture.

Large organisations are increasingly realising the value of SRE practices that help faster software delivery, quality delivery, and claim high reliability and availability, as follows:

- **Reliability will grow**: Evolving technology will push organisations to build more software applications. To be valuable to customers, software needed to be reliable. Users will have high expectations from software such as seamless experience, highly available, and highly performant. With the increase in user demand for software reliability, the SRE role will evolve. Organisations will need SRE engineers who can build reliable systems.

    Moreover, software systems are becoming distributed and complex, and reliability has become a critical concern. SRE engineers have acquired skills to help build reliability even for complex systems.

- **Evolving technology stack:** The technology landscape will continue to evolve and that will require building more tools, platforms and cloud-native solutions. SRE will have the opportunity to grow, learn, and build new tools.

- **DevOps and SRE collaboration:** Many organisations have blurred roles between DevOps and SRE. Sometimes they both overlap or maybe SRE adopts DevOps roles and is still called as SRE. In the future, DevOps and SRE roles will be blurred more and they might work as one team that bridges the gap between development and operations.

- **AI Ops:** Though AI is predictive to automate all the jobs, it is a long runway. Soon, AI engineers can build one-time automation for all manual tasks. SRE can adopt AI engineering to revolutionise SRE aspects such as identifying the root cause of failures, proactive measures to identify failures, auto-healing, and quick incident response, which will in turn increase the reliability and availability of the system. As SRE's future, AI and SRE can work together to build complex systems and also add intelligence to operations.

- **Focus on diversity:** SRE today has various roles to perform to keep complex systems up and running. In the future, organisations will focus more on diversity and inclusion. Diversity of skill sets, regions, ethnicities, and genders will help a team with a strong SRE skill set. With complex systems, SDLC teams will also grow it all the way become more important to collaborate and bring inclusion within teams.

- **Cultural shift**: Today also, we are in a cultural shift moving train. SRE has brought a culture of collaboration, blameless post-mortem, continuous improvement, and clear communication. It is still in the nascent phase, with organisations adopting SRE. In future, all SDLC teams will follow SRE practice to break all silos.

As a future career path, SRE will continue to evolve. Learn new tools and new programming frameworks, in-depth knowledge of the cloud, learn solution architecture, and enhance problem-solving.

Certifications that will help SRE to strengthen their skills professionals:

- o SRE Foundation Certification, will help beginners to learn and understand SRE practices.
- o Any Cloud Professional certification
- o SRE Certified Professional
- o SRE Practitioner
- o Certified Kubernetes Administrator
- o Red Hat Certified System Administration
- o Certified Automation Professional Associate Certificate

Some tips on how to find the right skills for SRE in your career:

- o **Clearly define your career goals**: List down the skills you want to learn and specialise in. Once you list down then determine the certification or course you would like to achieve.
- o Understand the role and responsibility of SRE and then map it to your current skill set.
- o Look for practical training available
- o Read and understand the SRE case studies available.

# Conclusion

This chapter explained some of the key features of SRE very briefly. In all previous chapters, you learned various facets of SRE and SDLC. This chapter will help you choose SRE as your career path and path forward. This being the last chapter of the book, we tried to visualise SRE in the real world. As technology grows daily, new methodologies are also coming up to enhance the software development process. SRE is also enhancing, and as you learned, there is no one solution to a problem.

In the previous chapters, you learned that SRE practices and approaches depend on various factors; however, by the end of this book, you will be able to apply the best practices of SRE in building efficient and reliable software.

To conclude, SRE is not just one team, and it is a methodology of best practices. Keeping reliability in mind from the initial stage of software building and measuring the performance at every milestone will help you achieve the goal of reliable software.

# Join our Discord space

Join our Discord workspace for latest updates, offers, tech happenings around the world, new releases, and sessions with the authors:

https://discord.bpbonline.com

# Index

www.ingramcontent.com/pod-product-compliance
Lightning Source LLC
Chambersburg PA
CBHW061811210326
41599CB00034B/6958